RICHARD RORTY'S POLITICS

Liberalism at the End of the American Century

Markar Melkonian

Humanity Books

an imprint of Prometheus Books
59 John Glenn Drive, Amherst, New York 14228-2197

Published 1999 by Humanity Books, an imprint of Prometheus Books

Richard Rorty's Politics: Liberalism at the End of the American Century. Copyright © 1999 Markar Melkonian. All rights reserved. No part of this publication may be reproduced, stored in a retrieval system, or transmitted in any form or by any means, electronic, mechanical, photocopying, recording, or otherwise, without prior written permission of the publisher, except in the case of brief quotations embodied in critical articles and reviews.

Inquiries should be addressed to
Humanity Books, 59 John Glenn Drive, Amherst, New York 14228–2197.
VOICE: 716–691–0133, ext. 207. FAX: 716–564–2711.

03 02 01 00 99   6 5 4 3 2

Library of Congress Cataloging-in-Publication Data

Melkonian, Markar.
 Richard Rorty's politics : liberalism at the end of the American century / by Markar Melkonian.
     p.   cm.
 Includes bibliographical references and index.
 ISBN 1–57392–724–4 (cloth : alk. paper). — ISBN 1–57392–725–2 (paper : alk. paper)
 1. Rorty, Richard—Contributions in political science. 2. Political science—Philosophy. 3. Liberalism—Philosophy. I. Title.
JC251.R59M45   1999
320.51'3—dc21   99–37145
                                                                    CIP

Printed in the United States of America on acid-free paper

It's hard to be cynical enough.
—Lily Tomlin

ACKNOWLEDGMENTS

In the course of writing these pages I have enjoyed the support and good counsel of a number of people. I want to thank Richard Rorty for his assistance, Ann Ferguson for her advice, and Eric Miller for much-needed assistance with revisions of an earlier draft. Special thanks, also, to Kanchana Mahadevan for her encouragement and ideas, and John Brentlinger for his considerable help at two stages of the development of this manuscript. And finally, I want to thank Suzy Melkonian for her considerable patience.

I dedicate these pages to Tamar and Narineh, in loving memory of their uncle Monte.

CONTENTS

Acknowledgments 7

Introduction 11

1. **Framing the Conversation** 21

   Three Anti-Isms 22
   Rorty's "We's" 30
   Strategic Considerations 35

2. Departures from Dewey   45

Dewey and the Public/Private Split   48
Dewey on Liberty and Democracy   55
Rorty on Liberty and Democracy   63

3. Freedom and Liberalism in Practice   85

Depicting the Apolitical Private Sphere   88
State Power and the Private Sphere   94
Privatization and Socialism   105
Private Selfhood and Ideology   116

4. Decency and Liberalism in Practice   135

Liberalism and Suffering   137
The Solemn Complement of Rorty's Ideals   143
Decency beyond Liberalism   155

5. Of Light Minds and Heavy Hands   167

A Circle without Circumference   167
Rorty's Incompatible Roles   181

Bibliography   203

Index   211

INTRODUCTION

Rorty's name, if not his opinions, is as well known outside divisional meetings of the American Philosophical Association as that of any other contemporary American philosopher. His name has appeared in public discussions about the curricula of liberal education, feminism, the "culture of human rights," and the state of "postmodern politics." Amnesty International and the AFL-CIO have invited him to speak, and his works have been translated into at least seventeen languages, including Chinese, Arabic, and Serbo-Croatian.

The fact that a living American philosopher's name is recognizable east of the Atlantic and at some remove from academia is remarkable enough to prepare us for analogies with John Dewey. Still, it would be easy to overstate his influence. As a *New York Times Magazine* interviewer put it, "Rorty is, in fact, about as widely esteemed as any American philosopher has been in the past forty years—which is to say, not very widely."[1]

Questions of name recognition and influence aside, what Rorty has had to say about social and political philosophy has resonated with the din of the collapsing Berlin Wall. The rhetoric of the victors in the cold war has been dominated by accolades to "the Market," Western-style democracy, and liberalism. Through constant conjunction and repetition, the terms *free market* and *democracy* have melded into one diphthong. Much of what Rorty has had to say about liberalism, in particular, corroborates the view of a well-known columnist, to the effect that "political philosophy is over. Finished. Solved."[2] Even after widespread disillusionment with "free-market reforms" in eastern Europe, a variety of commentators in the West still suppose that the liberal democracies have vanquished all contenders for all time, and that the final years of the American Century have deposited us at the threshold of a new millennium of Western-style democracy and free-market capitalism.

Rorty's writings on a range of topics also jibed with the views of some relatively influential writers years before the dissolution of the Warsaw Pact. In particular, a variety of writers who, like him, have been associated with the term *postmodernism* have for decades repeated the same pragmatist themes and rhetorical strategies that he has invoked. Examples that spring to mind include Thomas Kuhn, Stanley Fish, and in some respects François Lyotard. In his article "Postmodernist Bourgeois Liberalism," Rorty explicitly associated himself with the word *postmodernism*. In subsequent writings, however, he has regretted incorporating the word into his self-description. Extending pluralism across the panorama of cultural activities, he writes that he has "... given up on the attempt to find something common to Michael Graves's buildings, Pynchon's and Rushdie's novels, Ashbery's poems, various sorts of popular music, and the writings of Heidegger and Derrida."[3] Despite this gesture, however, commentators have continued to describe Rorty as a postmodernist.[4]

One obvious reason for uncertainty about Rorty's relationship to self-described postmodernists has to do with the fact that *postmodernism* is a word that has come to be invested with any of a number of different meanings, depending on the speaker and the audience. In a book published several years after "Postmodernist Bourgeois Liberalism," Rorty explained that when he briefly embraced the word *postmodernism*, he took it "in the rather narrow sense defined by Lyotard as 'distrust of metanarratives.'"[5] Postmodernists, by this account, are people who distrust certain metanarratives about the careers of such typically modern supersubjects as *homo humanus*, reason, and the proletariat. If we choose to take postmodernism in this sense—and if we charitably assume that it is not merely a fin de siècle subjectivism epitomized by the slogan *Il n'y a pas de hors-texte* (which might be loosely translated as "There's nothing beside[s] the text")—then Rorty (and the present author, too) may be counted as a postmodernist.

A related reason for uncertainty about Rorty's relation to postmodernism might have to do with his uneasy relationship to some of the most celebrated liberal philosophers of the past, philosophers who have considered themselves to be, or have been considered to be, continuators of the Enlightenment. Until recently, the best-known liberal thinkers from Locke to the present have imagined their preferred social orders as illuminated by the light of reason, grounded in natural law, and conformed to the intractable nature of the human individual. Their opponents, from Locke's divine-right adversary Robert Filmer to the luminaries of the Frankfurt School, have disputed this characterization. Critics both on the Right and the Left have endeavored to show that reason does not sanction the practices and institutions associated with liberalism and human nature does not legitimate them, the assumption being that this in itself constitutes a definitive indictment of liberalism. Rorty may be counted among the self-described liberals who themselves have abandoned the familiar philosophical rationales for their tradition. While conceding that liberalism is no more rooted in universal reason or human nature than any other political creed, they have nevertheless maintained their allegiance to liberal institutions and counseled others to do so, too.

This point is closely related to Rorty's distrust of metanarratives and supersubjects. He tells us he wants to "retain Enlightenment liberalism while dropping Enlightenment rationalism."[6] His defense of liberalism does not depend for its force on claims to be grounded in reason, or on epistemological guarantees or transcultural and ahistorical notions of human nature. Thus, what he has to say in defense of liberalism is likely to be received with sympathy by an audience that, having read lots of books by, say, Nietzsche, Heidegger, and Foucault, has come to doubt still-prevalent Enlightenment assumptions about human nature, community, historical progress, and so on—assumptions that traditionally have been deployed to repel attacks against liberalism. Moreover, if it turns out that Rorty's case against Philosophy with a capital *P*—that is, roughly, his case against foundationalism, representationalism, and essentialism, discussed in chapter 1—is incompatible with alternative political and social views, then so much the worse for those alternative views.

If, on the other hand, the discussion in the following pages succeeds in breaching Rorty's defense of liberalism, then readers whom he has convinced to abandon more traditional defenses might well register this as a blow against liberalism per se. What is at stake in the present discussion, then, is the defensibility of liberalism when it is stripped of its familiar Enlightenment rationales.

Analytic philosophers, at least as Rorty characterizes them, are the most visible heirs of the Enlightenment within Anglophone philosophy. Analytic philosophy, by Rorty's account, is the main contemporary tradition of epistemology-centered philosophy, a tradition that sees theories of knowledge, philosophy of language, and philosophy of science as providing foundations or guarantees for the truth of knowledge claims in all of the most important areas of culture. When we examine Rorty's objections to this notion of philosophy in the first section of chapter 1, it will become clear that he has launched an audacious flanking maneuver against the fully arrayed ranks of analytic philosophy. In *Philosophy and the Mirror of Nature* (henceforth *PMN*), published in 1979, he deftly identified the stakes of the battle and stated his aim: If philosophy since Descartes and Locke is the attempt to meet skeptical doubts concerning the problem of our knowledge of the external world or other minds, then we should abandon philosophy altogether.[7] In its place, Rorty offers a different conception of philosophy, notably in part 3 of *PMN* and in the essays published together as *Consequences of Pragmatism* (henceforth *CP*). This is philosophy as one form of literature alongside others, including poetry, novels, and literary criticism. Philosophy, by these lights, need be little more than "an attempt to see how things, in the broadest possible sense of the term, hang together, in the broadest possible sense of the term."[8] The cash value of philosophy so conceived is not to establish an unshakable foundation for the Tree of Knowledge, nor to adjudicate all knowledge claims from on high, nor finally to "get it right" after all these centuries. Its cash value, rather, is simply to "continue the conversation."[9] Philosophers, accordingly, should view themselves as all-purpose intellectuals, ready and willing to "kibbitz" on a wide range of topics.

Rorty hopes this different conception of philosophy, philosophy with a lowercase *p*, will eclipse philosophy as it has been practiced within the analytic tradition. In its place he envisions "a post-Kantian culture, one in which there is no all-encompassing discipline which legitimizes or grounds the others."[10]

Rorty's disparagement of the "traditional problems" of philosophy and his desire to thoroughly "de-divinize" culture in Western Europe and the United States provides a thematic and programmatic continuity, be it ever so tenuous, linking his sociopolitical writings with his views on epistemology, philosophy of mind, philosophy of language, and so on.[11] Beyond this, however, there does not appear to be much more to the manner in which his views on a wide range of topics "hang together."

This observation is fully in keeping with his intentions: He disparages what he calls "systematic philosophy" in favor of "edifying philosophy," conceived as philosophy "…designed to make the reader question his own motives for philosophizing rather than to supply him with a new philosophical program."[12] "Systematic philosophy," by contrast, is philosophy that aims to map the whole domain of knowledge of all of culture and provide an epistemological or ontological basis for such fields as ethics, politics, and art. In the following chapters, it will become clear that Rorty has sought to edify his readers on a number of presumably nonphilosophical topics, too, and in particular to preempt the suggestion that large numbers of people in the leading liberal democracies and elsewhere might need a new *political* program at the end of the American Century.

※ ※ ※

This discussion will focus on what Rorty has had to say about liberalism, selfhood, and community. His early books, written through the 1970s, and most, though not all, of his articles and reviews published between 1959 and the late 1970s do not take these "moral and social questions" as their first topic of discussion. Rather, the bulk of these early writings target the views of truth as correspondence[13] and knowledge as an assemblage of representations, together with the notions of reason and theories of meaning and reference that are parasitic on this view, as well as the notion of "system," which, in the post-Kant North Atlantic, at least, has been associated with it. However, Rorty has made known his opinions on "moral and social questions" at least as early as his 1960 review of David L. Miller's *Modern Science and Human Freedom*, and these opinions have become more explicit in later writings, notably in *Contingency, Irony, and Solidarity* (henceforth *CIS*) and his recent book, *Achieving Our Country* (henceforth *AOC*).

For Rorty, to "continue the conversation" in which our predecessors have engaged is a worthy end in itself. Indeed, if we are to believe him, it is the single most worthwhile activity remaining for philosophers today. Erudition for its own sake, however, may strike some of us as a rather poor incentive for plowing through the works of a prolific philosopher. I have hinted that a more compelling reason for taking his social and political views seriously is that, regardless of the merits of these views, many people invoke his name and reputation to bolster favorite themes that for years have been the stock-in-trade of writers on the winning side of the cold war. Since the prestige of Rorty's earlier writings, especially *PMN*, has transferred at least to some extent to his later social and political interventions, it would be a good idea to review some of his favorite nonpolitical themes. This will be the job of chapter 1.

In chapter 2, I will consider Rorty's claim to be a follower of Dewey. Focusing on social and political ideas, I will examine to what extent and in what sense this claim has merit. I will point out the significant differences between Rorty and his alleged progenitor, Dewey, notably when it comes to their respective conceptions of how to harmonize personal freedom with public responsibility.

Rorty understands a liberal to be a person who thinks that cruelty is the worst thing we do.[14] He also uses "liberal" and its cognates to describe certain actual and imaginary political setups. These include his preferred utopia, characterized by the public and private ideals introduced in chapter 2, as well as a number of existing institutions characteristic of contemporary Western Europe and the United States. Rorty holds these institutions to be paradigmatically liberal. In chapters 3 and 4 I will make the case that his proclaimed ideals conflict with the actual institutional practices of the "rich North Atlantic democracies."

Dewey once wrote that "all intelligent political criticism is comparative."[15] In chapter 3, I will compare some liberal assumptions about the relationship between the private sphere and political power to an alternative account that emphasizes the political character of the private sphere and private selfhood. I will argue that the existing liberal democracies Rorty is concerned with defending bear little resemblance to his democratic utopia, in which "the quest for autonomy is impeded as little as possible by social institutions." According to the alternative vocabulary I will introduce, political institutions, broadly conceived, traverse nearly the entire length and breadth of the private sphere in the North Atlantic democracies. This alternative description seriously compromises Rorty's evaluation of liberalism in practice.

With some key terms for an alternative conceptual vocabulary in hand, I will turn a critical eye in chapter 4 to Rorty's claim that the liberal democracies already contain institutions and practices well-suited to advancing the public ideal of ameliorating suffering. I will argue that existing liberal democracies fare little better with reference to Rorty's public ideal of ameliorating suffering than they did with reference to his private ideal of making room for self making. I will then suggest an alternative political setup, which I believe holds greater promise in relation to this ideal.

In the final chapter, I argue that, at the end of the American Century, Rorty's private role as ironist and his public role as self-described apologist for bourgeois liberal democracy are not so much incommensurable as they are incompatible. The better he fulfills one role, I will argue, the more seriously he compromises the other.

NOTES

1. L. S. Klepp, "Every Man a Philosopher-King: Richard Rorty of the University of Virginia," *New York Times Magazine,* December 2, 1990, p. 117.

2. Charles Krauthammer, "Decade Marks Triumph of Western Democracy," *Washington Post,* September 15, 1988, p. A31. Although Rorty has a hunch that "Western social and political thought may have had the last *conceptual* revolution it needs" (Richard Rorty, *Contingency, Irony, and Solidarity* [Cambridge: Cambridge University Press, 1989], p. 63 [hereafter cited as *CIS*]), he might have reservations about the claim that political philosophy is "solved." This point should become clear in the following pages.

3. Richard Rorty, *Essays on Heidegger and Others* (Cambridge: Cambridge University Press, 1991), p. 1 (hereafter cited as *EH*).

4. See, for example, Ray Bhaskar, *Philosophy and the Idea of Freedom* (Oxford and Cambridge, Mass.: Blackwell, 1991), p. 139; Sabina Lovibond, "Feminism and Postmodernism," *New Left Review* 178 (November/December 1989): 5; Kai Nielsen, *After the Demise of the Tradition: Rorty, Critical Theory, and the Fate of Philosophy* (Boulder: Westview Press, 1991), pp. 133, 139; Honi Fern Haber, *Beyond Postmodern Politics: Lyotard, Rorty, Foucault* (New York: Rutledge, 1994), p. 6; Gilbert Hottois and Maurice Weyembergh, eds., *Richard Rorty: Ambiguïtés et limites du postmodernisme* (Paris: Librairie Philosophique J. Vrin, 1994), pp. 10–11, among others.

5. Rorty, *EH,* p.1. For a further discussion of Rorty's credentials as a postmodernist and the ambiguity of the term, refer to Louis Dupré's contribution, "Postmodernité ou modernité tardive?" in Hottois and Weyembergh, *Ambiguïtés,* pp. 39–58.

6. Rorty, *CIS,* p. 57.

7. Refer, for example, to Richard Rorty, *Philosophy and the Mirror of Nature* (Princeton: Princeton University Press, 1979), pp. 180–81 (hereafter cited as *PMN*). Rorty has been accused of what Kant called "indifferentism," "the mother in all sciences of chaos and night" (Immanuel Kant, *Critique of Pure Reason,* trans. Norman Kemp Smith [New York: St. Martin's Press, 1965], p. 8). Pretending to reject all metaphysics, indifferentists fall back into metaphysical positions, while hiding their regression "by substituting a popular tone for the language of the Schools," and in this way excusing themselves from giving their metaphysical views the attention they deserve (Kant, *Critique of Pure Reason,* pp. 8–9). It should be noted, however, that in the first two-thirds of *PMN,* much of *Objectivity, Relativism, and Truth,* and other writings, Rorty does offer something in the way of reasons for advocating walking away from sticky epistemological problems—even if those reasons amount to little more than pointing out that, after centuries of futile endeavor, no one has come close to solving these

alleged problems (Richard Rorty, *Consequences of Pragmatism* [Minneapolis: University of Minnesota Press, 1982], pp. xvi–xvii [hereafter cited as *CP*]).

8. Rorty invokes Wilfred Sellars's nice phrase in *CP,* pp. xiv, 29, 226, and in *PMN,* p. 114.

9. Rorty, *PMN,* p. 391.

10. Ibid., p. 6.

11. As far as I am aware, the most comprehensive published bibliography of Rorty's work appears in József Niznik and John T. Sanders, eds., *Debating the State of Philosophy: Habermas, Rorty, and Kolakowski* (Westport, Conn. and London: Praeger, 1996), pp. 130–44. Also see Herman J. Saatkamp Jr., ed., *Rorty and Pragmatism: The Philosopher Responds to His Critics* (Nashville and London: Vanderbilt University Press, 1995), pp. 231–44.

12. Rorty, *PMN,* pp. 5–6.

13. According to the truth-as-correspondence view, truth is constituted by a relation between a belief, utterance, or statement and something not essentially mind-dependent, such as a fact, a state of affairs, a set of objects, a sequence of members of a domain, or a piece of spaciotemporal real estate.

14. Rorty, *CIS,* pp. xv, 74. Rorty thanks Judith Shklar for this formulation.

15. John Dewey, *John Dewey: The Later Works, 1925–1927,* ed. Jo Ann Boydston (Carbondale and Edwardsville: Southern Illinois University Press, 1984), p. 304.

CHAPTER ONE
FRAMING THE CONVERSATION

Before proceeding to examine Rorty's defense of liberalism, I will need to devote some pages to framing the discussion in relation to the larger body of his writings on other topics. In this chapter, I will do several things: First, I will indicate briefly in what respect I agree with Rorty's views about philosophy, and why. This will motivate the discussion in the pages that follow and help to narrow its scope. Remarks in the first section about his views on some chief concerns of analytic philosophy segue in the second section to related observations about his projected audience. Critics of Rorty's social and political views need to come to terms with these considerations if they are not to beg important questions he poses. The third and final section of the chapter is an attempt, by way of a preview of my strategy in the following chapters, to preempt the accusation that I beg important questions Rorty has posed.

THREE ANTI-ISMS

Rorty's salutary departures from Platonic and Cartesian perspectives may be appreciated by turning to three related positions he promotes in the first two-thirds of *PMN*. These are: (a) *antifoundationalism*, (b) *antirepresentationalism*, and (c) *antiessentialism*. Without claiming that these three "anti-isms" are in any way foundations of his thinking, I will devote space to an exposition of them simply because this is a convenient way of situating what he has to say about "moral and social questions" within the context of his larger body of writing.

(a) *Antifoundationalism*: In *PMN*, *CP*, parts 1 and 2 of *Objectivity, Realism, and Truth* (henceforth *ORT*), and elsewhere, Rorty has presented a strong case for abandoning the search for foundations of knowledge, or conditions for the possibility of knowledge, experience, and science. He has noted that most philosophers nowadays consider themselves to be antifoundationalist; nevertheless, he disparages analytic philosophers, in particular, for foundationalism, at least to the extent that they are still "…committed to the construction of a permanent and neutral framework for enquiry, and thus for all culture."[1]

Rorty's antifoundationalism depends crucially on what he has to say about *vocabularies*, in contrast to *sentences* or *beliefs*. Vocabulary shifts such as those Plato, Saint Paul, Newton, and Freud provoked amount to literalizations of new metaphors. Taking his cue from Donald Davidson, Rorty holds a view of metaphor as having no agreed-upon use, and hence no meaning other than the literal meaning of its constituent words, their prevailing normal use. A metaphor produces effects on its audience, and thus can be a *cause* of beliefs; nevertheless, it should not count as a *ground* or *reason* for beliefs.

Rorty views words as "nodes in the causal network which binds the [human] organism together with its environment."[2] When certain metaphors "catch on" or are adopted widely and become current, they eventually may become literalized. He cites the example of a *mouth* of a river or a bottle. The terms *private sphere* and *public sphere* are also likely candidates. The designation *sphere* in this context is one of a number of spatial metaphors, including "circle," "domain," "realm," and "arena," all of which have been used to differentiate the sum of public communities and activities from the sum of private ones. As should become clear in chapter 3, these metaphors, routinized in law and custom, have largely ceased to function as metaphors. Such metaphors, like the bread of the Eucharist in the orthodox doctrine of transubstantiation, have acquired a conventional use and are now dead.

When metaphors die, they cease to be merely *causes* and become *reasons* for beliefs.[3] Returning to Wittgenstein's slogan that the meaning of a word is its use, together with Davidson's definition of a (living) metaphor as a figure of speech that has no agreed-upon use, we may say that, as a dying metaphor gradually acquires a *meaning*, it comes to produce effects through that meaning.

Rorty views "rationality" as a name for "a suitable balance between respect for the opinions of one's fellows and respect for the stubbornness of sensation."[4] With this in mind, he has made a strong case, in *PMN*, chapter 1 of *CIS*, and elsewhere, that there is no way rationally to adjudicate vocabularies, in the manner that one may adjudicate sentences within a "normal" discourse or vocabulary. There is no such thing as an irrational nonlinguistic effect; there are only irrational justifications—that is, certain sentences with no use within a pre-given language game with set rules. Moreover, since any set of rules must be stated in an already existing vocabulary or language, it is futile to seek, as philosophers have, an overarching set of superrules adjudicating all language games for all time.

What distinguishes a metaphor from an inarticulate sound or mark is that the former is made up of *words*—that is, sounds or marks with literal meanings; sounds or marks that, in Rorty's terminology, are "about" something. Without literal meaning, there can be no metaphors. Thus, metaphor is parasitic on agreed-upon vocabularies or, to borrow a term from Thomas Kuhn, on *normal discourse*. Dead metaphors make up a large part of any given discourse, normal or abnormal. As metaphors are created, literalized, and killed, vocabularies change and supplant one another, and new physical theories, manners of versification, and moral and religious creeds eclipse incumbent ones. In this way, as a sympathetic commentator has described things, "progress in the cultural interests of poetry, science, philosophy, or politics results from 'the accidental coincidence of a private obsession with a public need.' "[5]

So it is not an exaggeration to say that for Rorty, "the motor of history, the chief vehicles of intellectual and moral progress" are the successive creation of new tropes and the literalization of metaphors.[6] When, for example, he urges readers to reject the political vocabulary of the Marxist Louis Althusser and to embrace that of the reformist Roberto Unger,[7] he is aware that such a shift not only registers a change in the political climate, but also contributes to such a change. He confirms this assumption when he salutes Unger's "many years of hard work here in North America, changing the curricula of many of our law schools and the self-image of many of our lawyers,"[8] and the

> thousands of recently graduated lawyers who [Rorty assures us, despite appearances to the contrary—MM], influenced by Unger and other members of the Critical Legal Studies Movement, are now helping make institutions in the United States slightly more flexible and decent.[9]

This example lends credence to an interpretation of Rorty according to which poets, in the extended sense as metaphor-makers, are "the unacknowledged legislators of the social world."[10] A commentator has summarized Rorty's "deflationary" account of the development of culture well:

> ...individuals who happen to have been born at certain times, who have been driven by certain obsessive states, who happen to have had neurons firing in response to certain random stimulations, happen to invent forms of words that are made public at the right time and place and catch on.[11]

This account resonates with Kuhn's case that scientific progress has less to do with discovering truth than adoption by a scientific community of new paradigms, or conceptual vocabularies. Rorty draws on Kuhn, among others, to make the case that the pronouncements of the hardest of the hard sciences have no epistemological privilege or priority over poetry. To call the set of descriptions hard scientists produce *more accurate* than the set of descriptions poets produce amounts to little more than the claim that the preferred set has paid its way better than the other set. As we know, however, there are different ways of paying one's way: Some ideas prove useful to many people for coping, for making life less difficult; others produce tingles in spines; and still others do lots of other things. Since the way the hard sciences pay their way is different from the way poetry pays its way, it does not make much sense to say that one of these fields of activity pays its way better than the other.

Still, hard scientists and poets do have some things in common. The romantic intellectual's impulse to create herself anew by redescribing and the humanitarian's imperative to mitigate the pain of others both depend on the creation of new final vocabularies. Both the poet and the humanitarian reformer set their faces against metaphysics, and both distinguish abnormal discourses from normal discourses, the invention of new metaphors from their literalization or social application.

Since, according to Rorty, the chief vehicle of intellectual and moral progress is the creation of new tropes, it is imperative that the scope of admissible alternative forms of words, descriptions, metaphors, literary genres, and final vocabularies be unlimited in principle. "It is central to the idea of a liberal society," Rorty writes, "that, in respect to words as opposed to deeds, persuasion as opposed to force, anything goes."[12]

It is worth noting, at least parenthetically, that this normative ideal has been espoused by lots of people, not just liberals. Rosa Luxemburg was every bit as adamant on this point as was John Stuart Mill.

(b) *Antirepresentationalism*: Rorty counts the tendency to treat vocabularies, or congeries of metaphors, as if they could be warranted like statements, beliefs, or propositions as the cardinal sin of traditional philosophy. This is because there are no reasons not already couched in some vocabulary that could establish once and for all that one had the *right* vocabulary. Correspondence of a belief with a nonlinguistic state of affairs, then, is not a criterion of knowledge or truth. Rorty's case against this representationalist account of knowledge appears in part 2 of *PMN* and his essay "The World Well Lost" in *CP*, among other places. A more fecund account of knowledge, according to Rorty, is one that does not view knowledge as a matter of getting reality right, but rather as a matter of acquiring habits of action for coping with reality. Antirepresentationalism, for him, is "the abandonment of a 'spectator' account of knowledge and the consequent abandonment of the appearance/reality distinction."[13]

Following Wittgenstein and Davidson, Rorty makes a particularly convincing case that the relation between language and the world is *causal*, rather than *representational*.[14] It is a mistake to treat vocabularies or languages in Tractarian fashion as a collection of representations, or as a medium more or less well-suited to the purpose of representing nonlinguistic objects. To say that a language such as, say, the language of modern chemistry, represents nonlinguistic objects and events is merely a way of paying that language a compliment.

What Rorty has to say about representationalism depends crucially on what he has to say about sentences or beliefs. Beliefs do not represent nonbeliefs. Like the unhyphenated coherentist, "The pragmatist recognizes relations of *justification* holding between beliefs and desires, and relations of *causation* holding between these beliefs and desires and other items in the universe, but no relations of *representation*."[15] Of course, the world causes beliefs to be accepted as true or rejected as false; nevertheless, these causes themselves cannot constitute *justifications* or *reasons* for retaining beliefs. Beliefs can be *caused* by any of innumerable nonlinguistic events or states of affairs; however, they can only be *justified* by other beliefs. Thus, there are no causes for the truth of beliefs.[16]

Rorty places himself squarely within the tradition of American pragmatism, represented by William James, who held that a true belief is more fruitfully viewed as one that "pays its way," rather than one that accurately represents reality. According to James, "*The true is the name of whatever proves itself to be good in the way of belief, and good, too, for definite, assignable reasons.*"[17] In a similar vein, Rorty writes that the "core of pragmatism" is "to replace the notion of true beliefs as representations of 'the nature of things' and instead to think of them as successful rules for action."[18] He advocates blurring the positivist distinction between the semantic and the pragmatic, theory and observation. Accordingly, in chapter 6 of *PMN*, among other places, he advocates abandoning all theories of reference, in favor of an everyday notion of "talking about" and "really talking about."

By this conception, truth has become, "...in William James' phrase, what is good for *us* to believe."[19] Like the ancient sophists, James and Rorty recognize that usefulness is always usefulness *for someone or some group*. Since something can be said to be useful or good in the way of belief only in relation to a given need or purpose, usefulness and goodness, and hence truth, depend upon "our" needs and aims. And this, in turn, depends upon who "we" are, since we are who we are, in large part at least, because we have certain needs. There is no usefulness or good, then, apart from usefulness for a given I or we. As one would expect and as we will see below, this observation, together with Rorty's account of selfhood and self-creation, has important ramifications when it comes to assessing his social and political views.

(c) *Antiessentialism*: Rorty's rejection of the notion of representation of an outer essence of nature or reality is symmetrical with his case against the notion of *expression* of an inner essence, or true self. "To abjure the notion of the 'truly human,'" he writes, "is to abjure the attempt to divinize the self as a replacement for a divinized world."[20]

However great his differences with Hume in other respects, Rorty lauds the Scotsman's redescription of selfhood as nothing but a loose bundle of preferences, fears, hopes, and other mental atoms.[21] For Rorty the nominalist, selfhood is not a thing with attitudes, but simply the set of attitudes themselves, "a network of beliefs, desires, and emotions with nothing behind it—no substrate behind the attributes,"[22] a network that is constantly reweaving itself, "a centerless web of historically conditioned beliefs and desires." These attitudes are not expressions or attributes of a self, but rather constituent elements of selfhood: Strip away the attitudes, and there is no self left. Selfhood is a tissue of contingencies, a concatenation of beliefs, desires, emotions, and other putative mental states. It is "centerless, an historical contingency all the way through," not the locus of a center, a divine spark, or a truth-tracking faculty called "reason." Thus,

> we do not need a categorical distinction between the self and its situation. We can dismiss the distinction between an attribute of the self and a constituent of the self, between the self's accidents and its essence, as "merely" metaphysical.[23]

By Rorty's lights, metaphysicians are people who are on the lookout for "... continuities—overarching conditions of possibility—which provide the space within which discontinuity occurs."[24] A prime example of such a continuity is the story of our alienation from and ultimate return to a universal and ahistorical human essence. Instead of human essence, Rorty wishes to substitute a characterization of the self as "the accidental tangle of compulsion, desires and roles that we crudely refer to with the pronoun 'I.'"

He favorably contrasts his view of the self as a historical product to the nonempirical self which Kant had to postulate in the interests of Enlightenment universalism.[25] This helps to explain his high esteem for Freud, or at least Donald Davidson's interpretation of the Austrian neurologist. According to Rorty, Freud corroborated a conception of the self as neither a discreet, integrated consciousness, a "natural kind with an intrinsic nature, an intrinsic set of powers to be developed or left undeveloped," nor as merely a "decentered machine."[26] In this way, Freud himself eschewed the very idea of a paradigm human being. Davidson and Rorty's Freud showed us how the more sublime creations of fantasts and poets may be traced not to an essence expressed, but to idiosyncratic events of the past, neuroses, infantile experiences, and the like. Strong poets, then, are not externalizers or expressers of an essence within. Their metaphors catch on not because they resonate with something universal and eternal within the human breast, but because for any of a number of reasons they just happen to meet the needs of members of a particular community at a particular time.[27] Proust's rusk biscuit was not so much a light turned inward for self-discovery as a catalyst for self-creation.

These observations subvert a line of criticism leveled against liberalism. This is the criticism, which Rorty associates with communitarians, that relies on the claim that political institutions presuppose a doctrine about the nature of human beings and that such a doctrine, unlike Enlightenment rationalism, must make clear the essentially historical character of the self.[28]

As we have seen, Rorty advises us to tell stories of our past as the saga of successive coinings of new tropes and the literalization of metaphors. Metaphor is the growing point of language.[29] Keeping in mind that metaphors are causes of belief, this amounts to advising us to view history as predominantly "cultural history," and cultural history as, in large part, the literalization of metaphor. This point, together with the observations about selfhood in the preceding paragraphs, lead Rorty to the conclusion that muzzling strong poets constitutes more than an attack on the freedom of some individuals: It amounts, more ominously, to promoting the "freezing-over of culture" and the "dehumanization of human beings."[30] Here, Rorty's precursor is J. S. Mill, who in chapter 2 of *On Liberty* famously argued that, to borrow Kuhnian terminology, if abnormal discoursers were one day to disappear, it would behoove normal discoursers to raise them up themselves.

At least one critic has challenged Rorty's view that acquiring beliefs is to a large or significant extent a matter of choice.[31] Although this critic does not deny that men and women may actively consider the sort of persons they want to be, she questions Rorty's emphasis on the contingency of self-creation. This line of criticism might lose some of its force, however, in view of Rorty's recognition that the strong poet is a rare individual, and even this rare figure depends for her existence on normal discourse, which is composed, in large part, of "unchosen belief." When Rorty characterizes the strong poet as one who is free to invent and move on to new and exciting forms of discourse, we should recall that for him freedom is the recognition of contingency. He recognizes that the strong poet has little or no choice when it comes to the forms of life into which she was born and the blind impresses that her behavings—including her discursive behavings—bear. Indeed, one thing that makes a strong poet strong is her refusal to try to escape this contingency.[32] Rorty has indeed produced an account of selfhood that assumes that acquiring some beliefs is a matter of choice; however, even when it is the strong poets' choice of descriptions that make up the story of her appearance on the scene, the chooser is always a finite, historically and culturally constituted subject, a chooser who is herself a tissue of contingencies.

Part of this finitude, this historical and cultural specificity, has to do with the array of choices perceived to be available, the range of "live options." Some commentators, problematizing the perception and range of these options, have identified what they have dubbed the problem of *adaptive preferences*. As Marx recognized, our preferences are often, and perhaps always, adaptations to natural, social, economic, and political circumstances beyond our control. What liberals typically assume to be free and voluntary consent may simply be adaptations to circumstances in which live options have been confined to narrow limits. In recent years some feminist writers have noted this problem and have deployed it in attacks against liberal notions of consent. Their claim is that what liberals take to be women's free and voluntary consent to various arrangements is spurious when and because it is based on preferences that are adaptive to circumstances over which they have little control.

The term *adaptive preferences*, however, might well be a pleonasm. As we have already noted, all beliefs have causes, even if they do not all have reasons. So in this sense, at least, even the most capricious or whimsical preferences conceivably could be described as adaptations to "nonsubjective" factors, biological, social, or otherwise.

RORTY'S "WE'S"

Long before Dewey, Jefferson made the connection between pragmatism and the experiment of democracy:

> [N]ature has constituted utility to man, the standard and test of virtue. Men living in different countries, under different circumstances, different habits and regimens, may have different utilities; the same act, therefore, may be useful, and consequently virtuous in one country which is injurious and vicious in another differently circumstanced.[33]

Jefferson also recognized that a particular description of institutions and practices that proves useful to some people may be worse than useless to others within the same country. It all depends on who "we" are. Recognizing this, as we have seen, his pragmatist successors, like his sophist predecessors, have shined a spotlight on "us" and directed the question of who "we" are to center stage.

Like Jefferson and James, Rorty acknowledges the nonuniversal, contingent, "historically situated" character of his own normative

FRAMING THE CONVERSATION

views: "[W]hat counts as rational or as fanatical," he notes, "is relative to the group to which we think it is necessary to justify ourselves—to the body of shared belief which determines the reference of the word 'we.' "[34] Educated inhabitants of what Rorty, following Roberto Unger, has dubbed the "rich North Atlantic democracies"[35] think it is necessary to justify themselves to various "we's" of different degrees of exclusivity. "We" in the broadest sense might correspond to one's *ethnos*, which "comprises those who share enough of one's beliefs to make fruitful conversation possible."[36]

Within the context of public affairs, then, it behooves seekers of truth to abandon the search for conditions of possibility of experience, and instead to foster as much intersubjective agreement as possible about what is good in the way of belief. Extending the reference of "us" as far as possible in this way may involve not only the persuasion of people with whom one already shares enough in common to engage in fruitful discussion, but also the attempt to make oneself understood to more and more people with whom one hitherto has not communicated. Accordingly, Rorty has urged setting aside such "Kantian questions" as "What should I do? What may I hope? What is man?" and fixing instead on "Deweyan questions," such as "Which communities' purposes shall I share?"[37]

Reviewing his references to the communities whose purposes he shares, it is possible to group them into two broad categories: On the one hand, there is a "private us," an "us insiders who share [Derrida's] background, who find the same rather esoteric things as funny or beautiful or moving as he does," "educated, comfortably off, cosmopolitan professionals" "who have read and pondered Plato, Newton, Kant, Marx, Darwin, Freud, Dewey, etc.," an "us for whom the discourse of philosophy actually *has* been important."[38] On the other hand, there is a "public us," as in "we social democrats," "we liberal intellectuals," "we modern inheritors of the traditions of religious tolerance and constitutional government," "we... liberal Rawlsian searchers for consensus," "us American liberals," and "we missionaries of the American Dream."[39] When he writes that "We should be more willing than we are to celebrate bourgeois capitalist society as the best polity actualized so far,"[40] Rorty is explicitly addressing the latter "us."

Presumably, the background "we" share with Derrida is first and foremost educational: What "we philosophy professors," "us middle-class intellectuals in American and European universities," or "we Anglo-Saxon philosophers" have in common with "we Western liberal intellectuals" is having read lots of books.[41] For Rorty, philosophy with a small *p* is one form of literature among others and should become or is in the process of becoming "culture criticism."[42] So, in keeping with his views on the aims of philosophy, Rorty's project would appear to consist, in large part, of "continuing the conversation" with contemporaries and precursors in philosophy departments, as well as in English departments and programs in comparative literature.

Education and the leisure time necessary to read lots of books, of course, are not universally accessible. Slum dwellers in Lima, longshoremen in Lagos, and working mothers in East Los Angeles are not likely to have the leisure time—let alone the acquired taste—for reading lots of books by Rorty's preferred authors. So whether or not "we powerful, discursive types"[43] are powerful because we are discursive, we certainly are discursive because we are powerful.

Rorty acknowledges this. As it turns out, "we" happen to be "the community of the liberal intellectuals of the secular modern West," "us relatively leisured intellectuals, inhabiting a stable and prosperous part of the world," "us—educated, leisured policy makers of the West," "people like ourselves—middle-class American and European readers of magazines like [*Dissent*]," "we American romantic secularists," "we rich North American bourgeois," and "we rich, fat, tired North Americans."[44] Rorty, then, is unlikely to dispute a critic's characterization of him as catering to

> a leisured elite—intellectual yuppies—neither racked by pain nor immersed in toil—whose lives may be devoted to the practice of aesthetic enhancement, and in particular to generating self, other and genealogical descriptions.[45]

From the perspective of its public role, this leisured elite would appear to correspond to Alastair MacIntyre's Managers, and perhaps to some of his Therapists, too. These, together with the Rich Aesthetes (Rorty's "private we's"), allegedly dominate "our culture," both civic and private.

According to this picture, then, there are private communities dedicated to aesthetic enhancement and there are public communities that dominate political culture. Community, however, is preeminently a public category. This is because, according to Rorty, the private sphere is the sphere of aloneness, narcissism, and idiosyncrasy: The point of private life in Rorty's liberal utopia, as he describes it in "The Contingency of Selfhood," is to have the opportunity to make oneself a creature that is not only new but unique. He denies that there is or should be any consensus about competing conceptions of the good life. Accordingly, he does not emphasize private "we's," except for "tiny circle[s] of initiates,"[46] small bands of kindred souls drawn together by the private projects they share.

Whether public or private, however, what Rorty's "we's" have in common evidently is a shared educational background, thanks to leisure, wealth, and freedom from censorship in the North Atlantic. Thanks to this common background, "we" have the freedom to run for office or write novels as we wish, depending on our idiosyncratic conceptions of personal perfection.

Self-identification and considerations of audience have a crucial bearing on the manner in which Rorty presents his views and on his evaluation of rational argumentation. He would not agree that he himself has provided a sustained argument against the old sort of philosophy.[47] Drawing on the arguments of Quine, Davidson, Sellars, and others whom he considers to be reductios of the analytic tradition, he wants to convince his audience that a *philosophical* defense of liberalism is unnecessary.

This is not to say, however, that he does not believe in *promoting* liberalism. He most emphatically does. Indeed, he describes himself frankly as engaged in *apologetics*, in the sense of "a circular justification of our practices" which "makes one feature of our culture look good by citing still another."[48] Mincing even fewer words, he has described his writings on moral and social questions as "a PR job"[49] for liberalism.

Noting that for him, as for Wittgenstein, language is a "tool," not a medium of communication open to rational analysis from a position outside of any particular language, David Hall has concluded that:

There is little to be gained from attempting to micromanage, fine-tune, disassemble, or deconstruct the account Rorty provides. The best one can do is to judge the relative attractiveness of Rorty's views by recourse to alternative visions.[50]

Unfortunately, Hall goes on to conclude that "Rorty's philosophy is closed to rational analysis, critique or dialectic."[51] This conclusion is precipitous. The fact that Rorty emphasizes rhetoric over argumentation and deploys a wide variety of rhetorical techniques in making his point does not imply that he has entirely eschewed argumentation, if we use the word as he does, in a sense in which the term *rational argumentation* is pleonastic.[52] As the reader might have guessed from remarks earlier in this section, Rorty's only criterion of rationality, if indeed it could be so viewed, is that it is "the way we do things around here."[53] And as the reader might have guessed from the preceding section, "around here" is, if not exclusively philosophy departments, then at least in large part academia—that is, an enclave inhabited by people unusually well prepared to produce sentence sequences that conform to the rules of formal logic; to engage in dialectic and criticism; to recognize "informal fallacies" when they encounter them, and so on.

At least one commentator is puzzled that in the course of making his positions look good Rorty appears to argue for them much as other writers do.[54] Rorty offers reasons for changing certain subjects; he respects logical consistency as well as the next philosopher, and he attacks opponents when they resort to such so-called informal fallacies as, say, ad hominem arguments directed against the philosopher Heidegger and the genetic fallacy with reference to the iniquitous origins of existing liberal democracies. As we can see, however, his recourse to philosophical argumentation remains justifiable on pragmatic grounds even though he does not address his writings of recent years exclusively to analytic philosophers but to a wider audience in various intellectual precincts. Because the educated intellectuals, philosophers, and professors with whom he identifies himself and to whom he thinks it is necessary to justify himself are specially trained to identify and defer to cogent arguments, philosophical argumentation of the sort one finds in

PMN and elsewhere is an especially effective rhetorical technique for bringing his audience around to his point of view.

True, Rorty's audience, however broadly we may describe it, is probably less impervious to flattery and *argumenta ad populum* than many members of that audience would like to admit. As Rorty points out in his paper "Philosophy in America Today,"[55] the way things are done in philosophy departments in the anglophone countries today typically resembles more closely the practice of a clever lawyer, juggling briefs, citing precedents and case law, and so on, than that of white-smocked laboratory researchers driven only by the passion for disclosing truth. Nevertheless, what distinguishes "us for whom the discourse of philosophy actually *has* been important" from a wider audience presumably is that members of the former community are more impressed by the sort of argumentation of which philosophers have long considered themselves to be exemplary practitioners.

So Hall may be right when he writes that

> Rorty's dependence upon metaphors rather than statements, pictures rather than arguments, and global interpretations, rather than internal analyses of the thinkers he employs, means that the persuasive dimension of his thinking is stressed above that of the strictly logical.[56]

He is mistaken, however, if he assumes that the persuasive dimension of Rorty's thinking can be promoted effectively without the "strictly logical" dimension. In view of his projected audience, the latter dimension is a pragmatically authorized instance of the former.

STRATEGIC CONSIDERATIONS

This last point might require more elaboration, in the form of a few words about my strategy in the following chapters. By way of preview, I should first summarize our political differences: Rorty describes existing liberal democracies as doing the best job of any comparable setup so far, and the best job of any setup for which we can realistically hope, when it comes to promoting two most precious ideals. These ideals are *personal freedom* and *ameliorating suffering*. According to my account, by contrast, existing liberal democracies do a singularly poor job of it on both scores. Without disputing Rorty's view that liberal institutions such as independent judiciaries, representative democracy, and a press free from direct state censorship are precious innovations, I make the case in chapters 3 and 4 that state power in the North Atlantic countries is pervasive and invasive, and that the "rich North Atlantic democracies" promote economic inequality and the political powerlessness of the majority domestically, and tyranny and misery outside of their cartographic borders. I then proffer an alternative to liberal democracy, one which I believe holds better promise for advancing freedom and ameliorating suffering.

More than one reviewer has felt that this line of criticism begs the question, since Rorty could always parry my attack by invoking the notion of incommensurable descriptive vocabularies: Without the criteria of correspondence to reality or expression of inner essence to appeal to, he could always take refuge in the claim that, outside of our respective vocabularies themselves, there is no court of appeal to adjudicate which set of descriptions of actual liberal practices better pays its way. For his purposes, his descriptive vocabulary is better in the way of belief than mine. End of story.

Admittedly, Rorty does provide plenty of fodder for this interpretation, or something like it. In his 1972 paper "The World Well Lost," and occasional comments in *PMN* and later works, he has, perhaps paradoxically, opined that there is no fact of the matter, and no way the world is. These formulations have led some readers to conclude that he wants to have his cake and eat it, too—that he wants to be a relativist (that is, a person who believes that every belief on a topic under discussion is as good as every other),[57] but he does not want to be identified as one.

It should not come as a surprise that Rorty denies these accusations. One problem, of course, has to do with the ambiguity of the term "vocabulary," and the ambiguity of other words that Rorty uses as near-synonyms, including "theory," "jargon," and "language." Unless one were able to distinguish one vocabulary, jargon, or language from another in the first place, it is not clear how one could pronounce two vocabularies, jargons, or languages incommensurable. Still, we do somehow distinguish alchemy from chemistry, Blake's manner of versification from Dryden's, and the language of Aristotelian physics from that of Newton. Rather than searching for some sort of formal criteria to account for how we make these distinctions, it strikes me as much more in the spirit of Dewey to look to the consequences or purposes of the language speakers. Thus, if Rorty's vocabulary and mine are incommensurable, then this is the case to the extent that his is useful for certain purposes which I do not share, and which are irrelevant to the purposes my vocabulary serves. This seems to be the case when we review the examples of incommensurable vocabularies Rorty cites: The fact that Newton's jargon helps us to predict and control the behavior of medium-sized objects better than Aristotle's jargon does not make the former better or truer than the latter, because (according to Rorty, at any rate) Aristotelians have not been primarily interested in this sort of prediction and control when they have described the order of things, but have had other aims foremost in mind. Likewise, Saint Paul's soteriological aims were not the same as Freud's, Blake's shiver-inducing purposes were not the same as Dryden's, and so on.

This observation, however, has a corollary: Although there is no relation of logical entailment here, it is reasonable to assume that, given communicative competence on the part of the interlocutors, it is to the point to compare two sets of descriptions when they are intended to serve the same purposes, or when in fact they do serve the same purposes. This seems to be the way "we," in some broad sense of the pronoun, tend to do things around here, and it is in the spirit of Dewey's search for consensus.

I should admit at least in passing that Rorty's manner of expression is not my favorite way of articulating a partisan view. When it comes to my own normative political expositions, I prefer to launch them from the perspective of *promoting workers as a class to state power*, rather than taking part in what strike me as somewhat vapid ventilations about ameliorating evitable suffering and promoting "freedom" in the abstract. Nevertheless, the following point bears emphasis: In the present discussion I have explicitly adopted Rorty's manner of expression—as well as the two aforementioned ideals or purposes he professes to hold highest —in order to avert the charge that I have merely juxtaposed an incommensurable vocabulary to his. The brunt of my argument in chapters 3 and 4 is that the existing liberal democracies which Rorty is concerned with defending do not in fact promote these ideals or purposes.

Starting with chapter 3, however, I also counterpoise an alternative vocabulary to Rorty's—a vocabulary that includes such key terms as *class struggle*, *political power*, and *ideology*. Aside from considerations of elaborating more comprehensive and elegant descriptions of social transformations, this vocabulary serves political purposes that admittedly are very different from Rorty's. In chapter 5, I argue that two distinct purposes exist side-by-side in Rorty's text, just as two purposes exist side-by-side in mine. Rorty's purposes are: (a) promoting freedom and ameliorating suffering, and (b) defending existing liberal democracies. My purposes, by contrast, are: (a) promoting freedom and ameliorating suffering, and (c) challenging bourgeois ideological hegemony, one contemporary instance of which is Rorty's neoliberalism. Rorty wants to convince his readers that in order to do (a) one should do (b); I want to convince my readers that in order to do (a) one should do (c).

Granted, Rorty's case for connecting (a) with (b) and my case for connecting (a) with (c) may themselves be posed largely in our respective incommensurable vocabularies. Moreover, if one focuses on (b) and (c), the vocabulary I counterpoise to Rorty's may be incommensurable with his. However, this does not change the fact that the brunt of my presentation is concerned with purposes and a vocabulary I have (temporarily!) adopted from Rorty.

Setting aside tedious debates about how to distinguish one vocabulary from another, we all admit that there is such a thing as different sets of descriptions which, though posed in the same vocabulary, are nevertheless factually or logically incompatible. Surely we should not take Rorty to be saying that, in an ordinary, nontranscendental, nonphilosophical sense of the term, there is no *fact of the matter* whether and to what extent, say, the private sphere is a genuine refuge from state power, or whether Uncle Sam has supported more tyrants and bankrolled more bloodshed than the Kremlin, or whether the publicized aims of the founders of the Alliance for Progress (which Rorty considers to be a salutary example of U.S. foreign policy) were consonant with their actions and their confidential intentions.[58] Rorty concedes that "the world contains the causes of our being justified in holding a belief."[59] To hold that there is no fact of the matter when it comes to such "ordinary, retail, detailed, concrete reasons which have brought one to one's present view"[60] is to qualify oneself as the sort of relativist Rorty has spilled much ink denying he is.[61] It also amounts to resorting to just the sort of maneuver Wittgenstein denounced when, in a widely misunderstood passage, he insisted that philosophy should leave everything as it is.

Rorty might wish to write off my descriptions of the rich North Atlantic, in good "metaphilosophical relativist"[62] fashion, as one philosophical jargon among many equally good or bad jargons. To do this, however, he would have to show why my descriptions, devoid as they are of transcendental conditions and epistemological heavy breathing, constitute a philosophical attempt to "ground" a scientific explanation, a morality, or some other practice, rather than, say, part of a first-level sociological, anthropological, or historiographical theory. And I do not think he can do this convincingly.

So Rorty appears to face a dilemma: If my characterization of existing liberal democracies in the following chapters is worded in a vocabulary or vocabularies commensurable with the vocabulary or vocabularies Rorty uses to defend them, then my criticisms need to be evaluated as logically or factually incompatible with Rorty's. If, on the other hand, the vocabulary of my attack is incommensurable with Rorty's vocabulary or vocabularies, then it is hard to imagine how anyone could ever engage Rorty in a genuine political debate. In such a case, Rorty would have indicted himself as an irrationalist, a charge against which he has protested more than once.[63]

※ ※ ※

So far, I have stated the problem to be taken up in this discussion, indicated what is at stake and located the problem in relation to the larger body of Rorty's published work, his audience, and his purposes. In the next chapter, I will turn attention to Rorty's liberal predecessors, focusing on his debt to Dewey and differences between the two pragmatists when it comes to their conceptions of democracy and liberty and their proposals for allaying the traditional opposition between the public and private spheres.

NOTES

1. Richard Rorty, *Philosophy and the Mirror of Nature* (Princeton: Princeton University Press, 1979), p. 8 (hereafter cited as *PMN*). At least one critic has argued that Rorty is himself a shamefaced foundationalist (refer to Ernest Sosa, "Nature Unmirrored, Epistemology Naturalized," *Synthese* 55, no. 1 [April 1983]: 49–72). Whether or not this criticism hits the mark, however, Rorty's case against foundationalism in *PMN* and elsewhere might yet withstand the occasional relapse into the view he is concerned with attacking.

2. Richard Rorty, "Relativism: Finding and Making," in *Debating the State of Philosophy*, ed. Józef Niznik and John T. Sanders (Westport, Conn. and London: Praeger, 1996), p. 38.

3. Richard Rorty, *Objectivity, Realism, and Truth* (Cambridge: Cambridge University Press, 1991), p. 171 (hereafter cited as *ORT*).

4. Richard Rorty, *Consequences of Pragmatism* (Minneapolis: University of Minnesota Press, 1982), p. 195 (hereafter cited as *CP*). This formulation, it will be noted, is not inconsistent with his occasional definition of rationality, mentioned below, as "the way we do things around here."

5. David L. Hall, *Richard Rorty: Prophet and Poet of the New Pragmatism* (Albany: SUNY Press, 1994), p. 17, citing Rorty.

6. Nancy Fraser, "Solidarity or Singularity?" in *Reading Rorty*, ed. Alan Malachowski (Cambridge, Mass.: Basil Blackwell, 1990), p. 306.

7. Richard Rorty, *Essays on Heidegger and Others* (Cambridge: Cambridge University Press, 1991), p. 189 (hereafter cited as *EH*).

8. Ibid., p. 177.

9. Ibid., p. 182.

10. Cf. Fraser, "Solidarity or Singularity?" p. 306. Fraser cites Rorty, who in turn is echoing Shelley.

11. Tom Sorell, "The World from Its Own Point of View," in Malachowski, *Reading Rorty*, p. 20.

12. Richard Rorty, *Contingency, Irony, and Solidarity* (Cambridge: Cambridge University Press, 1989), pp. 51–52 (hereafter cited as *CIS*).

13. Richard Rorty, introduction to *Pragmatism: From Peirce to Davidson*, by John D. Murphy (Boulder: Westview Press, 1990), p. 2.

14. Rorty, *ORT*, p. 60.

15. Ibid., p. 97, emphasis in the original.

16. Ibid., p. 121.

17. William James, *Pragmatism: A New Name for Some Old Ways of Thinking* (New York: Longman, Green, and Co., 1914), pp. 75–76, emphasis in the original.

18. Rorty, *ORT*, p. 65.

19. Ibid., p. 22; Richard Rorty, "Solidarity or Objectivity," in *Post-Analytic Philosophy*, ed. John Rajchman and Cornel West (New York: Columbia University Press, 1985), p. 5, emphasis in the original. Richard Miller, in his book *Fact and Method* (Princeton: Princeton University Press, 1987), has convinced me that what he has dubbed *deep causal explanation* plays a pivotal role in the nonaxiomatic sciences and workaday beliefs of good sense. I have other misgivings about pragmatism, but this point alone should disqualify me as a pragmatist in James's sense of the word. I may weigh in as a linguistic nominalist, an epistemological behaviorist, an antiessentialist, or an antidualist, or I may bear some other resemblance to one or another of Rorty's profiles of a pragmatist; however, I doubt that most professing pragmatists would welcome the likes of me into their fold. I wish to emphasize, however, that my dissension from James's notion of truth and the fact that I subscribe to a nonpragmatist account of scientific explanation will have no adverse bearing on my case against Rorty's social and political views. The brunt of my criticism in the following chapters is leveled against first-level, epistemologically unproblematic claims Rorty makes on behalf of existing liberal democracies.

20. Rorty, *CIS*, p. 35.

21. Rorty, *EH*, pp. 145–48.

22. Richard Rorty, "Postmodernist Bourgeois Liberalism," *The Journal of Philosophy* 80, no. 10 (October 1983): 585–86. The following citations in this paragraph are from Rorty, *ORT*, p. 192; Richard Rorty, "The Priority of Democracy to Philosophy," in Malachowski, *Reading Rorty*, p. 288. Also refer to ibid., p. 299 n. 24.

23. Rorty, "The Priority of Democracy to Philosophy," p. 289. Geras has complained that "Rorty sometimes writes as though people were simply what their society and culture make of them. They have no inherent nature" (Norman Geras, *Solidarity in the Conversation of Humankind: The Ungroundable Liberalism of Richard Rorty* [London and New York: Verso, 1995], p. 49). Geras does not discuss the possibility that one could deny that "socialization goes all the way down" (Rorty, *CIS*, pp. 64, 185), while at the same time denying an inherent human nature distinct from the biological makeup of *Homo sapiens*. This possibility occasionally appears to have been lost on Rorty, too, as when he recommends to us "a picture of human beings as children of their time and

place, without any significant metaphysical or biological limits to their plasticity" (the cited passage, from Rorty's article "Trotsky and the Wild Orchids," appears in Geras, *Solidarity*, p. 89).

24. Quoted passages in this paragraph are from Rorty, *CIS*, p. 25 n; L. S. Klepp, "Every Man a Philosopher-King: Richard Rorty of the University of Virginia," *New York Times Magazine*, December 2, 1990, p. 122.

25. Rorty, "The Priority of Democracy to Philosophy," p. 301 n. 39.

26. Rorty, *CIS*, p. 35. Refer to ibid., pp. 23–43, and Rorty's excellent paper, "Freud and Moral Reflection," included in *EH*, pp. 143–63. The Davidson-Rorty interpretation of Freud has not gone uncontested. By Martin Hollis's lights, for example, Freud does not reject human essence, but rather holds that "...poetically speaking, our glassy essence is an essence but not glassy" (Martin Hollis, "The Poetics of Personhood," in Malachowski, *Reading Rorty*, p. 246). Even if Hollis were right, however, Davidson and Rorty might well have produced a "productive misreading" of Freud that deserves to be taken seriously.

27. Rorty, *CIS*, pp. 34–35.

28. Rorty, "The Priority of Democracy to Philosophy," p. 282.

29. Rorty, *EH*, p. 12.

30. Rorty, *PMN*, p. 377.

31. Refer to Jane Heal's paper, "Pragmatism and Choosing to Believe," in Malachowski, *Reading Rorty*, pp. 101–14. In his contribution to the same book Charles Taylor echoes Heal's doubts (Malachowski, *Reading Rorty*, pp. 258–59). Also refer to Jurgen Habermas's comments in Niznik and Sanders, *Debating the State of Philosophy*, p. 23.

32. Refer to "The Contingency of Selfhood (Rorty, *CIS*, pp. 23–43).

33. Thomas Jefferson, *The Life and Selected Writings of Thomas Jefferson*, ed. Adrienne Koch and William Peder (New York: The Modern Library, 1944), pp. 639–40.

34. Rorty, "The Priority of Democracy to Philosophy," p. 281.

35. Refer to "Unger, Castoriadis, and the Romance of a National Future," in Rorty, *EH*, pp. 177–92.

36. Rorty, "Solidarity or Objectivity," p. 13. It is not clear that Rorty is willing to concede that "fruitful" conversation may take place without at least one of the parties to the conversation thinking it necessary to justify itself to another party.

37. Richard Rorty, "Dewey between Hegel and Darwin," in *Modernism and the Human Sciences*, ed. Doroty Ross (Baltimore: Johns Hopkins Press, 1994), p. 67.

38. Terms cited in this sentence appear in Rorty, *EH,* p. 120; Richard Rorty, *Achieving Our Country* (Cambridge and London: Harvard University Press, 1998), p. 87; Rorty, *CP,* p. 173; Rorty, *EH,* p. 108.

39. Terms cited in this sentence appear in Richard Rorty, "Thugs and Theorists," *Political Theory* 15, no. 4 (November 1987): 565; Richard Rorty, "Habermas and Lyotard on Postmodernity," in *Habermas and Modernity,* ed. Richard Bernstein (Cambridge, Mass.: MIT Press, 1985), p. 173; Rorty, "Solidarity or Objectivity," p. 12; Richard Rorty, "Pragmatism without Method," in *Sidney Hook: Philosopher of Democracy and Humanism,* ed. Paul Kurtz (Amherst, N.Y.: Prometheus Books, 1983), p. 272; Rorty, "Relativism: Finding and Making," p. 121.

40. Rorty, *CP,* p. 210 n. 16.

41. Terms cited in this sentence appear in Rorty, *CP,* p. 189; Richard Rorty, "The End of Leninism and History as Comic Frame," (unpublished), p. 4; Richard Rorty, "Signposts along the Way that Reason Went," *London Review of Books,* February 16, 1984, pp. 5–6; Rorty, *ORT,* p. 29; Rorty, "Solidarity or Objectivity," p. 12.

42. Hall, *Richard Rorty,* p. 19.

43. Rorty, *EH,* p. 182.

44. Terms cited in this sentence appear in Rorty, "Solidarity or Objectivity," p. 12; Rorty, *PMN,* p. 359; Rorty, *CP,* p. 203; Richard Rorty, "Movements and Campaigns" (unpublished), p. 4; Rorty, "Relativism: Finding and Making," p. 29; Rorty, "Postmodernist Bourgeois Liberalism," p. 588; Rorty, *EH,* p. 178.

45. Roy Bhaskar, *Philosophy and the Idea of Freedom* (Oxford and Cambridge, Mass.: Blackwell, 1991), pp. 134–35.

46. Rorty, *CIS,* p. xiii.

47. Cf. Rorty, *PMN,* p. 6.

48. Rorty, *CIS,* p. 57.

49. Klepp, "Every Man a Philosopher-King," p. 56.

50. Hall, *Richard Rorty,* p. 4.

51. Ibid., p. 6.

52. Rorty has defined philosophical argumentation as "the practice of playing sentences off against each other in order to decide what to believe" (Rorty, *EH,* p. 125 n). It is easier to distinguish argumentation from suasive rhetoric, however, if we view them as different sorts of language games with distinct goals: Deciding what to believe, after all, is not the same as convincing others to believe something.

53. Rorty offers this definition for the words *scientific* and *objective* (Rorty, *EH,* p. 101). It could as well apply to *rational,* however (cf. Rorty, "Solidarity or

Objectivity," p. 6; Rorty, "Relativism: Finding and Making," pp. 45–46). It is true that on other occasions he offers different definitions of rationality, including the attempt to make one's web of belief as "coherent" as possible (Rorty, *ORT*, p. 106; Rorty, *EH*, p. 30). One possible justification for this definition, however, is that seeking to make one's body of beliefs as coherent as possible, whatever that may entail, is just one of the ways things are done around here. Rorty has also defined rationality as "the habit of attaining our ends by persuasion rather than force" (Niznik and Sanders, *Debating the State of Philosophy*, p. 28). In chapter 4, however, I will make the point that persuasion rather than force very frequently is *not* the way Rorty's "we" does things.

54. Geras, *Solidarity*, p. 122.
55. Included in Rorty, *CP*, pp. 211–30.
56. Hall, *Richard Rorty*, p. 7.
57. Refer to Rorty's definition of relativism at Rorty, *CP*, p. 166.
58. As documented, say, by Gerard Colby and Charlotte Dennet in their book *Thy Will Be Done: The Conquest of the Amazon: Nelson Rockefeller and Evangelism in the Age of Oil* (New York: HarperCollins, 1995).
59. Rorty, *CIS*, p. 5.
60. Rorty, *CP*, p. 165.
61. Cf., for example, ibid., pp. 166 ff.
62. Ibid., p. 167.
63. Refer, for example, to relevant comments in "Pragmatism, Relativism and Irrationalism," in ibid., pp. 160–75.

CHAPTER TWO
DEPARTURES FROM DEWEY

Of the three main heroes of *PMN*, Rorty has written that he has come to feel the closest affinity to Dewey.[1] He wistfully appreciates Dewey and other engaged American philosophers of the New Deal era who played a significant role in articulating public policy and establishing the tone of public discourse in the United States.[2] Like Dewey, Rorty has been concerned with defending liberal institutions in the West—including "a free press, free universities, and enlightened public opinion," as well as an independent judiciary and electoral representation[3]—against their intellectual detractors. Indeed, he has described himself modestly as little more than an updater of his pragmatist predecessor.[4] Rorty's self-description would appear to be accurate, at least in view of the fact that he has offered little in the way of a positive political vision that Dewey, standing on the shoulders of Mill, Jefferson, and Locke, had not already proposed. Acknowledging this, Rorty, with equal modesty, has apologized for his "lack of imagination."[5]

Dewey, then, would appear to be a reasonable point of departure for an investigation of Rorty's social and political views. Comparing the two American pragmatists at close quarters, however, it becomes clear that Rorty is a more original thinker than his self-evaluation would lead one to believe. There are important differences between the two pragmatists.

One reason these differences might not be more apparent from a reading of Rorty alone is that his Dewey is, as one commentator has put it, "a surgically revised specimen, to be sure."[6] For one thing, the two philosophers differ sharply when it comes to their conceptions of the tasks of philosophers: True, both Dewey and Rorty hold that philosophy, if it is to be anything at all, should be an attempt to see how things, in the broadest possible sense of the term, hang together, in the broadest possible sense of the term. Beyond this, however, they offer divergent views of what the scope and ends of philosophy should be. Rorty disparages defenses of liberalism that rely on high theory—"philosophical liberalism" of the sort Kant is held to have provided. He prefers instead a defense of liberalism that casts a bright light on commonsense liberal beliefs, such as the belief that slavery is bad and the belief that people should be allowed to worship God as they please. "We should 'privatize philosophy,'" Rorty counsels, "and say that when it comes to the communal self-reassurance of the modern democratic societies, most of the work gets done not by deep thinkers...but by superficial dreamers."[7] Recognizing this, one commentator has noted that what is unique about Rorty's position on social and political questions is that it "manifests the insight that actually there is not much to be said that is distinctive!"[8]

Dewey, by contrast, had grander ends in view. As one Dewey scholar, J. E. Tiles, put it:

> The point of having a broad vision was for Dewey to have a vantage point from which to criticize, judiciously and sensitively, existing cultural institutions. Such criticism was for him the distinctive role of philosophy and it could not be conducted properly without an understanding of the methods of science. To mount such criticism effec-

tively, moreover, requires certain distortions in our conceptions of experience and of reality to be corrected, and it cannot be carried out without a sound grasp of the nature of the general goals of intellectual endeavor (such as "truth") and how these goals are progressively refined as our methods for pursuing them develop.[9]

On the same page, Tiles adds that, "All this leaves intact a great deal of what Rorty stigmatizes as 'Philosophy,' and moreover presents 'Philosophy' as instrumental to the proper conduct of 'philosophy.'"

If Tiles is correct, then he has made it difficult to imagine Dewey as authorizing Rorty's view of a "postphilosophical culture" and the vision of a liberal utopia presented in *CIS*. Tiles casts aspersions on Rorty's claims to Dewey's legacy:

> [Rorty] is in the end no more prepared to take seriously and develop the philosophic position for which Dewey argued than are those who remain firmly within the analytic tradition. He is no more able to see how Dewey's arguments might achieve what they set out to achieve than are those for whom pragmatism is "an outdated philosophical movement."[10]

Whatever the merit of Tiles's misgivings about Rorty's credentials as a Deweyan when it comes to the public role of philosophy, however, other differences between Rorty and Dewey are more relevant to the present discussion. Two such differences are the two pragmatists' divergent conceptions of liberty and their different attitudes toward democracy. The balance of this chapter will focus on Rorty's debt to and departures from Dewey when it comes to their conceptions of liberty, democracy, and alternatives to the diremption of public and private persons.

The first section of this chapter consists of a sketch of Dewey's account of the public-private split. This will prepare us in the second and third sections to appreciate Rorty's debt to him and to take measure of the distance separating the two pragmatists on these issues. As we shall see, these differences have an important bearing on how the younger pragmatist conceptualizes and defends his brand of liberalism.

DEWEY AND THE PUBLIC/PRIVATE SPLIT

In at least one important respect, Dewey shared a crucial assumption with his best-known liberal predecessors: All agreed as to the most basic constituents of society. "Society," Dewey wrote, "is composed of individuals: this obvious and basic fact no philosophy, whatever its pretensions to novelty, can question or alter."[11]

This "basic fact" notwithstanding, it is a mistake, according to Dewey, to think that humans are what they are independently of living in association with others, or to think of humans as creatures who only enter into association as a means of getting what they are quite capable of wanting regardless of whether they live socially or in isolation. Humans both make up *and have been formed by* "societies, associations, groups of an immense number of kinds, having different ties and instituting different interests."[12]

To appreciate the last point more fully, it will help to be more specific about these "societies, associations, and groups." Dewey's inventory of latter-day examples includes

> gangs, criminal bands; clubs for sport, sociability and eating; scientific and professional organizations; political parties and unions within them; families; religious denominations, business partnerships and corporations; and so on in an endless list. The associations may be local, nation-wide, and trans-national.[13]

Of course, none of these groups and associations have existed in their present form from time immemorial. Dewey noted that defunct forms of association that existed three to four centuries ago restricted trade and shackled inquiry.[14] The latter point is easy to discern in the cases of, say, guilds, the apprenticeship system, and ecclesiastical education. Those who struggled against the old restrictions formulated their opposition to existing institutions by appeal to the sacred authority resident in the protesting individual. These appeals gave rise to "a theory which endowed singular persons in isolation from any associations, except those which they deliberately formed for their own ends, with native or natural rights."[15]

Dewey could see no reason why the political appeal should have been to the individual's rights rather than to the right of "some primary groupings," except that similar battles were being fought on several fronts, religious and intellectual as well as commercial and political, and the individual was the lowest common denominator for the protesters on all fronts to make common cause. Thus arose the belief in "the naked individual," to whom "all associations [were] foreign to his nature and rights save as they proceeded from his own voluntary choice, and guaranteed his own private ends."[16]

As shall become clear below, the activities of individual members of consensual associations figure prominently in both Dewey's and Rorty's characterizations of liberal communities. Nevertheless, they both opposed the picture of the "ready-made and complete individual" making choices and forming these associations, preferring instead to characterize individuals as socially produced, historically variable, and unfinished. Both pragmatists would have agreed with George Herbert Mead's view that, at least in large part, the self is a social creation. Furthermore, Rorty would agree with Dewey that "Individuality in a social and moral sense is something to be wrought out," and that social arrangements, laws, and institutions are means of creating individuals.[17]

Observing that the lines drawn between the activities of different individuals, as well as between their activities and those of public officials, are redrawn as circumstances change, Dewey advised against attempting to trace such lines before examining the particular historical circumstances within which the public-private split is inscribed. This reasonable advice, presumably, is an instance of Dewey's "historicism," which Rorty applauds.[18]

Dewey stressed that language makes it possible for interactions to take the form of collective actions with anticipated consequences or ends, and that these ends often inform or are present in the various stages of collective activity leading up to their achievement. To the extent that individuals in a group hold such ends in common, they are united into a group with an identity of interest. The anticipation in common of particular consequences of conjoint activity, the possession of a *common interest*,[19] is what makes participants in a collective activity a *community*, rather than a mere aggregation of individuals who happen to be working toward the same end without realizing it. "The planets in a constellation would form a community," Dewey wrote, "if they were aware of the connections of the activities of each with those of the others and could use this knowledge to direct behavior."[20] When such a common interest obtains,

> there is generated what, metaphorically, may be termed a general will and social consciousness: desires and choice on the part of individuals in behalf of activities that, by means of symbols, are communicable and shared by all concerned.[21]

Dewey sensibly recognized that persons more and more are joined together not so much because they have voluntarily chosen to be so united, but because "vast currents are running which bring men together."[22] Still, unless and until prison inmates, refugees, or bonded laborers came together to form gangs, resistance organizations, unions, or other formally organized and more-or-less voluntary associations, he was not prepared to count them as communities. Conversely, community does not obtain when only one member of a group is aware of what events mean and manipulates them in furtherance of personal, private interests and goals. Thus, child-labor contractors, Elmer Gantrys, and imperious gurus do not qualify as community leaders, since those over whom they wield authority do not constitute proper communities. Nor does community obtain when one member of a group forces others to surrender their interest, as in the cases of slavery, forced religious conversion, or dictatorship. To the extent that neither egregious manipulation nor forced renunciation of self-interest takes place within an organized group, however, associated life therein constitutes community life, however rudimentary.

Of course, it may be futile to attempt to draw a sharp line of demarcation between voluntary and involuntary acts of association or to try to quantify coercion or consent. Although there may be no neat way to draw a line between coercion and consent, nevertheless, as Rorty has noted, "the distinction is no fuzzier than most."[23] As with many other things, one often can distinguish greater or lesser degrees of coercion. One way to do this, for instance, might be to compare particular cases, with an eye to the extent to which members of a group share common ends, and the extent to which collective activity is conducive to these ends. Accordingly, a convent may be said to be less coercive than a prison.

When people act in association with one another with certain ends in view, their actions often have unintended or unforeseen consequences. Sometimes these consequences, for all practical purposes, are confined only to those who share in the association. At other times, cooperative actions considerably affect people who are not directly engaged in them. Dewey tied his distinction between *public* and *private* to the distinction between people who are directly affected by some cooperative activity and others who are indirectly, but enduringly and extensively, affected by it.[24]

This distinction between public and private, it should be noted, is not the same as that between *social* and *individual*. Dewey recognized that many cooperative (and in this sense *social*) activities do not have serious indirect consequences for many people. In this sense, these activities remain merely *private*. On the other hand, people who are not directly engaged in a given activity often recognize that they have an interest in it. Those who are not direct participants in a transaction but nevertheless are seriously affected for good or evil may constitute a *public*.[25] By this account, a public comes into being as the result of the recognition of a common interest in relation to the *indirect consequences* of conjoint activity, notably the activities of private associations. So, for example, an association consisting of concerned residents in the vicinity of an oil refinery constitutes a public group, if they are indirectly affected by the refinery's operation in an enduring and extensive manner, such as, say, air quality, local tax base, or property value assessment. On the other hand, the board of directors and top echelons of management of the oil company constitute a private group directly engaged in ownership and management of the refinery.

It is clear that one and the same act—say, a decision by executive officers to increase production or to close the refinery down—can have both a public and a private character. Furthermore, the line between public and private, which is to be drawn on the basis of "the extent and scope of the consequences of acts which are so important as to need control, whether by inhibition or by promotion,"[26] would appear to be highly variable. For one thing, the notion of "indirectly and seriously affecting for good or evil" may, of course, be interrogated further: Whether or not a collective activity may be judged to affect seriously for good or evil may depend crucially on one's final vocabulary. Jefferson's assertion that "it does me no injury for my neighbor to say there are twenty gods, or no God,"[27] for example, clearly is at odds with the Hebrew scriptural account of the judgment of nations by a jealous God.

This last illustration underscores the importance of consensus to Dewey's vision of community, and the importance to him of a common interest or a common final vocabulary as explicitly acknowledged ties that hold the members of a public together. According to him, when individuals are not aware that they share a common interest in the indirect consequences of some activity that affects them, these individuals constitute only a *potential* public. When they are aware but lack any institutional means to control such consequences, they constitute what Dewey called an *inchoate* public.[28]

To regulate the activities that affect its interests, a proper public must have some institutional means, however rudimentary or ill-adapted they may be. An institution that possesses any form of organization allowing some degree of regulation of the indirect consequences of private activities constitutes a public organization. These consequences, of course, are controlled and regulated not by "the public" as "something *per se*, something intrinsically manifesting a general will and reason,"[29] but by individual persons acting conjointly. Those who are invested with the duty of controlling these consequences in a manner responsible to the public are *officials*. These officials, taken together, constitute a *government*, and the public thus organized thereby becomes a form of *political state*. "Government is not the state," Dewey stresses, "for that includes the public as well as the rulers charged with special duties and powers."[30]

According to Dewey, then, a state is a politically organized public. It is "the organization of the public effected through officials for the protection of the interests shared by its members."[31] His state, moreover, is not an all-inclusive entity that incorporates the entire life of the community, as does Hegel's state: Dewey recognizes that one may be a member of many associations, and in most instances these associations do not have consequences requiring regulation.

DEPARTURES FROM DEWEY

In chapter 3, we will see that there is room to doubt some of the formulations in the preceding paragraphs. In the meantime, we will notice that, since Dewey defines a public in terms of indirect consequences of conjoint behavior, what public we define depends on what consequences we have in mind. Accordingly, a state conceived as the politically organized public will also depend on what consequences we have in mind.

It might be noted in passing that this picture has prompted complaints to the effect that Dewey flattens out qualitatively different types of association and ties them all together under the heading "the public." According to one critic,

> Such a theory of free-floating and equally graded publics might have had a certain semblance of plausibility in reference to a small trading and farming community of the nineteenth century like Burlington, Vermont [Dewey's home town—MM], where property was more or less evenly distributed and distinctions of wealth and social standing were not too glaring. But it ignores the fundamental fact of life in the highly centralized monopoly capitalism today.[32]

The question then arises how these various voluntary associations, communities, or publics are to coexist as components of larger national communities. Dewey hoped for a community of communities or "partial publics" in which pulls and responses of different groups reinforce one another and their values accord. For him, the ideal of such a Great Community—a community in which harmony has been achieved without coercion, manipulation, and domination—is the idea of "...a society in which the ever-expanding and intricately ramifying consequences of associated activities shall be known in the full sense of that word, so that an organized, articulated Public comes into being."[33] This ideal was intended to meet a need to resolve a conflict of interests, to find a framework of purposes that incorporates each conflicting interest and reveals thereby how far each reasonably may be pursued. It is the hope for compromise, class peace, piecemeal reform, experimentation, and open debate.

Dewey claims that his conception of the state and the public "gives a criterion for determining how good a particular state is: namely, the degree of organization of the public which is attained, and the degree in which its officers are so constituted as to perform their function of caring for public interests."[34] In the same essay, he acknowledges that "The forms of associated action characteristic of the present economic order are so massive and extensive that they determine the most significant constituents of the public and the residence of power."[35] Thus, at times of widespread domestic conflict, it would seem, by Dewey's account, that a large "constituent of the public" could be transformed into a community opposed to the public interest, as defined by much less numerous but more "significant constituents of the public and the residence of power." As the wave of broadly supported strikes in western Europe in 1995 and 1996 remind us, such a scenario is not entirely hypothetical, even within the rich North Atlantic democracies. Although Dewey surely did not intend it as such, his vocabulary lends itself to those who would claim that one or another state that is well-organized enough to defeat a more numerous but less efficiently organized opposition is a *good* state, protecting the interests shared by its members, and thus acting in the public interest.

For Dewey, as for Rorty, human communities bring together those who, by virtue of the contingency of their circumstances, happen to be susceptible to persuasion of the desirability of the community's aims or guiding purpose. Conscious and voluntary choice, then, is a necessary (though not a sufficient) condition for community.

It is significant that Dewey appears to view membership in an economic class not, in the first place, as inclusion in a social group identifiable with reference to its relationship to appropriation of the social surplus, ownership and control of means of production, or some other criterion independent of consensual association, but rather as membership in a particular community with shared ends in view. According to this view, in an era of dwindling union membership and declining support for explicitly working-class political initiatives, wage earners would constitute at most an inchoate public.

Dewey's emphasis on the consensual character of political association has important implications when we turn to the rationales he and Rorty have offered for liberalism. Before counterpoising a different vocabulary to that which they share, we should register several significant differences separating the two American pragmatists.

DEWEY ON LIBERTY AND DEMOCRACY

Traditional English liberalism from Locke through Mill has rested on a fairly simple "negative" conception of liberty as freedom from the constraints of the state, conceived of as a system of public institutions. This is the liberty of classical liberalism, a liberalism that did not go much further than setting its face against absolutism to demand religious freedom, central national authority with well-defined and limited powers, and at least some degree of control by the ruled. In his *Two Treatises of Government*, Locke defined liberty as a state that an individual enjoys when he is under no other legislative power but that established by consent in the commonwealth, and as the progressive elimination of the arbitrary from political and social regulation.

Mill, who is often represented as one of the most consistent advocates of negative liberty, mapped the domain exempt from public intervention in broad strokes:

> It comprises, first, the inward domain of consciousness, demanding liberty of conscience in the most comprehensive sense, liberty of thought and feeling, absolute freedom of opinion and sentiment on all subjects, practical or speculative, scientific, moral, or theological.[36]

He added that "the liberty of expressing and publishing opinions" is inseparable from liberty of thought itself, as is the "liberty of tastes and pursuits, of framing the plan of our life, to suit our own character, of doing as we like," as well as the liberty of "combination among individuals; freedom to unite for any purpose not involving harm to others."

Mill's "inward domain of consciousness," free from political and social legislation, corresponds to the classical liberal representation of the private sphere, what Isaiah Berlin called the "inviolable private sphere," the domain of Rorty's strong poets. Many liberals have viewed this inward domain of consciousness as something invaluable in itself, not just as a means to anything else. For them, government regulation of the private sphere is undesirable, since it is pointless at best to regulate or interfere in activities that do not have serious indirect effects for good or evil outside the circle of a voluntary association.

Although classical liberals believed, like the decidedly nonliberal Hobbes, that the liberty of particular men depends on "the silence of the Law,"[37] they were a far cry from anarchists. Classical liberal proponents of negative liberty viewed state institutions as a necessary evil, securing what Locke called the "civil interests" of "Life, Liberty and property."[38] These civil interests include law and order at home, defense against foreign invasion, and security of possessions. Even Mill—who insisted that "...the only purpose for which power can be rightfully exercised over any member of a civilized community, against his will, is to prevent harm to others"[39]—conceded that the state may invade the private domain in order to promote education, hygiene, social security, or justice.

English liberals have maintained that the law can also extend the liberties of subjects by curbing and limiting the executive. Like subsequent liberals including Dewey and Rorty, they held that the law should properly reflect a public concern that the public sphere not encroach on the private sphere. Thus, they promoted laws of habeas corpus and bail, and legal restrictions on police entry and arrest.

The traditional form of English political liberalism went hand in hand with the classical economic doctrine of laissez-faire. In his first inaugural address of 1801, Locke's most illustrious American follower summed up this doctrine in a well-known passage:

> ...a wise and frugal government, which shall restrain men from injuring one another, which shall leave them otherwise free to regulate their own pursuits of industry and improvement, and shall not take from the mouth of labor the bread it has earned. This is the sum of good government, and this is necessary to close the circle of our felicities.[40]

Although Dewey admired Jefferson, he found much with which to disagree when it came to Jefferson's belief that that government governs best that governs least, and to the related Lockean conception of liberty. Dewey's differences with Locke and his followers become especially acute when it comes to the relationship between *liberalism* and *democracy*. The American philosopher acknowledged that some public institutions may involve each member of the public in every decision taken; more commonly, however, decisions will be taken by official representatives of the public on its behalf. In either case, we have what he is prepared to call a form of *political democracy*. Dewey defined a democratic state as "a public articulated and operating through representative officers."[41]

Locke and Burke, as well as James Mill and Bentham, viewed political democracy in this sense as one of the chief "immoderate" threats to the common weal. Locke did not propose to make the people into the governing authority, nor to raise the people to the level of coequal with the monarch; rather, he was concerned with providing a criterion, namely collective community consent, by which to gauge the right of a political authority to rule, while at the same time providing guarantees against "the credulous superstition of the giddy multitude."[42] Even more famously, the younger Mill identified "the tyranny of the majority" as one of his chief concerns in *On Liberty*. Montesquieu and the Whigs, as well as such classical liberals as Tocqueville, the Mills, and their conservative liberal successors, all warned of the danger to "the public welfare" when democracy is extended too far, in the form of universal adult suffrage.

These early liberals or protoliberals, then, did not portray democracy as an end in itself, or something intrinsically good. According to some of the best-known early and classical liberals, if the governors judge democracy to be less efficacious than other means of securing the public welfare, or what Mill called the "interest and will of the nation," they could be forgiven for limiting democracy, or jettisoning it altogether, as needs arise. In *The Life and Times of Liberal Democracy*, C. B. Macpherson has pointed out that liberals only began to espouse egalitarian democracy—the sort of democracy that could be summed up by the slogan "One man one vote"—when, well within the industrial era, it gradually became clear that extending the franchise did not threaten the propertied classes. As it has turned out, of course, representative democracy with full adult franchise has proven itself, in England, the

United States, and elsewhere, to be a particularly effective means for securing the consent of the ruled, and hence the property and prerogatives of the rich and powerful.

On the eve of the French Revolution, as we know, Rousseau entered the stage as Locke's foil. Rousseau's followers looked forward to an egalitarian democracy in which the state was not viewed as a necessary evil, but as a servant for the common well-being, an instrument of collective betterment. They embraced a conception of liberty as freedom of opportunity to develop one's individual capacities, and they viewed the state as a positive instrument for attaining liberty thus conceived. This conception of liberty is conducive to Rousseau's civic republicanism, Jefferson's civic humanism, and Dewey's "community." The word *autonomy* sometimes has been used interchangeably with "liberty" so conceived.

Subsequent liberals, embracing such a "positive" conception of liberty or autonomy, have portrayed participation in democratic institutions not merely as an instrument for attaining the good life, but as part of the good life itself. Like Hannah Arendt, they view citizen participation in the affairs of the political community as a characteristically free and human activity.

Judging from passages such as the following, Dewey also may be counted prominently among these nonclassical liberals:

> Liberty is that secure release and fulfillment of personal potentialities which take place only in rich and manifold association with others: the power to be an individualized self making a distinctive contribution and enjoying in its own way the fruits of association.[43]

Reading this passage in the light of what has already been said about Dewey's conception of the public, it becomes clear that what is described here is not the negative liberty of the classical liberals, the freedom of the individual from the state, but something more akin to the Rousseauians' positive liberty.

Furthermore, Dewey distinguished between political democracy as a system of government and democracy as what he called a "social idea." As he explained,

> The idea of democracy is a wider and fuller idea than can be exemplified in the state even at its best. To be realized it must affect all modes of human association, the family, the school, industry, religion.[44]

Regarded as an idea, the author states, democracy is not an alternative to other principles of associated life. Rather, as Dewey put it, "It is the idea of community life itself."[45]

There are ways to draw a connection between liberty and democracy without invoking the notion of autonomy in the public sphere. According to a familiar liberal rationale for American-style representative democracy, for example, experience has taught us that unless there are some widely accepted and enforceable constraints on individual behavior, individuals, each pursuing her or his own irreducibly unique vision of personal perfection, are likely to come into conflict with one another. Thus, individuals find they must have some form of recognized government to adjudicate and ameliorate conflicts among private parties, for the good of the larger public. Unfortunately, people in positions of authority, including government officials, have an advantage over others when it comes to procuring the means to realize their nonpolitical, private aspirations and aims, while those without authority may find their aspirations thwarted by venal magistrates who take advantage of their positions. Thus, leaving institutions of government in the hands of people who do not have to answer for what they do invites abuse. The most effective way so far found to prevent such abuse is to make the institutions of government answer ultimately to everyone. When everyone is subject to the same constraints, at least formally, and those constraints are enforced by authority widely deemed to be answerable to everyone equally, the governed recognize themselves in the government, or at the very least do not consider government to be hostile or externally imposed. Under such a regime of political democracy, government takes place peacefully, with the consent, however passive or tacit, of the governed. Political democracy, thus conceived, is an instrument for resolving conflicts between individuals pursuing their own private aims, and liberty is the classical liberal freedom from excessive government.

Whatever the merits of this rationale, Dewey rejected it.[46] In contrast to many of his liberal predecessors, he viewed participation in democratic institutions not as a mere means to an end, but as something intrinsically good, and good not only for the community as a whole, but for each individual member of the community: For Dewey, public institutions as well as the family and friendships are part of being not only a responsible citizen, but also a fulfilled private individual. As he put it,

> Law, state, church, family, friendship, industrial association, these and other institutions and arrangements are necessary in order that individuals may grow and find their specific capacities and functions.[47]

Dewey is well known for having viewed elementary education as a creative experience in its own right, rather than exclusively as a preparation for adulthood. Similarly, he viewed participation in democratic institutions as an autonomous activity in its own right. In this respect, then, the inextricably related institutions of democratic participation and public education are as much components or instances of the good life as they are instruments for attaining it. By participating in these and other noncoercive public institutions and identifying herself with policy, the individual-as-citizen becomes a person more securely in possession of capacities and resources that these institutions have helped to foster. Since, as we shall see, Dewey's evaluation of public life contrasts sharply with Rorty's, it is worth quoting him at length on this point:

> When a state is a good state, when the officers of the public genuinely serve the public interest, this reflex effect is of great importance. It renders the desirable associations solider and more coherent; indirectly it clarifies their aims and purges their activities. It places a discount upon injurious groupings and renders their tenure of life precarious. In performing these services, it gives the individual members of valued associations greater liberty and security: it relieves them of hampering conditions which if they had to cope with personally would absorb their energies in mere negative struggles against evils. It enables individual members to count with reasonable certainty upon what others will do, and thus facilitates mutually helpful cooperations. It creates respect for others and for one's self. A measure of the good-

ness of a state is the degree in which it relieves individuals from the waste of negative struggle and needless conflict and confers upon him positive assurance and reinforcement in what he undertakes. This is a great service, and there is no call to be niggardly in acknowledging the transformations of group and personal action which states have historically effected.[48]

Dewey disputed the view of means and ends that permits us to treat public democratic institutions merely as external means adopted to ensure a fulfilled private life. According to him, the relationship between means and ends is thoroughly reciprocal: What individual human selves desire constrains and provides the standard of adequacy for means; means, as they are hit upon, refine and enlarge ends. Ends are not pregiven: They are constituted in the course of pursuing means. Nor are there "genuine" or "authentic" ends, in view of which all means, past, present, and future, may be evaluated with respect to how conducive they are to realizing those ends. Dewey urged us to treat our ends as open, so that our means can become "genuine instruments"—that is, constituents of our ends. Participation in democratic institutions constitutes a particularly important body of shared experience which, in turn, bolsters those institutions, extending and deepening democratic participation. Treating our ends as open helps us to adapt to the contingencies of our existence, thereby helping us to act freely.

If Dewey's view of the relationship between means and ends on the one hand and freedom on the other appears to be tenuous, this is because of a set of presuppositions underlying the familiar rationale, presuppositions that he viewed as distortions of important facts. These presuppositions represent individual human selves and what they desire as something given, something already there. These givens then function as absolute constraints on inquiry, which in turn give rise to fruitless conceptions of our relationships as individuals to political institutions and the larger communities of which we are a part. Thus, for example, debates about psychological egoism versus altruism, about whether or not people always or usually pursue their self-interests and what those self-interests are, quickly lead into familiar philosophical cul-de-sacs. Recognizing this, one Dewey scholar has noted that,

> The individualism of "classic Liberalism" has bequeathed to us an opposition between self-regarding and other-regarding, egoism and altruism, neither of which is satisfactory and between which we should not feel we have to choose.[49]

Dewey refused to enter into such debates. He abandoned the problem of "the celebrated modern antithesis of the Individual and Social, and the problem of their reconciliation."[50] For him, as the previously cited source noted,

> The choice is not between a self-regarding person and an other-regarding person, but between a person whose regard for self is regard for something narrow, trivial, transient and exclusive, and a person whose regard for self is for something wide and inclusive enough to embrace the interests of other people and permanent and significant enough to flourish only in an environment sustained by shared values and cooperative action.[51]

As we have seen, Dewey's conception of liberty as autonomy, and his evaluation of democratic participation and public education as ends in themselves, represent significant departures from classical liberalism. In few other places is this departure clearer than in his refusal to endorse the opposition of public and private persons.

On the other hand, Dewey's use of key terms such as *interest, government, political state*, and *political democracy* is not noticeably inconsistent with Rorty's vocabulary. The same is true, also, with reference to *community*, as in Rorty's question, cited above, "Which communities' purposes should I share?" And, as we shall see, Rorty agrees with Dewey insofar as both rejected descriptions of the narrowly self-regarding egoist and the exclusively other-regarding citizen as irreconcilable opponents.

In the following pages, however, it should become clear that Rorty's way of averting the clash of public and private persons differs significantly from Dewey's. It should also become clear how much weight the public and private spheres must bear as repositories of altruism and egoism, respectively, to sustain Rorty's view.

RORTY ON LIBERTY AND DEMOCRACY

One well-known controversy among classical liberals concerned J. S. Mill and his father, James Mill. The younger Mill came to feel that the liberalism of Bentham and the elder Mill one-sidedly focused on "external culture"—reason and truth—and did not take proper account of "internal culture"—the individual's feelings, passions, impulses, natural inclinations, and idiosyncrasies. The author of *On Liberty* was convinced that individual freedom was increasingly threatened by "the tyranny of the prevailing opinion and feeling," as well as the tyranny of magistrates. His reaction was to insist on reserving as large a space as possible exempt from the intervention of magistrates and the majority. This space is Mill's "appropriate region of human liberty," which we encountered in the previous section.

J. S. Mill's liberal successors have thought of themselves as standing in defense of individuality and self-creation, of maximizing and defending the region of individual liberty against others, whether singly or organized as governments or nongovernmental associations. At the same time, however, liberals have also stood for the containment of individuality and self-creation. Thus, for liberals like Benjamin Constant, the task of liberalism is to protect against personal politics and the chaos of unconstrained self-expression.

Like Mill, Rorty also prizes idiosyncrasy and individuality, as well as the idea that freedom creates room for self-creation, as ideals that his liberal utopia is bound to count as its chief purpose. For Rorty, as for Mill, freedom from the tyranny of prevailing opinion and feeling is a precondition for pursuit of one's self-perfection. Consider, for example, Rorty's approving description of Dewey:

> He assumed that no good achieved by earlier societies would be worth recapturing if the price were a diminution in our ability to leave people alone, to let them try out their private visions of perfection in peace. He admired the American habit of giving democracy priority over philosophy by asking, about any vision of the meaning of life, "Would not acting out this vision interfere with the ability of others to work out their own salvation?"[52]

According to Mill's "one very simple principle," "The sole end for which mankind are warranted, individually or collectively, in interfering with the liberty of action of any of their number is self-protection."[53] Rorty would agree with Mill that the authority of law should intervene only when it becomes clear that one person's pursuit of private perfection is interfering extralinguistically with another's—only when strong poets and revolutionaries make life harder for others by deeds, rather than just words. For Rorty, the ideal liberal community is one in which "...the only sort of human liberty which is hoped for is Isaiah Berlin's 'negative liberty'—being left alone."[54]

Like many liberals since Constant, however, Rorty also worries about the dangers of one-sidedly focusing on this ideal. These dangers are not limited to whatever cost the community may have to bear for withdrawal or aloofness from public affairs on the part of aesthetes and visionaries. Strong poets may well pose a greater threat when they make politics an arena for heroic or messianic self-display. By placing inordinate or exclusive emphasis on individual self-assertion, we invite into the public arena passionate visionaries intent on realizing their utopian obsessions *by any means necessary* (to borrow an expression popularized by one such visionary in the second half of the twentieth century).

Like Plato, St. Paul, and Kant, Marx allegedly tried in his own way to produce a single vocabulary capable of serving two different purposes, namely making oneself a new creature and establishing justice on Earth.[55] And at a point, it seemed he succeeded:

> Marxism has been the envy of all later intellectual movements because it seemed, for a moment, to show how to synthesize self-creation and social responsibility, pagan heroism and Christian love, the detachment of the contemplative with the fervor of the revolutionary.[56]

Marxist revolutionaries, and other revolutionaries besides, have viewed the public sphere as an arena within which to do two things simultaneously: In the course of building the revolution, the revolutionaries reinvent themselves in the image of the New Socialist Man. "The discontent of messianic radicals," as Yack describes it, is so intense partly because they believe that the redemption of the world hastens their own redemption. The fate of the institutions they hate determines the success of their pursuit of psychic health. The destruction of the old order redeems their souls as it cleanses the world. The end of the old world ends their dissatisfaction with themselves.[57]

Dr. Wolfgang Huber, of the Psychiatric Neurological Clinic of Heidelberg University, provided a caricature of this view when, at the height of the activity of the *Rote Armee Fraction* (the so-called Baader-Meinhof gang), he counseled his patients to "Bomb for mental health!"

After herculean efforts in this century, however, attempts thus to fuse public and private aims have ended in debacle. Self-proclaimed Marxist regimes in the East have either collapsed in the face of popular discontent or, as in the case of China, have thoroughly capitulated, if not to Western-style democracy, then to the profit motive and the "free market." This record of failure in practice is the best argument against attempting to fuse public and private aims in theory. Accordingly, Rorty urges us to

> stop looking for a successor to Marxism, for a theory which fuses decency and sublimity. Ironists should reconcile themselves to a private-public split within their final vocabularies, to the fact that resolution of doubts about one's final vocabulary has nothing in particular to do with attempts to save other people from pain and humiliation.[58]

As Constant's heirs are quick to point out, the means visionaries in the public sphere have deemed to be necessary have often included cruelty and the violent obstruction of the self-creative acts of others. This is why Nancy Rosenblum has claimed that the romantic sensibility is safe under no other system but liberalism, with its "regular and pacific liberty."[59] When politics becomes the terrain of sublimity, narcissism, and the romantic impulse to make it new, and visionary self-asserters are tempted to merge politics and sublimity, then large numbers of people may be swept up into the romance of history and deposited at the slaughter bench. Thus, where private projects conflict with minimizing the possibility of humiliation, these projects should be privatized, depoliticized.

Rorty's examples of dangerous self-asserters prominently includes such "nonpoets" as Lenin, Stalin, Hitler, and Mao.[60] The list is noticeably skewed against Uncle Sam's bêtes noires, and at least one commentator views Lenin's inclusion on it as little more than a gratuitous anti-Marxist political gesture.[61] In spite of misgivings about his choice of illustrations, however, Rorty's warning is clear enough: When the aesthetic obsessions of a strong public figure prevail over tolerance and all other ideals as the chief values in public discourse, the stage is set for evitable cruelty on a grand scale.

For Rorty, as for Dewey, thinking of oneself as a member of a community is a necessary part of being a member of a community. Rorty has defined a liberal community as one with no ideal or purpose other than making life easier on strong poets, allowing them to continue to change language.[62] In this way he registers his concern with averting the tyranny of the majority. It is difficult to imagine any additional ideal or purpose (with the possible exception of protection of property rights), whether emanating from a public or a private impulse, which would not at least to some extent encroach on Mill's "internal culture." Accordingly, Rorty has sometimes defined a liberal community as "one which has no purpose except freedom,"[63] the freedom that makes room for self-creation.

On other occasions, however, he has defined a liberal as a person for whom cruelty is the worst thing we do, and insisted that no goal, public or private, is more important than ameliorating suffering. Despite manifest problems with utilitarianism, he sees no better way of stating duty to others than the greatest happiness principle. Vocabularies of public decency in the West are concerned with the alleviation of cruelty, most notably with that peculiarly human form of cruelty, humiliation, or "forced redescription." In Rorty's book, ameliorating this sort of cruelty is the defining ideal of liberals.[64] This manner of putting things underscores his emphasis on the efficacy of linguistic practices, sometimes at the expense of nondiscursive causal processes. At times, this emphasis has resulted in far-fetched formulations, exemplified by his endorsement of "a Whitmanesque sense that our democratic community is held together by nothing less fragile than social hope."[65]

By philosopher Nancy Fraser's lights, Rorty at one time made the case that these two ideals, making the world safe for strong poets and ameliorating suffering, complement each other: The romantic poet and the pragmatic reformer are "natural partners."[66] By de-divinizing things about which they are concerned, both figures encourage us to cease pinning our hopes on God, reason, human nature, and the moral law, and in this way they direct us away from objectivity to ungrounded solidarity, to clinging together against the night. By redescribing our situation in various and unfamiliar ways, strong poets teach us to view life as a tissue of contingencies, ourselves as finite, and liberal institutions as fragile human inventions. This earlier Rorty, according to Fraser, has emphasized that we only see the practices of earlier ages as cruel and unjust because the poets have taught us how to redescribe them using metaphors and vocabularies they invented. Moreover, by redescribing and re-redescribing hitherto familiar objects, they teach us tolerance of alternative perspectives and accommodation to the opinions of our fellow citizens. In this light, the freezing-over of culture is a threat to a far broader constituency than just romantic intellectuals. Thus, by making society safe for strong poets, we make it safe for everyone—except perhaps those who aspire to become Orwell's O'Brien.

Fraser's periodization of Rorty's views on the usefulness of the romantic poet to liberal democracy may be too tidy: Even in more recent work he sounds in some respects like an advocate of the "natural partners" view.[67] In any case, events since the collapse of the Berlin Wall have brought home very graphically the dangers posed when romantic poets—in Russia, the Baltic republics, the Caucasus, Central Asia, the former Yugoslavia and, yes, even the Czech Republic—are propelled into high political office. Not so long ago Rorty wrote that "...in contemporary Russia and Poland, poets, playwrights and novelists serve as the best examples of certain...moral virtues."[68] As soon as the former dissident novelists and poets became the *acknowledged* legislators of the social world, however, the result has often been tyranny and misery worse than the worst of their immediate "nonpoet" predecessors. In the course of a few short years, the Gamsekhurdias, Sharanskys, and Elchibeys, the Karadzics, the Talibanis, and a long list of other former dissident intellectuals (in a broad Gramscian sense of the word *intellectual*) have embezzled billions of dollars, expelled or imprisoned a new generation of dissidents, vindicated the cruelest forms of misogyny, bulldozed homes, tortured and killed detainees, assassinated political opponents, pauperized tens of millions of their compatriots, turned millions of others into refugees, and presided over ethnic-cleansing campaigns in a dozen locales, from Tajikistan to the Trans-Dniester. Examples could be multiplied almost at will. Not even Rorty's liberal hero Vaclav Havel has remained unsullied: The playwright and first president of the Czech Republic has given his imprimatur to repressive legislation that was objectionable even to the editors of the *Wall Street Journal*, who complained that he "...just signed a new law calling for up to two years in prison for anyone convicted of 'defaming' the government, parliament or the constitutional court."[69]

Developments since the early 1990s, then, have made it ever more difficult to view cultural innovators and seekers of social justice as "natural partners." By Rorty's lights, the production of imaginative literature is "...the principal means by which bright youth gain a self-image."[70] Even before it became clear to the syndicated columnists that the balance of power in Eastern Europe had irreversibly shifted in favor of Bonn and Washington, D.C., he had come to discern what Fraser has described as a "'selfish,' antisocial motive in Romanticism, one that represents the very antithesis of communal identification."[71] On the one hand, as Mill has reminded us, solely focusing on the public welfare or the greater good can lead to the tyranny of the majority and Rorty's "freezing-over of culture." On the other hand, as we have seen, the romantic impulse to make it new, when unleashed in public, can lead to evitable pain and humiliation. Thus, to take either public welfare or self-creation alone and elevate that single ideal to the status of sole definitive purpose of a liberal community is to invite disaster. One of the most difficult tasks of liberal utopians is to negotiate some sort of modus vivendi for these two liberal impulses, these two ideals of liberal society.

To claim, as Rorty does, that freedom for self-assertion and alleviation of cruelty both deserve equal claim to our allegiance, while at the same time acknowledging that there is a constant tension between the two, is entirely in keeping with a long-standing self-image of liberals as promoters of tolerance and compromise. Like Constant, Rorty can think of no better way to achieve a compromise between equal opportunity and the freedom that makes room for self-making than to distinguish carefully between private and public spheres of life as the spheres of altruism and self-perfection, respectively. As he emphasizes, with reference to his book *CIS*,

> The core of my book is a distinction between private concerns, in the sense of idiosyncratic projects of self-overcoming, and public concerns, those having to do with the suffering of other human beings.[72]

The distinction between public and private concerns, Rorty hastens to add in the same note, is emphatically not "the distinction between the domestic hearth and the public forum, between *oikos* and *polis*."

For Rorty, the private sphere is the space within which idiosyncratic projects of self-overcoming take place, and the public sphere is the realm of shared concerns of the community. For the latter-day Rorty of what Fraser calls the "partition position," it is imperative to keep these two spheres apart. It is not surprising, therefore, that he envisions political institutions that will foster public indifference to such issues as theology and metaphysics, the nature of the self, the nature of God, the point of human existence, and the meaning of life, while putting no restriction on private discussion of them.[73]

These most precious liberal institutions include the institutions we have already mentioned: independent judiciaries, free universities, a free press, and so on.[74] A liberal democracy will not only exempt opinions on such matters as theology, metaphysics, and the meaning of life from legal coercion, but will also aim at disengaging discussions of such questions from discussions of social policy. In this respect, he is indeed a continuator of Jefferson, who, in Rorty's words, held that citizens

> must abandon or modify opinions on matters of ultimate importance, the opinions that may hitherto have given sense and point to their lives, if these opinions entail public actions that cannot be justified to most of their fellow citizens.[75]

Part of the originality of Rorty's position is his use of an antiessentialist vocabulary to defend Jefferson's compromise between an individual's opinions on matters of ultimate importance and her public actions. The best—if not the *only*—way to ensure that the romantic urge for "total revolution" remains unavailable for political exploitation is to ensure that the ideal of noninterference with the self-creation of strong poets will not be the one and only purpose of a community, but to temper it with the ideal of ameliorating suffering. And a good way to check the tyranny of the majority is to promote the freedom that makes room for self-making. It is not surprising, then, that in Rorty's liberal utopia, the optimal political synthesis of love and justice may turn out to be what he has described as "an intricately-textured collage of private narcissism and public pragmatism."[76]

It is, of course, unremarkable for the decent citizen and the strong poet to be combined within one and the same biography: If, as Whitman put it, "I contain multitudes"—many selves, more or less transient and incomplete—we may expect that members of liberal communities typically will comprise both public and private selves. Furthermore, as we have seen, it is possible and desirable to imagine a liberal utopia that would serve both figures. This utopia would place no ideal higher than the pursuit of self-perfection and the amelioration of suffering. Moreover, thanks to the public/private split, there would be no need, within such a utopia, to elevate one of these two ideals above the other.

Despite occasional appearances to the contrary, then, Rorty refuses to define a liberal community—that is, a public in the broadest sense of the word—in terms of one overarching goal (such as, say, the glorification of God, the greatest happiness for the greatest number, or making room for self-making). This reluctance, presumably, is a feature of his "pluralism." Instead, he upholds the idea of a community that strives after both intersubjective agreement and novelty. To strive for intersubjective agreement on the need to ameliorate cruelty is to seek liberal consensus, in Shklar's sense of the word "liberal." To strive for consensus, when it comes to granting every private self unlimited freedom of opportunity to produce novel tropes, is to strive to ameliorate humiliation in the public sphere, while at the same time promoting toleration of humiliation in words, but not in deeds, in the private sphere.

Rorty praises Howe for having taught, during his editorship of *Dissent*, "how one could combine the contemplative and the active lives without trying to synthesize the two."[77] He advocates abandoning the invariably unsuccessful attempt to devise an algorithm for determining from case to case which ideal will prevail. In the utopian future this task of determination will have to take place as it has in the past, by "muddling through" as the need arises, with the institutions and practices at hand. The closest thing to a guideline he proffers is his recommendation that the strong poet not be hindered from striving as much as he likes for self-perfection—as long as he does it on his own time. In an interview, he sloganized this ideal as follows: "Always strive to excel, but only on weekends."[78]

Rorty insists on the radical separation of the public and private spheres. Referring to historicist writers concerned with private perfection and those concerned with promoting more just and free human communities, he writes:

> We shall only think of these two kinds of writers as *opposed* if we think that a more comprehensive philosophical outlook would let us hold self-creation and justice, private perfection and human solidarity, in a single vision.[79]

Rorty, of course, is at the farthest remove from those who have held that the private ideal of self-creation and the public-spirited ideal of greatest happiness for the greatest number are realizations of eternally pregiven potentialities latent in humankind, but only recently released, thanks to the Renaissance, the Reformation, the French Revolution, or the Romantic movement. For him, these and all other ideals, purposes, and goals are historically and culturally specific discursive productions. Since his antiessentialism prohibits him from positing a genuine human essence to be expressed, repressed, or liberated, these goals have no foundation in universal reason. Rorty cannot imagine what a non-question-begging argument in favor of these ideals would be like: They have long been part of a form of life prevailing in the North Atlantic, and as such they are elements of what it is to be *us*. Contemporary inhabitants of liberal democracies would be inclined to dismiss anyone who would deny these ideals—in words, if not in deeds—as irrational, rather than taking them seriously.[80] To deny these ideals—again, in words, but not necessarily in deeds—is just not the way things are done around here.

Moreover, Rorty adds, public debate should not problematize these ideals. If there is one thing one should not allow oneself to be ironic about in public, it is such ideals of justice. To the extent that ironism is the stock-in-trade of the strong poet, this returns us to the injunction to exclude the strong poet from the public square. And, to the extent that the strongest theorists are ironist theorists, Rorty concludes that political theory is not very useful to contemporary liberals.[81]

For the mature Rorty of Fraser's "partition position," all attempts to merge public altruism with private egoism into one all-encompassing theory are either futile or inadvisable or both. The separation of public and private persons, of public altruism and private sublimity, should also be a separation in "theory." In the absence of a universal essence that members of a community share, an essence that can bridge the public/private split, it is futile to try to do justice to these two figures, decent citizen and strong poet, within one integrated theory, or to try, as the stoics and their successors have tried, to combine inward tranquillity and duty to others within one and the same ethical system.

Indeed, the attempt is ill-conceived at the outset. Since, as we have seen, Rorty denies the value of any notion of human nature independent of what our latest vocabularies put in play, there can be no such thing as grounding a human community in a correct view of human nature. If the notions of an intrinsic human nature from which to be alienated and of authentic needs to be fulfilled fall by the wayside, then it is pointless to reproach institutions and practices because they allegedly defy this nature or these needs.[82]

By Rorty's nominalist lights, language amounts to little more than human beings using marks and noises to get what they want. One of the things we human beings want to get with language, in addition to food, shelter, and sex, is an enhanced sense of solidarity with other humans; still another may be to create or enlarge oneself by developing one's own private, autonomous language. The latter two items are distinct purposes, proper to public and private concerns, respectively.

Our concern for negative liberty and self-enlargement is backed up by a picture of the self as a space of self-elaboration which can freely generate new self-interpretations—and hence new ways of being human—by creating new vocabularies, new forms of "abnormal discourse." On the other hand, our community-oriented sense of being "one of us" is backed up by the recognition that abnormal discourse is possible only at the margins, only against a background of normal discourse that defines our shared identity.

These observations have prompted Rorty to conclude that his own antiessentialist vocabulary is more useful to contemporary liberalism than the essentialist rhetoric of natural rights, reason, and so on, which has hitherto been associated with liberalism. As we have seen, it is not very useful to *theorize* liberalism, to ground it in a correct view of human nature; however, it is useful to *articulate* liberalism, to make it attractive to the next generation, not by pretending to ground political practices but by expressing political hopes.

When it is possible to bring together elements of a given discourse under a set of rules that will tell us how rational agreement can be reached on what would settle the issue on every point where statements seem to conflict, Rorty describes these elements, in terminology he borrows from Thomas Kuhn, as *commensurable*. Normal and abnormal discourses are incommensurable. Rorty's claim that the private vocabularies of strong poets and abnormal discoursers are incommensurable with the public vocabularies of decent reformers allows him to deny the necessity of placing one ideal above the other, or claiming that one reduces to the other or logically entails the other.

For this reason, he agrees with Dewey that we should not feel we have to choose between public altruism and private egoism, in the form of the striving for self-creation. In contrast to his best-known liberal predecessor, however, he believes both are satisfactory, as long as laissez-faire and individualism are reserved for the private sphere, and equality, democracy, and solidarity are reserved for the public sphere. Normal discourse, Rorty continues, is discourse in which commensuration works. This happens when both parties to a conversation treat their discursive exchanges in accordance with agreed-upon conventions. Abnormal discourse, by contrast, occurs in periods of transition from one theory to another. In this transitional or "revolutionary" stage, old terms take on unfamiliar meanings and new words are introduced. Public discourse, the discourse of the dutiful citizen, or discourse which is useful for ameliorating suffering, is incommensurable with private discourse, the discourse of the strong poet seeking self-perfection.

To conflate the two sorts of vocabularies is to run together two distinct language games. Rorty illustrates this with reference to Nabakov's disdain for Orwell: The Englishman might or might not have tried and failed to fuse decency with sublimity in his writing. What he is rightly praised for, however—and what appears to have made little impression on Nabakov—was the manner in which he brought our attention to evitable suffering, and in particular, to officially sanctioned humiliation. Similar misunderstandings abound on the other side, too, as when engaged writers condemn their aestheticist colleagues as irresponsible for describing the color of the dying man's lips.[83]

Rorty agrees with Dewey that we should not feel as though we have to choose between either the role of a community-spirited, dutiful public person or a narcissistic private person. Like Dewey, the younger pragmatist rejects the hoary antithesis of the individual and the social. He disagrees with Dewey, however, when it comes to the attempt to break down the distinction between duty to self and duty to others, the private and the public imperatives, respectively. Dewey's attempt, described toward the end of the previous section, is characteristic of a long-standing tradition in social philosophy since Plato, a tradition which sees the *polis* as man writ large.[84] By Rorty's account, however, one of Dewey's illustrious contemporaries showed us how to break with this tradition:

> Freud gave up Plato's attempt to bring together the public and the private, the parts of the state and the parts of the soul, the search for social justice and the search for individual perfection.... He distinguished sharply between a private ethic of self-creation and a public ethic of mutual accommodation. He persuades us that there is no bridge between them provided by universally shared beliefs or desires—beliefs or desires which belong to us qua human and which unite us to our fellow humans simply *as* human.[85]

Pragmatists, in contrast to Plato's heirs, promote the use of both vocabularies of private self-creation and vocabularies of public welfare, without trying to reduce the one to the other. Accordingly, Rorty proposes a division of labor that a sympathetic commentator has described as follows:

DEPARTURES FROM DEWEY

> The scientists, technicians, and engineers, with the exception of those very few who are able to serve as paradigms of self-creation, are accorded the task of easing the pains of social existence; the poet and novelist are to provide new vocabularies which can serve as models of private perfection.[86]

Rorty's assignment of distinct stations and duties to public and private persons allows him to shunt the dutiful citizen and the divine egoist off to separate and incommensurable spheres. In the course of so doing, he boldly redraws the line between altruism and egoism that Dewey tried to efface.

Of course, he does not deny that public and private persons coexist within the same body: One and the same biography may contain the story of a dutiful citizen, concerned with ameliorating pain and humiliation of his fellows, and the story of a strong poet, striving for personal perfection. Moreover, he does not deny that private obsessions occasionally coincide with public needs; on the contrary, he acknowledges that when a private fantasy finds an audience, the result is sometimes great art.[87] Nevertheless, he does deny the assumption that duty to others and duty to self can or should be combined into one multipurpose normative vocabulary, that self-creation and justice can be brought together at the level of philosophical theory.

Rorty agrees with Dewey that there need not be any opposition between duty to self and duty to others, but he differs with his predecessor when it comes to the manner in which he wishes to avert this opposition. As we have seen, the elder pragmatist believed that public education and democratic participation could and should play a decisive role in promoting a broader, more inclusive, and permanent sense of selfhood, and hence a convergence of self-interest with common interests of a larger public. Rorty also wants a more inclusive *ethnos*; nevertheless, he does not challenge the continuity of narrow individualism. He merely urges us to keep the romantic desire for self-creation and "total revolution" out of the public domain, out of politics. He associates those who yearn for revolutionary movements, both political and cultural, with self-surrender and the self-deceptive slogan: "Not my will, but the movement's, be done."[88] Rorty wishes to shunt self-assertion and narcissism to the private sphere, while holding that "we consciousness" is more appropriate to the public sphere. The exceptions—tiny circles of kindred souls involved in the same private projects as we are ourselves—only prove the rule, by virtue of their isolation and elitism.

Rorty also differs from his pragmatist mentor when it comes to their respective conceptions of autonomy. As we have seen, Dewey denied that autonomy is something that all human beings have within them and that society can release by ceasing to repress them. In this sense, then, he is indeed waiting at the end of the road Michel Foucault was treading.[89] Nevertheless, Dewey held that public institutions, notably public schools and democratic institutions, should be viewed as "genuine instruments" for creating individuals with more inclusive common interests, and hence a stronger "we consciousness."

This conviction contrasts sharply with Rorty's. "We consciousness," for the younger pragmatist, is principally a public concern, not a private one.

> If you accept the distinction between the public and the private realms which I draw in *Contingency, Irony, and Solidarity*, then [the question of which kind of human being you want to become] will divide into two subquestions. The first is: with what communities should you identify, of which should you think of yourself as a member? The second is...: what should I do with my aloneness?[90]

Autonomy, the sort of thing some people actually achieve in their aloneness and on their own time, is a private concern, not a public one:

> The sort of autonomy which self-creating ironists like Nietzsche, Derrida, or Foucault seek is not the sort of thing that *could* ever be embodied in social institutions. Autonomy is not something which all human beings have within them and which society can release by ceasing to repress them. It is something which certain particular human beings hope to attain by self-creation, and which a few actually do. The desire to be autonomous is not relevant to the liberal's desire to avoid cruelty and pain—a desire which Foucault shared, even though he was unwilling to express it in those terms.[91]

For Rorty, then, autonomy is *private* autonomy, autonomy synonymous with self-creation. Autonomy is something self-creators in the private sphere seek to achieve, and that some rare individuals actually do achieve. Such rare individuals are the results of incalculable contingencies, accidents, and cosmic rays scrambling neurons. This being the case, public institutions cannot embody autonomy and should not be expected to do so.

Participation in democratic institutions and public life has no special place in Rorty's vision of private perfection, either. And in this respect, too, he differs from Dewey. David Hall has noted that, compared to Dewey,

> Rorty's democratic sentiments (or, at least, his democratic expectations) are seriously qualified. Democracy is the vehicle for the rise in the minimum standards of life—increased freedom and autonomy. But the freedom is a formal freedom, empty in the sense that only a very few will be able to exercise it in a meaning creating and, therefore, meaningful manner. And the autonomy is, for most, a blind autonomy, unguided by a sense of relevance.[92]

For Rorty, as for Hegel and Sidney Hook, democracy, nowadays, is little more than one of the most efficient ways of selecting candidates for government office and conferring legitimacy on them. It should not be surprising, then, that Rorty would describe his democratic utopia, uninspiringly enough, as one in which "the quest for autonomy is impeded as little as possible by social institutions."[93]

༉ ༉ ༉

As we have seen in this chapter, Rorty differs from Dewey when it comes to their respective views on autonomy, liberty, and democracy. These differences have to do with the very different manners in which the two American pragmatists view the relationship between the public and the private. For Dewey, public institutions, notably public education and democratic institutions, are indispensable from the perspective of positive liberty or autonomy, as he used these words. Rorty, on the other hand, has reverted to a classical liberal conception of private autonomy and liberty as exemption from state intervention. Autonomy, for him, does not entail merely a duty to self, but a duty to self that, even at those copacetic moments when it happens to coincide with duty to others, is necessarily *in contrast to others.*

Though Rorty might refuse the neoliberal tag, he—like other contemporary neoliberals, but unlike Dewey—views democracy not as an end in itself, but as a means for securing other ends. In Rorty's case, as we have seen, these ends are amelioration of suffering and making the world safe for strong poets. The alleged fact that Dewey's vision of democratic community advances liberal ideals suffices to legitimize it.

We have noted that Rorty subscribes to the idea that freedom makes room for self-making. But what of the freedom from want and humiliation which is the concern of his decent, dutiful citizen in the public sphere? Thugs and the secret police, obviously, are impediments to this freedom. So are corporate managements that promote "lean production," thereby eliminating the leisure time and energy required for self-creation and autonomy. In the latter case, it is clear that some of Rorty's celebrated "institutions of large market economies" stand in the way of freedom.[94] Rorty recognizes this, of course, but can think of no better remedy than constant adjustment and compromise between state intervention and the market.

He also acknowledges more than once that poverty is an impediment to autonomy. Nevertheless, his stress on the role of one particular liberal institution, the institution of "large market economies," in promoting freedom has prompted one sympathetic commentator to write:

> I wish Rorty had included in his discussion of political theory some reflections upon the relationship between liberal democracies and their economic determinants.... Rorty's failure to treat these issues in any argumentative detail makes his reflections on political life seem somewhat detached. Viewed in the light of his endorsement of the idea that "cruelty is the worst thing we do," his programmatic interests come off as rather thinly urgent at best.[95]

We will return to the question of Rorty's programmatic interest in ameliorating suffering in chapter 4. Before that, however, we should turn our attention to his defense of liberal institutions with reference to the ideal of impeding the quest for autonomy as little as possible. This will be the focus of the next chapter.

NOTES

1. Richard Rorty, *Consequences of Pragmatism* (Minneapolis: University of Minnesota Press, 1982), p. 49 (hereafter cited as *CP*); Richard Rorty, "Relativism: Finding and Making," in *Debating the State of Philosophy: Habermas, Rorty, and Kolakowski,* ed. József Niznik and John T. Sanders (Westport, Conn. and London: Praeger, 1996), p. 32.

2. Rorty, *CP,* pp. 63, 207. Rorty repeats this theme throughout *Achieving Our Country* (Cambridge and London: Harvard University Press, 1998; hereafter cited as *AOC*).

3. Richard Rorty, *Contingency, Irony, and Solidarity* (Cambridge: Cambridge University Press, 1989), p. 63 (hereafter cited as *CIS*); Richard Rorty, "Thugs and Theorists," *Political Theory* 15, no. 4 (November 1987): 567.

4. L. S. Klepp, "Every Man a Philosopher-King: Richard Rorty of the University of Virginia," *New York Times Magazine,* December 2, 1990, p. 122.

5. Richard Rorty, *Essays on Heidegger and Others* (Cambridge: Cambridge University Press, 1991), p. 184 (hereafter cited as *EH*).

6. David L. Hall, *Richard Rorty: Prophet and Poet of the New Pragmatism* (Albany: SUNY Press, 1994), p. 84. Also refer to John Rajchman and Cornel West, eds., *Debating the State of Philosophy: Habermas, Rorty, and Kolakowski* (Westport, Conn., and London: Praeger, 1996), p. xxviii, n. 7. Rorty's interpretation of Dewey may be culled from "Overcoming the Tradition" and "Dewey's Metaphysics," in Rorty, *CP,* pp. 37–59 and 72–89, respectively; "Pragmatism and Post-Nietzschean Philosophy," in Rorty, *EH,* pp. 1–5; and Richard Rorty, "Dewey between Hegel and Darwin," in *Modernism and the Human Sciences,* ed. Dorothy Ross (Baltimore: Johns Hopkins Press, 1994), pp. 54–68, 317–21.

7. Richard Rorty, "Posties," *London Review of Books,* September 3, 1987, p. 12.

8. Jo Burrows, "Conversational Politics: Rorty's Pragmatist Apology for Liberalism," in *Reading Rorty,* ed. Alan Malachowski (Cambridge, Mass.: Basil Blackwell, 1990), p. 327.

9. J. E. Tiles, *Dewey* (London and New York: Routledge, 1988), p. 4. Similarly, Kai Nielsen has noted that "For Dewey (pace Rorty), considerations of

method were central" (Kai Nielsen, *After the Demise of the Tradition: Rorty, Critical Theory, and the Fate of Philosophy* [Boulder: Westview Press, 1991], p. 168).

10. Tiles, *Dewey*, p. 5. The citation within the quoted passage is from Rorty, *CP*, p. xvii. Also consider David Hall's doubts about Rorty's "strong misreading" of Dewey as a hero of antifoundationalism (Hall, *Richard Rorty*, p. 116).

11. John Dewey, *Reconstruction in Philosophy* (Boston: Beacon Press, 1957), p. 187. I subscribe to a very different conception of society, according to which its constituents are not individuals but rather practices of production (refer to Markar Melkonian, *Marxism: A Post–Cold War Primer* [Boulder: Westview Press, 1996], pp. 27–46). To avoid confusion, I will refrain from using the word *society* in the present discussion, except in citations or when the word is bracketed by quotation marks or appears in such terms as "civil society" and "political society," as these are discussed below. The qualifier *social*, as I shall use it in this discussion, should be taken as interchangeable with "collaborative" or "cooperative." This usage is not inconsistent with Dewey's: "In the broad sense any transaction deliberately carried on between two or more persons is social in quality" (John Dewey, *John Dewey: The Later Works, 1925–1927*, vol. 2, ed. Jo Ann Boydston [Carbondale and Edwardsville: Southern Illinois University Press, 1984], p. 244).

12. John Dewey, *Intelligence in the Modern World: John Dewey's Philosophy*, ed. Joseph Ratner (New York: Random House, 1939), p. 382.

13. Dewey, *John Dewey*, pp. 278–79.

14. The discussion in this section draws from Dewey, *John Dewey*, especially the chapter entitled "The Public and Its Problems," pp. 235–372, and from the discussion in Tiles, *Dewey*, pp. 204–27.

15. Dewey, *John Dewey*, p. 289.

16. Ibid., pp. 289–90.

17. Dewey, *Reconstruction in Philosophy*, p. 194. At *CIS*, p. 63 and elsewhere, Rorty reveals his debt to Mead on the topic of selfhood and community (refer to Mitchell Aboulafia, "George Herbert Mead and the Many Voices of Universality," in *Recovering Pragmatism's Voice: The Classical Tradition, Rorty, and the Philosophy of Communication*, ed. Lenore Langsdorf and Andrew R. Smith [Albany: SUNY Press, 1995], pp. 179–94).

18. Refer, for example, to Richard Rorty, *Philosophy and the Mirror of Nature* (Princeton: Princeton University Press, 1979), pp. 9–10 (hereafter cited as *PMN*); Rorty, *CIS*, pp. 57–58.

19. I am not convinced that it is useful to distinguish between true, authentic, or objective interests on the one hand, and false or illusory interests

on the other. At any rate, for purposes of this discussion it will suffice to use the word *interest* in a sense in which the term *perceived interest* is redundant. By this usage, there is no such thing as an interest of which no one is aware. For an alternative view, refer to Raymond Geuss, *The Idea of a Critical Theory: Habermas and the Frankfurt School* (Cambridge: Cambridge University Press, 1981), pp. 45 ff.

20. Dewey, *John Dewey*, p. 251.
21. Ibid., p. 331.
22. Ibid., p. 301.
23. Rorty, *CIS*, p. 48.
24. Dewey, *John Dewey*, pp. 243–44.
25. Ibid., p. 257.
26. Ibid., p. 245.
27. Thomas Jefferson, *The Life and Selected Writings of Thomas Jefferson*, ed. Adrienne Koch and William Peder (New York: Modern Library, 1944), p. 274.
28. Dewey, *John Dewey*, p. 317.
29. Ibid., p. 278.
30. Ibid., p. 253.
31. Ibid., p. 256.
32. George Novack, *Pragmatism versus Marxism: An Appraisal of John Dewey's Philosophy* (New York: Pathfinder Press, 1975), p. 206.
33. Dewey, *John Dewey*, p. 350.
34. Ibid., p. 256.
35. Ibid., p. 302.
36. John Stuart Mill, *On Liberty* (New York: Penguin, 1987), p. 71.
37. Thomas Hobbes, *Leviathan* (London and New York: Penguin, 1985), p. 271.
38. John Locke, "A Letter Concering Toleration," in *Treatise of Civil Government and a Letter Concerning Toleration* (New York: Irvington Publishers, Inc., 1979), p. 172.
39. Mill, *On Liberty*, p. 68.
40. Jefferson, *Life and Selected Writings*, p. 323.
41. Dewey, *Intelligence in the Modern World*, p. 379.
42. Locke, "A Letter Concerning Toleration," p. 219.
43. Dewey, *John Dewey*, p. 329.
44. Ibid., p. 325.
45. Ibid., p. 328.

46. Refer to the discussion in ibid., pp. 282–304.
47. Dewey, *Reconstruction in Philosophy*, p. 188.
48. Dewey, *John Dewey*, pp. 279–80.
49. Tiles, *Dewey*, p. 223.
50. Dewey, *John Dewey*, pp. 289–90.
51. Tiles, *Dewey*, p. 219.
52. Richard Rorty, "The Priority of Democracy to Philosophy," in Malachowski, *Reading Rorty*, p. 294.
53. Mill, *On Liberty*, p. 68.
54. Richard Rorty, "Habermas, Derrida, and the Functions of Philosophy" (unpublished), p. 17.
55. Rorty, *EH*, pp. 127–28. The attribution of this aim to Marx is disputable. Admittedly, however, some Marxists have seen "their own inner transformation as auguring the transformation of the human world" (ibid., p. 137).
56. Rorty, *CIS*, p. 120.
57. Bernard Yack, *The Longing for Total Revolution: Philosophic Sources of Social Discontent from Rousseau to Marx and Nietzsche* (Princeton: Princeton University Press, 1986), p. 25.
58. Rorty, *CIS*, p. 120. It is worth noting that on at least one occasion Rorty has appeared willing to concede that Marxism, like Foucauldianism, might still retain some usefulness as a private vocabulary, as a way of tracing "the blind impresses our behavings bear" (refer to Richard Rorty, "Review of Jacques Derrida's *Specters of Marx: The State of the Debt, the Work of Mourning, and the New International*" [unpublished], p. 13).
59. Nancy L. Rosenblum, *Another Liberalism: Romanticism and the Reconstruction of Liberal Thought* (Cambridge, Mass. and London: Harvard University Press, 1997), p. 25. Other liberals, however, have opposed romanticism to liberalism (refer, for example, to Karl Popper, *The Open Society and Its Enemies*, vol. 1 [Princeton, Princeton University Press, 1963], p. 168).
60. Refer, for example, to Rorty, *CIS*, pp. 66, 157; and Richard Rorty, "The End of Leninism and History as Comic Frame" (unpublished), p. 2.
61. Nancy Fraser, "Solidarity or Singularity?" in Malachowski, *Reading Rorty*, p. 320 n. 5.
62. Rorty, *CIS*, p. 41.
63. Ibid., pp. 60–61.
64. Ibid., pp. xv, 65.
65. Rorty, *EH*, p. 48.

66. Fraser, "Solidarity or Singularity?" p. 304–305.

67. As when he states: "To sum up, poetic, artistic, philosophical, scientific, or political progress results from the accidental coincidence of a private obsession with a public need" (Rorty, *CIS*, p. 37).

68. Richard Rorty, *Objectivity, Relativism, and Truth* (Cambridge: Cambridge University Press, 1991), p. 62.

69. Editorial. "Post-Communist Press," *The Wall Street Journal*, November 26, 1993, p. A8. Also see: *"Decommunization" Measures Violate Freedom of Expression and Due Process Standards,* Human Rights Watch seventeen-page report on the Czech Republic (April 1992). With reference to the persecution of Gypsies under the Havel regime, refer to *Czechoslovakia's Endangered Gypsies* (Human Rights Watch, August 1992).

70. Rorty, *CP,* p. 66.

71. Fraser, "Solidarity or Singularity?" p. 309.

72. Rorty, "Habermas, Derrida, and the Functions of Philosophy," p. 1 n.1.

73. Rorty, *ORT,* p. 182 n.

74. Refer to n. 3, above.

75. Rorty, *ORT,* p. 175. It is interesting to note that Rorty left his last philosophy department in 1983 to become Kenan Professor of Humanities at the University of Virginia in Charlottesville—Jefferson's "bantling of forty years' growth and nursing" (Jefferson, *Life and Selected Writings,* p. xlii), and the first North American university free from official church recognition.

76. Rorty, *ORT,* p. 210.

77. Richard Rorty, "Movements and Campaigns" (unpublished), p. 7.

78. Quoted in Klepp, "Every Man a Philosopher-King," p. 122.

79. Rorty, *CIS,* p. xiv.

80. Richard Rorty, "Solidarity or Objectivity," in *Post-Analytic Philosophy,* ed. John Rajchman and Cornel West (New York: Columbia University Press, 1985), p. 12.

81. Refer, for example, to Rorty, "The Priority of Democracy to Philosophy," pp. 279–302; Rorty, "The End of Leninism"; Rorty, "Movements and Campaigns"; and Rorty, *AOC.*

82. Rorty, "The Priority of Democracy to Philosophy," pp. 282–83.

83. Rorty's discussion of Nabakov and Orwell, entitled "The Last Intellectual in Europe: Orwell on Cruelty," appears in Rorty, *CIS,* pp. 169–88. Ruskin's image of the dying man's lips appears in Rosenblum, *Another Liberalism,* p. 98.

84. Robert Westbrook has criticized Rorty for ignoring the communitarian side of Dewey and overemphasizing "negative liberty" (Robert Westbrook, *John Dewey and American Democracy* [Ithaca, N.Y.: Cornell University Press, 1984], pp. 541–42). With reference to Westbrook's claim that Dewey believed, as Rorty does not, that "the springs of private fulfillment and of human solidarity are the same," Rorty states parenthetically: "I am not sure whether or not Dewey thought this and would urge that there is a lot of evidence on both sides" (Rorty, "Dewey between Hegel and Darwin," p. 320 n. 43); cf. Rorty, *AOC*, p. 149 n. 15).

85. Rorty, *CIS*, pp. 33–34.

86. Hall, *Richard Rorty*, p 121.

87. Rorty, *CIS*, p. 37.

88. Rorty, "Movements and Campaigns," p. 8. The citation is from an approving discussion of Irving Howe's alleged repudiation of "movement politics." (See also Rorty, *AOC*, p. 124.) Rorty appears to be unaware that, though Howe disparaged the Black Power movement and the New Left, he came to embrace one especially brutal messianic-redemptive movement all the more enthusiastically. Zionism, both as a body of doctrine and as a colonial settler project, epitomizes "movement politics" and the sort of yearning Yack disparages. To acknowledge the Zionist predilections of Howe and other contributors to *Dissent* is to cast doubt on Rorty's characterization of them and on the motives he imputes to their selective denunciations of some political movements.

89. Rorty, *CP*, p. xviii; Rorty, *EH*, p. 207.

90. Rorty, *ORT*, p. 13.

91. Rorty, *CIS*, p. 65. Cf. Yack, *The Longing for Total Revolution*, p. 365.

92. Hall, *Richard Rorty*, p. 37.

93. Rorty, "Habermas, Derrida, and the Functions of Philosophy," p. 4. More recently, Rorty writes that "Even someone like myself, whose admiration for John Dewey is almost unlimited, cannot take seriously his defense of participatory democracy against Walter Lippmann's insistence on the need for expertise" (Rorty, *AOC*, p. 104).

94. Recent figures from the Bureau of Labor Statistics bear out United States Labor Secretary Robert B. Reich's view that U.S. workers, struggling to maintain their standard of living in the face of declining wages, are working longer hours at more jobs to make ends meet (cf. "Employees Get a Real Workout," *Los Angeles Times*, September 4, 1992, pp. 1, A22).

95. Hall, *Richard Rorty*, p. 113.

CHAPTER THREE
FREEDOM AND LIBERALISM IN PRACTICE

One of the most common representations of modern states—a representation that has gained even more force since the proclaimed end of the cold war—depicts political power chafing at an external limit posed by the private sphere. As I indicated in the previous chapter, Rorty subscribes to this conventional model of the relationship between the private sphere and political authority. This is most evident when, as we have seen, he celebrates existing liberal democracies as setups which "leave people alone, to let them try out their private visions of perfection in peace."[1]

This conventional model may have been an accurate picture of the relationship between the private sphere and political authority in Eastern Europe in the final years of the cold war; however, I will argue in this chapter that it is not an accurate representation of the state of affairs in the rich North Atlantic. In the latter case, as the sanctity of the private sphere has been proclaimed ever more vociferously, the scope of surveillance, regulation, and control by agencies of political authority has become ever more efficient and has extended ever further into the private sphere.

One account of the latter development immediately presents itself: The accessibility of private life to surveillance and control by state agencies requires a relatively high level of development of information collection, retrieval, and management, a level that is attainable only at a relatively advanced stage of technological development and centralization of economic practices. A medieval king in his castle cannot make decisions about how his peasant subjects will live when he has no way of even knowing how many subjects he has, or where they live, let alone their birth and death rates and levels of productivity. As Marx pointed out, it is capitalism that first develops the forces and relations of production in ways that make a high degree of centralized control possible. Since Poland or Russia, with their "precapitalist" economies, lacked much of "the power that modern technology makes available to thugs,"[2] it is unsurprising that regimes there would not have been able to mount the sort of massive invasions and manipulations that are standard operating procedure in, say, Germany, Japan, and the United States.

This account, of course, has more than an element of truth to it. Certainly, simple access to the technical means of surveillance and manipulation will go a long way in accounting for the greater scope of authoritarian control in, say, Pakistan—formerly a U.S. cold war ally that, until the end of the Najibullah regime in Kabul, was a beneficiary of relatively unimpeded computer technology transfers—as compared with Pakistan's erstwhile "nonaligned" neighbor to the east.

A narrowly technological account of the expansion of state control, however, ignores problems that should not be ignored. For one thing, by portraying innovations in the technologies of surveillance and control as more or less unilaterally determining the scope of state intervention, we risk understating the role of state institutions in promoting or squelching the large-scale deployment of certain technologies. In a state such as the former Soviet Union, for example—where guards were posted at fax machines, where telephone directories were classified secrets, and where mimeograph machines, photocopiers, and even typewriters were required to be registered with one or another ministry—it is not surprising that the productivity of labor would have fallen far below that of the advanced capitalist economies, and that citizens would be deprived of consumer goods and services available to many people in the West.

Aside from the devastation of the Second World War, there were at least three reasons for the lack of development and widespread application of these new technologies in the Soviet Union: (a) a technology and trade embargo enforced by the West deprived the Soviet Union of credit, foreign capital and labor and consumer markets, and of the opportunity to emulate Japan, the Six Tigers of the Pacific Rim, or China, whose nascent high-tech industries have relied in large part on copying foreign designs; (b) a constant push to increase the productivity of labor through automation would only have made it harder to maintain the charade of constitutionally guaranteed full employment; and (c) new technologies, notably telecommunications and computers, fueled the official fear of the dissident press, the *samizdat*, the audience for which was burgeoning—thanks in large part to high literacy rates, state subsidization of intellectuals on a scale unknown in the West, and what, paraphrasing Nabakov, we might call capitalist propaganda, disseminated through Radio Liberty, the Voice of America, black-marketed videocassettes, and so on.[3]

The officially imposed fetters on the productivity of labor had a predictably disastrous impact on the All-Union economy. Ironically, what happened in the first workers' state was exactly what Marx expected would happen when dominant relations of production persistently retard the development of the productive forces.

In the rich North Atlantic, by contrast, the story has been very different. There, the rhetorical apotheosis of the private sphere has proceeded in lockstep with increased surveillance, manipulation, and control by institutions both public and private in that very same sphere. In the democracies of this region, we have witnessed an expansion of regulation in almost all aspects of life, while at the same time odes to the inviolable private sphere have become louder and found an ever larger audience.

This strikes me as remarkable, and in need of a sort of explanation that the narrowly technological approach cannot provide. In considering how it is that these two trends have taken place, surely we ought to consider whether, and if so in what manner, the degree of violability of the private sphere on the one hand and the efficiency of political authority on the other hand are related by more than just the common preconditions provided by development of the instruments of production, narrowly conceived along technocratic lines. This is the problem to be broached in the balance of this chapter. It will be helpful to begin by examining at closer quarters representations of the triumph of the inviolable private sphere.

DEPICTING THE APOLITICAL PRIVATE SPHERE

In an oft-cited article, Francis Fukayama suggested that we "might" have reached the end of history: Western liberal democracy, lately universalized on the stage of world history, is to be "the final form of human government," while in the domain of the economy (which evidently has to do with little more than the selection and consumption of commodities that inexplicably pop up on display shelves and showroom floors), "easy access to VCRs and stereos" is the actualized ideal of the universal homogeneous state.[4] For Fukayama, then, economic liberalism amounts essentially to the satisfaction of ever more sophisticated consumer demands by a market which is free, presumably in the sense that buying and selling, investment, hiring, and resource allocation decisions are largely in private hands.[5] Accordingly, when control and ownership of the means of production are wrested from the state and returned to private hands, the absolutely free will has taken a stride forward in its career of self-actualization.

Similar paeans to the private sphere have been voiced by contemporary figures who might be thought to have little in common with Fukayama. Rorty, for example, approvingly quotes Milan Kundera's announcement that what is most precious about European culture is "...its respect for the individual, for his original thought, and for his right to an inviolable private life."[6] The hallmark of Kundera's "European spirit of freedom," we are told, is the sanctity of a sphere of conscience, a private sphere protected against incursions by the state.

These paeans have not been limited to the usual anti-Communist millenarians of the New World Order, either. In his address to the 1989 congress of the Communist Party of Great Britain, Martin Jacques, editor of *Marxism Today*, suggested that in both the East and the West, "We live in a society which is increasingly driven by civil society rather than the state."[7] As evidence for this development he invites us to "Think of the enormous membership of environmental groups, or the range of cultural activity, or the massively enhanced role of the media." This postwar development has been a source of crisis for the left, says Jacques, because leftists have always seen the state as the centerpiece of political change. However, if the state at one time used to represent politics in a concentrated form, it should no longer be seen like that: Power has shifted from the state to civil society. According to this picture, then, it would seem that civil society, whatever else it may be, is a pluralistic domain of political power that, at least for the most part, lies somewhere safely beyond the reach of the state.

In order to execute its constitutionally mandated function of preserving the peace and securing property, even Mill, as we have seen, conceded that government must periodically make limited forays into the private sphere. For the sake of preserving freedom, however, these forays must be checked by a vigilant public, a free press, free universities, an independent judiciary, and other agencies independent of the government.

A recent émigré writer restated the conventional paradigm well when he claimed that the distinction between the public and private spheres is determined by "the actual intrusion of the state or other organizations into the activity of groups and individuals."[8] In the case of "authoritarian societies like the Soviet Union in which the state controls all major spheres of social life," the distinction between the public and private spheres lies in "the degree of individual autonomy from government interference." Thus, in both the authoritarian East and the liberal democracies of the West, activities that belong to the private sphere—which include a person's choice of occupation and place of work, marriage partner, religious convictions, and consumption habits—are distinguished from public activities in that the former enjoy a larger degree of independence from intervention by the state and "other organizations."

It is evident, then, that the conventional paradigm admits degrees of privateness: The circle of family and friends, for example, is held to be more private by virtue of being less intruded upon by other institutions, governmental or otherwise, than the sphere of such voluntary associations as, say, chambers of commerce, unions, and sports clubs. The distinction between public and private, then, is not absolute: The picture of a continuum is more appropriate in the application of this paradigm to social analysis.

According to this paradigm,

> With an aggressive state like Stalin's or Mao's, private life in a society can be reduced to almost zero, with family and other small groups almost completely exposed to the regular intervention of state agencies, usually the political police.[9]

In the liberal democracies of the West, by contrast, there is supposedly less intervention by state agencies in individuals' activities, family and friends, and voluntary associations.

In the vocabulary of this paradigm, when the government or the state supposedly divests itself of whole domains that it had previously controlled or supervised directly, it is said that *privatization* has taken place. The degree of privatization that has taken place is "a leading indicator of dynamics in democratic and nondemocratic societies."[10] In view of how widespread this paradigm is, it is not surprising that the decisions of central authorities to privatize the Russian and Chinese economies have been hailed by some as the dawn of a new era of democracy, while the same sources have denounced popular victories in Guatemala, Chile, and Nicaragua as totalitarian when they have involved the nationalization of foreign-owned corporate holdings.[11]

As already noted, and as should become even clearer below, Rorty subscribes to this picture of the relationship between the private sphere and governmental institutions in the liberal democracies. I will argue, by contrast, that private individuals, as well as "primary" and "secondary" groups, in the rich North Atlantic democracies are controlled and defined to an unprecedented extent by dominant political forces that project power far beyond the institutions of the state proper.

The notion of privacy as a distinct right originated in English and colonial American opposition to arbitrary police intrusion and search and seizure. Louis Brandeis notwithstanding, no such right is mentioned in the U.S. Constitution. Nevertheless, according to a common assumption which contrasts sharply to the view I defend, the legal right to privacy, like the right to property, is a natural relation that has finally come to be respected and protected by the liberal democratic state. In this regard, we may refer to an exemplary "expert opinion" which appears in an anthology published by a prestigious university press:

> One basic finding of animal studies is that virtually all animals seek periods of individual seclusion or small-group intimacy. This is usually described as the tendency toward territoriality, in which an organism lays private claim to an area of land, water or air and defends it against intrusion by members of its own species.[12]

The author proceeds to expatiate about meadow pipits, three-spined sticklebacks, and the long-suffering laboratory rat. Then the cultural anthropologists are trotted out on cue to testify to the universal need for privacy among the Tikopia, the Tlingit, and the Tuareg. Thus, in the figure of the savage we discover once again the requisite link between nature and civilization.

The author of this passage has given academic imprimatur to a pervasive prejudice that Karl Marx excoriated a century and a half ago. Referring to the political revolution that resulted in the foundation of the secular democratic republics of his day, the twenty-five-year-old Marx wrote:

> Its attitude to civil society, to the world of need, to work, to private interests, private law is that they are the foundation of its existence, its own presupposition that needs no further proof, and thus its natural basis.[13]

As recent interpreters of "animal studies" confirm, it is still a widely held belief today that natural man is the precondition for civil society, which in turn is the basis of the bourgeois state. Today, as in 1843, we are invited to draw the conclusion that bourgeois social relations and the relations of domination that they inscribe are as immutable as the natural order.

One need do little more than state these assumptions explicitly in order to cast doubt on them. It is tempting to suspect, for example, that the whole history of our species has been retrospectively reconstructed to conform to a historically contingent contemporary prejudice.

One would expect Rorty, the historical nominalist, to support Marx's view. After writing—perhaps with some degree of naiveté—that "There is not, in fact, much naiveté left these days," he adds: "Tell a sophomore at an American college that something is only a social construct, and she is likely to reply 'Yeah, I know. So are you, Mac.' "[14] Since Rorty views humanity as a product of luck and chance, presumably he views the public/private split, as it is institutionalized in the liberal West today, the same way. When he is explicit about the contingency of the self and community, he does sound like one of what he has called the "historicist, including Marxist, critics of 'liberal individualism.'"[15] At crucial junctures, however, he occasionally writes as though he has slipped back into the view Marx criticized. This is apparent, for example, when, as we saw in the previous chapter, he reinstates the egoistic private person alongside the altruistic decent citizen as perennial and ineradicable members of any remotely attractive polity (any polity, that is to say, that is conducive to Rawls's two principles of justice).[16] It is also apparent, though perhaps less obviously so, in his approval of what Berlin and Kundera have referred to as the inviolable private sphere.

Whether or not we reject the assumption that the private sphere was ordained by nature, however, we are still confronted with the impression that, in the modern period at least, it certainly appears to be ineradicable. After all, it has reasserted itself time and again, with almost irresistible tenacity, both in contemporary reality and in the works of the great dead modern political thinkers in the West, from Hobbes and Locke to Constant, Tocqueville, the Mills, and Dewey.

One reason Hegel has attracted renewed attention from liberal thinkers such as Fukayama might be that, while he acknowledged the historical specificity of the private sphere, he also emphasized the inevitability of its appearance. Hegel also provides insights into the relationship between the notions of the private sphere and civil society, and between the latter and political institutions. In his *Philosophy of Right*, the author contrasted "the family," as the embodiment of abstract particularity, to *burgerlich Gesellschaft*, conceived as a "system of needs." Within civil society, that welter of particular wills, some persons recognize that their particular interests are consonant with the interests of others. On the basis of this recognition of common interests, an association is formed that resembles Dewey's Great Community.

What Hegel calls the *political state*, as an "objective organization" distinct from civil society, presents itself to the immediate observer in the form of specialized public institutions and arrangements that typically are subsidized through "public funds," chiefly in the form of tax revenue. In contemporary terms, a system of such institutions is composed of a wide variety of institutions, including: the head of state; the legislature; the administration (which now extends far beyond the traditional bureaucracy of the state to take in a large variety of ministries, committees and other bodies such as central banks, policy planning groups and regulatory commissions); the judiciary; subcentral, regional, prefectural and municipal governments; the military, police, courts, and penal systems; and such ancillary setups as postal services, social services and welfare bureaucracies, public school systems, and so on.

The public sphere is sometimes thought of as encompassing the state, conceived as the sum total of these institutions in their specific global organization and interaction, plus all other social institutions not included in the private sphere. Returning to Dewey's advice encountered in chapter 1, it might not be worth the trouble to attempt to draw a more precise line between public and private spheres, before examining particular historical circumstances. In any case, we need not attempt to do so for present purposes. (For present purposes, we also need not examine the otherwise momentous transmogrification of state institutions, as both a consequence and a contributing causal factor in a number of interrelated processes we may abbreviate here with the word *globalism.*)

Now that we have at least the rough contours of the "political state" in view, we are in a position to compare the preceding sketch of the private sphere as a refuge from political authority to an alternative description of the relationship between the system of state institutions we have identified and the private sphere. My aim in the next section is to present, in as brief a space as possible, some key terms of an alternative vocabulary for conceptualizing this relationship.

STATE POWER AND THE PRIVATE SPHERE

Let us begin with an underacknowledged but empirically verifiable observation: In the countries of the rich North Atlantic, among other places, a large part of the social surplus is systematically appropriated by owners and controllers of means of production who themselves are not producers. In a Marxist sense of the term, then, these communities are *class-divided*.[17]

This would not appear to be a terribly difficult position to defend, particularly in view of the enormous and increasing gap between rich and poor, both globally and within the richest countries themselves. The UN Human Rights Development Committee released a report in early June 1997 that concluded that, despite fifty years of phenomenal economic growth, the gap between haves and have-nots has also grown. Not only is one-quarter of the earth's human population living in "severe poverty," but, according to the report, the gap between rich and poor in the most highly industrialized countries is wider than it has been since the 1930s. In the last quarter of the twentieth century, the North Atlantic countries have witnessed burgeoning gross domestic products, record-high corporate profits, skyrocketing stocks and bonds markets, gigantic mergers, and eight-digit salaries for top CEOs. They have also witnessed feverish "downsizing," massive capital flight in search of cheap labor markets, escalating antiunion campaigns, slipping wages, and slumping living standards for the working population.

Even the "press of record" in the United States has acknowledged the latter trends, however infrequently and grudgingly. According to a series on downsizing that appeared in the *New York Times* in March 1966, for example, the percentage change in real income for four-fifths of the U.S. population from 1990 to 1994 was between −1 and −5 percent, while the top 5 percent registered a 15 percent rise. Annual median family income, adjusted for inflation in 1994 dollars, decreased from 1990 to 1993, and only slightly rebounded in 1994 to approximately the 1992 level. Assuming a positive correlation of consumption and income levels, and assuming furthermore that consumption levels play an important role in the determination of living standards, these figures confirm that living standards for a large part of the United States are indeed slipping, and that the enormous gap between rich and poor in America is growing.[18] Clearly, these trends are instances and effects of well-organized and invigorated corporate capitalist forces wresting concessions and higher rates of exploitation from disorganized and demoralized workers.

In view of these trends, the fact that Rorty has only rarely acknowledged the class-divided character of existing liberal democracies should count as something of a virtuoso feat of insouciance. For him, it seems, wage earners must explicitly identify themselves as a class in order to count as a class at all. This interpretation is consistent with the Deweyan view mentioned in chapter 2. According to this view, we should recall, a group of wage earners who lack a commonly accepted ends-in-view embodied in distinct institutions could constitute at best only a potential or inchoate public. Viewed in this light, the only properly identifiable class that exists in the rich North Atlantic is "the business community," or the monopoly capitalist class, with its multitude of active trade agreements, regulatory commissions, business associations, lobbies, cartels, government connections, research and policy-planning institutes, interlocking directorates, and so on. Regardless of how class-conscious, well-organized, and compact capitalists are—or, more accurately, *because* of this—and regardless of aggravated social divisions, there can be no struggle between classes as long as wage earners remain disorganized, fragmented, and confused. So, for example, when Rorty discusses liberalism as "the attempt to fulfill the hopes of the North Atlantic bourgeoisie,"[19] there is no suggestion that these attempts are tied up with the exploitation of workers, class conflict at home, or imperialism internationally. By Rorty's lights, the qualifier *bourgeois* in the term *bourgeois liberalism* designates little more than unspecified "historical, and especially economic, conditions."

This helps to explain how, despite formidable evidence of class divisions and antagonisms in the rich North Atlantic,[20] Rorty has suggested that talk of class divisions is "clumsy" or otherwise not worth the trouble.[21] Indeed, if one is committed at the outset to defending the proposition that in liberal communities there is a "harmonization of diverse impulses into common purposes," then talk of exploitation, class conflict, and state power may well be *worse* than clumsy. When he has anything to say about class struggle at all, he typically speaks of it as a thing of the past. At one point, for example, he likens what he takes to be "nostalgia" for the class struggle to nostalgia for *les rois faineants*, idle kings.[22]

Once we problematize Rorty's assumption of harmony among diverse impulses, however, a dark shadow begins to fall over his liberal vision. For one thing, assuming that most workers have not chosen to be exploited, his Deweyan picture of a liberal community composed of a multitude of voluntary associations united by common ends-in-view begins to appear either far-fetched or trivial, depending on what one wishes to mean by the adjective *voluntary*.

In his justly influential essay, "Ideology and Ideological State Apparatuses,"[23] Louis Althusser has noted that the institutions that make up the state operate, in large part, by violence or the threat of violence, however attenuated or symbolic the threat may be. Althusser has advanced the following description of the state from a perspective of its coercive function:

> The state is a "machine" of repression, which enables the ruling classes . . . to ensure their domination over the working class, thus enabling the former to subject the latter to the process of surplus-value extortion (i.e., to capitalist exploitation).[24]

This emphasis on the coercive character of the state has a long pedigree in anarchist literature, as well as such Marxist classics as the *Communist Manifesto*, the *Eighteenth Brumaire*, and *Class Struggles in France*, and *Lenin's State and Revolution*. Even "mainstream" political theorists come close to certifying the state as a constellation of repressive apparatuses when they represent it as monopolizing legitimate violence.

Althusser's formulation, as general as it is, would of course have to be reformulated in an even more general way to cover most noncapitalist states. A broader formulation from the same functional perspective might be stated as follows: *A state enables at least one class, the appropriating class or classes, to subject other classes to one or more forms of appropriation, which tend to increase the appropriating class or classes' share of the surplus product or its value relative to other social groups.* This process of subjection takes the form of coercion, both with respect to internal discipline, censorship, and so on within a given institution, as well as coercion projected outward, beyond the institution itself.

The institutions of the "political state" mentioned above play a role in maintaining or extending class domination by enabling one or more classes to subject other classes to extortion of the social surplus. When particular classes are able, thanks in large part to the state, to appropriate a relatively large share of the social surplus, those classes may be described as *ruling classes*. By virtue of its relationship to the state as a whole,[25] a ruling class may be said, metaphorically, to "wield" *state power*. Accordingly, state power may be thought of as a special case of political power: It is the power of one or more classes exercised over other social groups through the state as a whole. James Madison alluded to this political function of the state when he argued at the Constitutional Convention that the proper aim of government is to protect "the minority of the opulent" against the majority.

Of course, the individual agents whose actions directly secure the dominance of a given class typically have remained unaware of their role, and are not even for the most part members of a ruling class. This is confirmed by the drama that workers play out hour by hour, day by day, in the capitalist West, and it was especially poignant in the case of Polish workers, who enthusiastically sacrificed much in the early years of Lech Walesa's tenure to bring to power a capitalist regime that has rewarded them with lower wages, job insecurity, and the dismantling of social programs taken for granted in the past.

When state institutions on the whole have ensured social relations conducive to more than one mode of appropriating the surplus, we may speak of a *ruling class alliance*. Slaveholding planters and northern industrial capitalists, for example, formed a precarious ruling class alliance in the antebellum United States. Moreover, certain social strata and factions often may ally themselves with a given class alliance. In the years leading up to the Civil War, for example, church leaders, publishers, and other professional intellectuals in the North allied themselves ever more closely with the northern industrialists. These considerations complicate the picture, but they do not change the fact that there are ruling classes and subaltern classes.[26]

State institutions often survive transferal of state power to incipient class forces. This observation, needless to say, does not apply solely to the postal system and elevator inspectors. One may readily discern this point by considering the continuity of a large part of the bureaucratic and military machinery of the former Soviet state in the wake of Yeltsin's fall 1991 countercoup and the final, full disenfranchisement of Russian workers under Yeltsin's tenure.

Nevertheless, in order to extend their own organization and to hamstring incumbent ruling alliances, newly ascendant class forces have frequently been pushed to restructure, dismantle, gut, and destroy old state institutions and create new ones in their own image.[27] I take it the point is obvious enough to allow us to forego historical illustrations: When a new class alliance achieves state power, it does not as a rule simply take over the helm of a preexisting state that remains the neutral terrain of class struggle.

It is also important to note here that individual state institutions are themselves sites of class struggle, however unequal that struggle may be. It might suffice as an illustration of this point to consider that in the final hours of waning class rule, even the ranks of the praetorian guards may split, part of them going over to the side of the insurgency. Moreover, in less tumultuous times, representatives of subaltern classes may capture positions in municipal, regional, and national legislatures, governments, and ministries. Indeed, we have witnessed instances—most recently in Japan, Brazil, Italy, India, and National Assembly elections in France—in which representatives of normally militant working class organizations have occupied the highest legislative and executive offices in nonrevolutionary periods of governmental or parliamentary crisis.

The fact that a ruling class does not monolithically dominate every institution of a modern state, however, does not imply that its political power is any less effective or emphatic. For one thing, as we have already emphasized, state power, though exercised in large part through state institutions, is not confined to those institutions. One might com-

FREEDOM AND LIBERALISM IN PRACTICE

pare here the discipline enforced within the ranks of a police department to the violence the police force projects beyond its own ranks. Key institutions of the modern state have projected state power ever further, over an ever wider array of nonstate institutions, including "private enterprise," the church, and the family.

It is important to recognize, moreover, that extending the power of a ruling class is not exclusively the function of state institutions. Many nonstate institutions, both public and private, also mediate conflicts among ruling class elements and enhance their coordination, compactness, and agility, while thwarting, hamstringing, and fragmenting subaltern classes and strata. Obvious examples in the latter category may include such "private" economic associations as chambers of commerce, cartels, interlocking directorates, and international lending institutions.

As I have already indicated, and as should be clear in any case, violence and repression are not the only forms that political domination takes. As Gramsci has emphasized, even the most repressive ruling class would not be able to maintain the social order for long if it were to rely solely on violence and the threat of violence. Without securing at least some degree of consent from subaltern groups, class rule cannot be maintained. To gain a more panoramic view of political power and class rule, we need to cast a glance, however briefly, at some of the noncoercive institutions and practices that have assumed great importance in the contemporary West.

Gramsci proposed an alternative conception of the state,

> which is usually thought of as political society—i.e., a dictatorship or some other coercive apparatus used to control the masses in conformity with a given type of production and economy—and not as a balance between political society and civil society, by which I mean the hegemony of one social group over the entire nation, exercised through so-called private organizations like the Church, trade unions, or schools.[28]

Elaborating on this train of thought, Althusser has provided a vivid picture of the role of a wide variety of institutions in the reproduction of the social order. He has noted that such institutions as spectator sports, churches, and even the family—forms of association which in the secular North Atlantic are represented as paradigmatically distinct from the state—have in fact played a crucial role in the reproduction of the skills of labor power and labor power's subjection to the established order.[29]

With reference to the complex and variegated contemporary states of the North Atlantic, then, it does not appear to be possible to distinguish between state and nonstate institutions solely on the basis of the function of ensuring the reproduction of prevailing relations of production. Aside from the many seamless connections between the state and "private enterprise," another reason for this difficulty is that, as noted, individual state institutions are themselves strategic positions in the class struggle, positions that have been contested and captured by opposing class forces even when state power and the class character of the state as a whole has not faced a serious challenge.

The observation that there is no hard-and-fast line of demarcation between the modern state and nonstate institutions is instructive when it comes to evaluating the conventional paradigm of the relationship between the private sphere and the state. As Gramsci has noted and Althusser has repeated,[30] the state itself is the precondition of any distinction between the public and the private. The distinction between the public and private spheres is, among other things, a distinction between categories of bourgeois law within what Marx metaphorically referred to as the *superstructure*. It is a distinction, moreover, which is an effect of political power—which in turn is always, at least to some extent, contested. In this regard, one might consider the early clashes of the bourgeoisie with the ancien régime around demands for the separation of church and state, protection of personal property rights, habeas corpus, and probable cause. Or one might consider later struggles over public education, labor legislation, regulation of industry and banks, antitrust laws, and civil rights legislation.

We should keep in mind that the distinction between categories of bourgeois law does not have an immaterial, ideal existence. On the contrary, beyond the material embodiments of this legal distinction—in legislation and case law, in public school curricula, architecture, and urban design, in the institutional practices and normalization techniques that Foucault describes in *Discipline and Punish*, in the actual discourses of biologically and socially formed subjects—there is nothing else to point to, outside the realm of theology and idealist metaphysics, as an instantiation of the public/private split.

The diremption of public and private spheres accompanied (but of course does not neatly correspond to) the progressive separation of the state from the economy in the transition from feudalism to capitalism in parts of Europe.[31] Peasants were forced into the cities as land was capitalized; political power was centralized as it shifted from the countryside to the city; labor markets developed; the guilds were transformed; constitutional rights and obligations replaced traditional allegiances; the individual's conscience replaced priests and confessors; and simultaneously the private sphere evolved as a legal category.

In the rich North Atlantic, at least, the public/private distinction is not a horizontal partition of a community into a lower private realm and a higher public realm; rather, it is present at the "individual" and "primary group" levels, just as much as at the level of the judiciary and the legislature.[32] Indeed, as Althusser and others have argued, the public/private split is a component of individuality itself: One and the same individual human being is both legal subject, accountable to the law, and private subject, accountable to her creator, her conscience, and the market. Unions, chambers of commerce, sports clubs, fraternal associations, schools, churches, and political parties—each of these voluntary associations exists by virtue of constituting or reproducing individual humans as subjects, that is, by constituting or reproducing a given mode of subjectivity or selfhood—either as mother or father, union member, alumnus, religious believer, or something else. In the absence of religious believers, of performers of certain rituals, after all, there is no religion.

This observation, as far as it goes, resembles the claim, which we have already attributed to Dewey, that individuals both *form* and *are formed by* social groups. When we turn to involuntary associations, however, differences between the two views become significant. According to the view presented, political institutions and practices of class rule, including *in*voluntary associations, play a crucial role in reproducing individuals as legal subjects, wage earners, felons, and so on.[33] State institutions, in particular, prescribe not only the character of public selfhood, but also to a large extent the character of private, nonvoluntary associations, and hence the character of private selfhood. By enforcing the separation of church and state, for example, judiciaries, legislatures, tax authorities, and so on have been instrumental in making religion "purely a matter of conscience." And this has had a profound impact on the character of "the religious personality,"[34] which in turn has bolstered the Jeffersonian compromise and enhanced the stability of bourgeois social relations.

In chapter 2, we noted that Rorty has abandoned Dewey's hope that members of a democratic community could be reconstructed to efface the contrast between private selfhood and community-spirited public selfhood. In view of the preceding observations, it is easy to agree with the critic who wrote that, "Rorty's assumption that there is a private self which can be formulated *independently* of the public one neglects the social origins and implications of the self."[35] This is as true of the strong poet as of the decent citizen.

In post–cold war eastern Europe, as in the rich North Atlantic, political power has been reinvested in private associations and nonstate public associations (notably mafias and, to a far less extent, the much-ballyhooed nongovernmental organizations), all the while augmenting the power of the new ruling classes. As I have emphasized in this section, however, one important reason for this is the role that nonstate institutions play, including mass media and the "free press," churches, schools, reformist unions, and the bourgeois family, at least in some of its permutations. Even domestic drug-trafficking gangs could count as highly "functional" associations in the latter category, considering their demoralizing and demobilizing effect on working-class neighborhoods.

On the other hand, it should be stressed that discourses and activities that subvert prevailing relations of domination are not all the result of dysfunctional public institutions. To take some obvious examples, the most consistently militant workers' parties, unions, national liberation movements, and Christian base communities have not been public institutions that just did not do what they were "supposed" to do. These institutions have been characterized by internal organizational structures and practices geared for battle against the state and ruling class alliances. These structures and practices may have included clandestineness, democratic or bureaucratic centralism, abstention from elec-

FREEDOM AND LIBERALISM IN PRACTICE

toral politics or the use of elections for merely "pedagogical" purposes, and a preparedness to resort to such militant tactics as general strikes, land seizure, armed struggle, and so on. Such organizations have come into conflict with coercive institutions of the state when they have done what they were "supposed" to do.

It would seem that the demands of a subaltern group cannot be launched from a platform beyond the sanction of the state without at least posing a threat to the dominant position of the ruling class force. As long as Jim Crow remained on the books, police and FBI officials viewed even the avowedly nonviolent civil rights movement of the 1950s and 1960s as a threat to "national security." By contrast, when legal and extralegal impediments to the activism of subaltern groups are removed and the political struggle is transferred to terrain within the compass of state surveillance and control, the political struggle, however heated, takes place on a playing field which as a rule is steeply inclined in favor of the ruling class alliance.

These observations are all the more poignant when it comes to accounting for the resilience of capitalist class rule in the West. In "the most advanced states," Gramsci noted, "'civil society' has become a very complex structure, and one which is resistant to the catastrophic 'incursions' of the immediate economic element (crises, depressions, etc.)."[36] The modern state and what Gramsci referred to as civil society break up opposition the way a prism breaks up white light. Both state and nonstate institutions channel dissent into myriad legal institutions, and in this way they absorb the shock of opposition into themselves. Gramsci described this process well:

> The massive structures of the modern democracies, both as state organizations, and as complexes of associations in civil society, constitute for the art of politics as it were the "trenches" and the permanent fortifications of the front in the war of position: they render merely "partial" the element of movement which before used to be "the whole" of war, etc.[37]

In the East, by contrast (and evidently Gramsci had Russia foremost in mind), "the general-economic-cultural-social conditions [and] the structure of national life are embryonic and loose, and incapable of becoming 'trench or fortress.'"[38]

It would seem, then, that within the context of the contemporary north Atlantic, both the public and the private spheres must be brought, at least in large part, under the sway of dominant political institutions, state or nonstate, or the continuity of prevailing relations of production and class rule will be at risk. If, for instance, a ruling class attempts to maintain its political domination by proscribing the contest for control of representative institutions from the arena of legal political activity, this struggle may then take the form of a military siege by an enemy which is then, by definition, opposed to the state.

According to the account presented so far, we will notice, both the private and the public are political constructs. The private sphere is itself, at least in large part, an *effect* of politics, conceived broadly not as tinkering aimed at consensus and amelioration of suffering, but as a struggle among classes, the highest stakes of which are state power.

Proceeding a step further, one may even describe the self to whom the strong poet recognizes a duty as itself largely an effect of state institutions and other public institutions. Thus, one may conclude, pace Rorty, that autonomy, or lack thereof, is to a large extent an effect of social institutions. It should be noted, moreover, that one may accept this conclusion without thereby subscribing to the view against which Rorty convincingly polemicizes, to the effect that autonomy is "something which all human beings have within them and which society can release by ceasing to repress them."[39]

So far, I have sketched a picture of the state as inseparable from the reality of class domination, of state power as a stake of political struggle, of state institutions as sites of class struggle, and of political power as an effect of nonstate institutions as well as state institutions. This sketch contrasts sharply to Dewey's picture of the state as "the organization of the public effected through officials for the protection of the interests shared by its members," to Rorty's picture of "social institutions as experiments in cooperation," and to Dewey's assumption, which Rorty shares, that "politics is a matter of everyone pulling together to solve common problems."[40]

We are now in a better position to compare Rorty's account of the apolitical private sphere, presented in chapter 2, with the account of the

FREEDOM AND LIBERALISM IN PRACTICE 105

state and the private sphere sketched in this section. A convenient way of doing this would be to evaluate the very different ways in which the two accounts allow us to compare the defunct nominally socialist states of eastern Europe with the liberal democracies of the North Atlantic.

PRIVATIZATION AND SOCIALISM

I will begin by making hay of headlines in an admittedly distasteful manner: As late as 1987, Rorty wrote that "...time seems to be on the Soviet side,"[41] and in a paper published two years later, he wrote, with reference to the "spectacularly successful Communist oligarchs" in the Soviet Union:

> Orwell was not the first person to suggest that small gangs of criminals might get control of modern states and, thanks to modern technology, stay in control forever.[42]

A mere two years after Rorty disparaged the "unchanging second World run by an impregnable and ruthless Inner Party," this "world," its "intractable," "monstrous" regimes, and its "ruthless" leaders, collapsed like a circus tent, scattering less debris in Moscow than settled on the streets of Los Angeles the following spring.[43] Since then, the victorious "reformers" and "democrats" apotheosized by cold war liberals have presided over the impoverishment and disenfranchisement of their populations, the worst political repression in Europe in half a century, and blood baths on a dozen killing fields from Kosovo to Tajikistan.

Surely it is bad taste to toss an author's political forecasts in his face from the unfair vantage point of eight-year retrospection. After all, Rorty could easily rally a legion of equally embarrassing prognostications from the same period authored by erstwhile admirers of "existing socialism." Moreover, he provides us with evidence that he was not entirely oblivious to the changes taking place around him: In a footnote presumably added for the 1991 republication of a text first published in 1989, he acknowledged that what two years earlier he had referred to as "the unbreakable grip of the KGB in the Russian people and of the

Soviet army on a third of Europe" has been broken, thanks in large part to Mikhail Gorbachev, "the Abraham Lincoln of Eastern Europe."[44]

Sometimes, however, bad taste is warranted. There are two reasons why I permit myself to use Rorty's political prognostications of a nearly a decade ago to motivate the discussion in this section.

First of all, he engages in this sort of maneuver himself, and turn-about is fair play. Not only has he gainsaid socialist triumphalists retrospectively, in the light of developments at the beginning of Gorbachev's tenure, but he also has condemned writers who, twenty years earlier and more, clung to the hope that the Soviet Union could have been reformed.[45]

Secondly, and more significantly for the present discussion, he shares something important with socialist triumphalists in the West: Whether lamenting the prospect or exalting in it, both sides confidently subscribed to an image of "existing socialism" that was at least in one respect a projection of the image of the liberal political systems within which they lived. According to this image, the Soviet regime was stable, in control, and in possession of lots of resources to stay in control. Nontriumphalists to the left of Rorty could also be indicted for the same offense, including the Frankfurters and Foucault, who, by casting both East and West into the same "technological," "postindustrial," or "carceral" pot, greatly overstated the flexibility and resources of the regimes in the East, and in this respect greatly underestimated the differences between East and West.

The question we will raise for Rorty, then, must also be directed to many of his critics on the left: How could a person who "has read lots of books" have been so far off the mark as late as 1989 when it came to assessing the stability of the rapidly disintegrating regimes of the Eastern Bloc?

A possible response might be that these cosmopolitan academics have tended to underestimate the central role that virulent nationalism played in their "velvet revolutions." Faithful heirs of the Enlightenment, including Gorbachev himself, preferred to think of their allies against the old guard as fellow democrats with "normal civilized" goals, rather than as the opportunists, obstreperous megalomaniacs, and ethnic cleansers they so often turned out to be.

Another possible response to this question, one that is more relevant to the present discussion, might entail defending the following claim: Whether or not the Soviet leadership was a gang of criminals in some special but unspecified sense in which the leadership of, say, the United States is not,[46] the Soviet Union most certainly did not exemplify a "modern state," at least with reference to institutions that generate the consent of the governed.

This last point is particularly evident with reference to private forms of association under "actually existing socialism." Past claims of the Novosti Press Agency to the contrary, it does not appear that in Eastern Europe private life had been made public. On the contrary, as a previously cited source has noted,

> Since the late 1950s the Soviet people have gradually but unswervingly diverted their interests from the state to their primary groups (family, friends, and lovers) and to semi-legal and illegal civil society as well as to illegal activity inside the public sector.[47]

As is well-known, this process of privatization had been taking place for a long time, at the individual, family, and friendship levels, at the level of the so-called mass organizations, and even at the level of the highest apparatchiks. Ample evidence of this trend could have been collected by almost anyone with even casual contact with the woefully inefficient state-owned industrial enterprises, or the cooperative and state farms, or the venal state functionaries and party officials who regularly took advantage of their positions for personal gain.

Because of their corruption and inefficiency, the old regimes of Eastern Europe were forced to augment their more directly repressive state institutions, even to the point of resorting to foreign military intervention to quell popular uprisings, as in Hungary in 1956 and Czechoslovakia in 1968. Predictably enough, these and other repressive measures had the opposite effect. As Nicos Poulantzas wrote at least thirteen years before 1991:

> Not only does authoritarian statism fail to enclose the masses in its disciplinary web or to "integrate" them in its authoritarian circuits; it

actually provokes general insistence on the need for direct, rank-and-file democracy—a veritable explosion of democratic demands.[48]

These regimes did not just provoke democratic demands, however; they also created the space both within state institutions and outside them for the formation of subversive associations. What rendered state institutions in Eastern Europe highly dysfunctional was not just inefficiency within their domains of authority, but also the limited scope of their operation. In some cases, such as widespread black marketeering within state-owned enterprises, state power did not even saturate important state institutions, let alone private associations. Rather than being controlled and regulated to a great extent by state institutions, as in the West, the private sphere came to be determined in large part by fissiparous and increasingly assertive institutions lacking state sanction. These included organized crime syndicates, the church, the samizdat, human-rights watch groups, and later, independent trade unions, nationalist fronts, and full-blown opposition parties.

Even the most intimate primary groups were transformed at least partially into subversive institutions. Surveys conducted in the final years of the Soviet period indicate the prevalence of private institutions—including that sanctum sanctorum of the private sphere, the family—over public ones, including state institutions, in forming the value systems of the respondents.[49] Smaller families, a growing desire for economic independence on the part of the younger generation, and rejection of cohabitation with parents after marriage—all of these developments, and many more besides, testify to increased "privatization within private life," while at the same time they provide further impetus for extended privatization.[50]

Similar observations apply to other areas of the private sphere, as well as to other Eastern European states. In one case after another, the private sphere was first a refuge from state power, then a fortress, and then a secure rear base for a frontal assault against the state.

However accurate this model of the relationship between the state and nonstate associations may have been with reference to Eastern Europe, however, it does not fit well with reference to the advanced capitalist West. In the liberal democracies, even the most intimate realms of activity play an important role in maintaining dominant social relations of production. For example, Althusser and others have emphasized the role of the nuclear family in reproducing prevailing relations of class domination.[51] This view may well have been too unilateral with reference to the French bourgeois family under the Fifth Republic, let alone the transmogrified family structures of the contemporary United States, where, thanks in part to a 50 percent divorce rate, the patriarchal nuclear family consisting of a male breadwinner and a female housewife accounts for only 12 percent of the households. Also, the importance of the nuclear family in this context has diminished relative to public schools and television. Nevertheless, to the extent that the institution of the family in the liberal democracies has, in large part, been spared exposure to direct and overt incursions by state agencies, it may simply be because the bourgeois family itself has not required much state intervention to function as a guarantor of the continuity of ruling class power. When, for any of a number of reasons, a particular family structure no longer reproduces dominant social relations efficiently (as, for example, in the case of France in the closing years of the nineteenth century, or the United States in the final years of the twentieth century), it has been subject to the increased intervention of state institutions.[52]

Poulantzas has argued that the state's ability to reproduce itself depends on the institutional integration of power relationships. Ironically, in the case of the highly centralized states of the East these power relationships were far less integrated than in the liberal democratic states of the advanced capitalist West. In view of the diminishing power of subversive institutions in the advanced capitalist West, Poulantzas's observation carries even more weight today than when it was first made:

> [There is] no limit *de jure* or in principle to the modern State's encroachment on the private. However paradoxical it may seem, the very separation of public and private that is established by the State opens up for it bound-less vistas of power.[53]

If in Eastern Europe the private sphere was continually violated by a handful of enormous and enormously unwieldy, corrupt, and incompetent bureaucracies, in the West it is supervised not by one or two centralized bureaucracies, but by multiple networks of overlapping institutions, both state and nonstate, public and private, which are not limited to such narrowly repressive state agencies as the FBI, the Immigration and Naturalization Service, and the Bureau of Alcohol, Tobacco, and Firearms. Consider, for example, such private sources of information as employment records, telephone accounts, academic transcripts, credit reports, actuarial projections, medical records, psychodiagnostic assessments, background checks by insurance agencies and private investigators, and omnipresent electronic monitors in the labyrinthine panopticons of shopping malls, parking lots, white-collar work sites, and cyberspace. In his book *The Naked Consumer*, Eric Larson describes the formidable private sector information networks that monitor, track, and manipulate consumers. The profusion of examples testifies to the pervasiveness of nonstate surveillance, regulation, and manipulation of private life in the rich North Atlantic.

To complicate matters, it is not always a straightforward task to distinguish state from nonstate agencies of surveillance and control. This is true particularly in the West, where, as we have already noted: (a) the administration of the state extends far beyond the traditional bureaucracy, to encompass central banks, regulatory commissions, lobbies, nonprofit corporations and foundations, policy planning institutes, and other agencies, each of which has its own resources for information-gathering and control, and (b) the power of big business has merged seamlessly with the state.

Furthermore, as we have indicated, the scope of state intervention and the compass of state power have been anything but fixed. One generalization to be drawn from a survey of the labor history of the United States is that multiple sites on terrain contested by state power have been flashpoints of class conflict. Working-class leaders and organizations have fought long and hard to expand state supervision in the areas of union recognition, minimum wage laws, corporate taxes, regulation of industry and commerce, social security, occupational safety, environmental safeguards, and social programs. At the same time, some of the same individuals and organizations have fought bitter battles for a rigorous implementation of the Bill of Rights, to restrict the operation of state agencies, especially repressive ones, in the private sphere. And in each of these battles, they have encountered much resistance from ruling-class forces. The character and compass of state and nonstate public institutions have been a bone of contention vis-à-vis both institutions of the "private sector" and the "primary groups" of the private sphere. The first category would include conflicts over regulation, antitrust legislation (which in any case have amounted to little more than pro forma concessions to widespread discontent),[54] use of public lands, environmental degradation and corporate liability, subsidies to industries, health care, social security, and so on. The second category would include contention over freedom of speech, reproductive rights, due process, sodomy laws, the separation of church and state, "family values," and so on. In recent years the battle zone has expanded to cyberspace, as opponents have clashed over the Telecommunications Bill, the future of the so-called information superhighway, surveillance of the Internet, and control of the content of multimedia programming.

These examples underscore the observation already made, to the effect that the border between state and nonstate institutions and between the public and private spheres are blurry, elastic, discontinuous, and shifting lines of scrimmage which are often, though not always, located on political terrain defined by state institutions. Moreover, at the risk of further complicating a picture that is already exceedingly complex, it is important to keep in mind the class character of the terrain itself and the fact that it also undergoes constant transformation.

As the foregoing considerations would suggest, it is inaccurate to depict the negative rights embodied in documents such as the Bill of Rights as somehow carving a sphere of freedom away from the mechanisms of class rule and political domination. To paraphrase Foucault, we must not think that by saying yes to the private sphere we say no to political power.

The contrast-term for *private sphere* is *public sphere*, not *the state*. Moreover, as I have indicated, state power far overreaches state institutions. It would seem, then, that Jacques's picture of a power shift from the state to civil society is inaccurate, or at least stated in a misleading manner. True, many functions that, at least at the official level, used to be reserved for public institutions of the state have indeed shifted squarely to the nonstate institutions of what he calls civil society, and to more intimate realms. Far from detracting from the power of the ascendant ruling class alliance, however, this shift has greatly enhanced that power.

Let us recall the instances Jacques cites to illustrate his claim: the burgeoning membership in environmental groups, the "range of cultural activities," and the massively enhanced role of the media today. As it turns out, each one of these instances could be turned convincingly against Jacques's claim. One might note, for starters, the co-optation and political neutralization of events such as Earth Day by corporations and state commissions; the futility of the Rio Summit; or the political use of the rain forest issue by the IMF to inhibit the development of more independent capitalist economies in the South, to the benefit of the G-7. With reference to cultural activities, one might consider the monotonous, soporific, and demoralizing effects of increasingly corporate-sponsored cultural activities in the rich North Atlantic,[55] or recall John Foster Dulles's prescient observation that culture is the leading edge of U.S. foreign policy. Edward Said's remark might also be relevant in this context:

> I would like to suggest that many of the most prominent characteristics of modernist culture, which we have tended to derive from purely internal dynamics in Western society and culture, include a response to the external pressures on culture from *imperium*.[56]

Moreover, with reference to the enormous influence of the media today, Jacques would do well to consult Ben Bagdikian's book, *The Media Monopoly*, for documentation of the rapid and massive concentration of ownership of the electronic and print media in fewer and fewer hands, and the ever closer connection between the corporate media and the government.

These observations bring us back to the conclusion that in the advanced capitalist West, the private sphere conforms to and bolsters the liberal democratic state and capitalist class rule: Almost all domestic political opposition is loyal opposition; the content of the omnipresent and increasingly corporate-owned press and entertainment industries meshes ever more finely with state policy; and nearly all "cultural expression," including supposedly subversive art, has been tolerated and even subsidized by the state. As Foucault and Poulantzas have indicated each in his own way, surveillance in a "pluralist society"—that is, a setup in which there is a broad mix of functions of public and private institutions—reins in nearly the entire panorama of life.

Ironically, then, Rorty's ominous prognostications about some twentieth-century states miss his intended target. If there are regimes that have stayed in power thanks in large part to modern technology, they were not the member-states of the Warsaw Pact, but rather the rich North Atlantic democracies, including Rorty's own liberal democratic experiment, the United States of America. The private sphere is not a realm of freedom insulated from political power—least of all in the liberal democracies of the West, where it is thought to be freest. Like American bison in a theme park, what Rorty has referred to as "Emerson's American sense of a new kind of social freedom"[57] survives in a much-diminished form, as a simulacrum of a sentimentalized past, within a well-circumscribed and controlled domain. Thus, Orwell's question, which Rorty approvingly repeats,[58] is aimed one hundred eighty degrees in the wrong direction: The question whether one can remain free inside should be directed in the first place to the rich North Atlantic, where the private sphere functions very efficiently to ensure the hegemony of a small minority of exploiters.

Leninists have been accused of postulating the absence of civil society. Indeed, the apparent reassertion of civil society, and the intractability of the private sphere in Eastern Europe seem to be chief reasons why Jacques and other leftists have claimed that Leninism "has had its day." It may well be true that what distinguishes the Leninist view of state power from other perspectives is the repudiation in theory of the notion of civil society, as well as skepticism as to whether it is at all meaningful to speak of a private sphere in the absence of the state.[59] What has been said so far, however, would suggest that by at least one possible interpretation, Lenin was affirming a great truth when, speaking of the Bolsheviks, he once said "We do not recognize anything 'private.'"[60] To the extent that the private is a legal category instantiating the system of ownership of the means of production, and to the extent that the state stands above the law (except, of course, in the imaginations of some political philosophers, their popularizers, and the many under their sway), Lenin's rejection of the notion of a nonpolitical private sphere may well be an advantage for descriptive purposes other than apologetics for bourgeois liberalism.

This, however, does not imply that, despite appearances, everything is really public "deep down." I have presented a case for concluding that nothing is naturally or intrinsically either public or private. Nevertheless, as I have emphasized, the private sphere is not a pure illusion produced by false consciousness, either. It is, rather, an important component or aspect of contemporary social relations, an element that public policy makers ignore at their own risk.

The proposals advanced during the period of perestroika confirm the view that Soviet leaders were compelled to acknowledge that a pervasive and vigorous private sphere had long ago become an established fact in the Soviet Union. It is instructive to consider several of their more sweeping proposals, with reference to public institutions of the state:

- Dismantle the unwieldy central planning bureaucracy and attempt to develop some sort of market mechanism to conform costs of production more closely to consumer prices—hopefully, within the context of economic planning. (As we know, however, Gorbachev's economic initiatives terribly undermined the well being of direct producers, while at the same time depriving workers of the old mechanisms for redress of grievances.);

- Decentralize production by eliminating state subsidies to inefficient enterprises and legalizing forms of "personal property" and cooperative enterprises which would effectively amount to private ownership of the means of production (though it would not necessarily amount to large-scale exploitation, as long as cooperatives would be prohibited from hiring large numbers of direct producers);

- Foster independent workers' unions and legalize the right to strike;

- Scrap the scores of prohibitions and security measures obstructing access to new technologies, information, foreign travel, and resource allocation;

- Separate the Party structure from that of the state, and inaugurate a multiparty candidate-selection system;[61]

FREEDOM AND LIBERALISM IN PRACTICE

- Distinguish sharply between the property, rules, norms, and organizational principles of voluntary political organizations and those of state institutions;
- Develop an institutional framework of representative democracy—preferably, as a foundation upon which to build some form of participatory democracy, workers' and consumers' councils, and mass organizations;[62]
- Put in place more effective guarantees for the negative rights of liberal democracy, while deemphasizing such "positive rights" as workers' self-management and the right to a job;
- Strengthen and regularize mechanisms for oversight and accountability, to enforce strict legality both within state institutions and within the Party;
- Inaugurate a looser All-Union federal arrangement (perhaps along lines proposed in the democratically ratified March 17, 1991 referendum), granting a greater degree of self-determination to nations within the multinational state, and permitting much greater latitude for economic, cultural, and political initiatives at the republic level.

Admittedly, this list is selective: Various constituencies advanced other demands that were less compatible with the point argued here. However partial this list may be, however, I believe it is representative of one dominant trend within the Soviet Communist Party in the late 1980s, a trend that used to be associated with the name of Mikhail Gorbachev.[63]

It would be accurate to characterize the proposals on this list as part of a sweeping movement towards privatization. As I have attempted to indicate, however, it would be incorrect to conclude from this that they amount to moves to diminish the extent of state power. True, most of the proposals listed involve expanding the private sphere at the expense of the public sphere, and state institutions in particular; nevertheless, none of them requires a retreat of state power from the private sphere. On the contrary, implementation of some of these proposals has arguably intensified and expanded the terrain of political domination by giving state sanction to large areas of private life previously ignored on the official level, while simultaneously bringing these areas under the authority of the state. Consider, for the sake of illustration, the myriad enterprises which have constituted so-called shadow economies in Eastern Europe: As these enterprises are forced to function aboveboard, they will in time probably become subject to greater state regulation and taxation.

From the fact that these economic and political reforms proved to be too little, too late for the Soviet Union, it does not follow that they are, in principle, incompatible with socialism. Indeed, as I have suggested, prospects of alternatives to this sort of privatization would appear to be poor in the foreseeable future: If workers are to retain state power after winning it through political struggle, they will have to transform private forms of association into mechanisms of workers' power, instead of attempting to proscribe them by means of repression.[64]

In the next section I will bolster the case against Rorty's account of the inviolable private sphere by elaborating on the proposition that social institutions and practices, including *in*voluntary associations and state institutions, play a crucial role in defining not only the character of public selfhood, but also to a large extent the character of private selfhood. My aim is to dispute Rorty's claim that it is not fruitful to take as a topic of conversation how one's notions of community and how even private self-descriptions facilitate or inhibit prevailing relations of exploitation and political domination. In the course of doing this I will argue for a conception of ideology which is immune from his criticisms of *Ideologiekritik*.

PRIVATE SELFHOOD AND IDEOLOGY

David Hall has noted that "The grounds for Rorty's hope and Foucault's hopelessness lie in the different attitudes of these two thinkers toward the relations of the public and private sphere."[65] Hall is repeating a theme of, for instance, the last two-thirds of *CIS*, as well as the final section of Rorty's paper entitled "Method, Social Science and Social Hope," included in *CP*. Hall continues:

FREEDOM AND LIBERALISM IN PRACTICE

Insisting upon distinguishing the public and private spheres risks begging what for both Rorty and Foucault is the essentially empirical question of whether there is an efficacious private life for individuals, in liberal democratic societies.[66]

Rorty answers this essentially empirical question in the affirmative, of course. As one might guess by now, however, this answer follows almost trivially from his definition of a liberal society as one which guarantees Kundera's right to an inviolable private life.

In this chapter we have encountered a very different view of the private sphere. I have suggested that the state is a condition of actuality of both the public and the private spheres, and that private institutions as well as public ones play crucial roles in bolstering relations of exploitation consonant with capitalist class rule. While I have pointed out good empirical reasons for rejecting Rorty's picture of an apolitical private sphere, I also have indicated that the private sphere is not a pure illusion of false consciousness, either.

So if Hall takes the modifier *efficacious* in the passage just cited to signify that the distinction between public and private life makes a big nonlinguistic difference, then his "empirical question" may be answered as follows: Yes, of course there is an efficacious private life for individuals in liberal democracies. After all, the sphere of private life and private property is instantiated in architecture and urban planning, individual behavior, patterns of consumption and production, and so on, as well as in thousands of constantly reenacted legal procedures, institutional routines and norms, and so on.

It seems more likely from the context of Hall's passage, however, that he holds that private life is *efficacious* to the extent that it is somehow self-sealing, or is prior to politics or separable from institutions of the state. If this is a correct interpretation of his view, then, as I have indicated, there are good reasons not to answer his question in the affirmative. If we take *efficacious* in this sense, then apparently Hall has failed to distinguish between the public sphere on the one hand and institutions of political domination on the other hand as distinct analytical categories. This would account for his and Rorty's assumption that wherever there is an efficacious private sphere there is also freedom and the possibility of autonomy, as they use these terms.

For Foucault and many Marxists, by contrast, extensive state recognition of a private sphere is not synonymous with the expansion of negative freedom and the opportunity to achieve autonomy. On the contrary, if private associations and practices play such an important role in securing near-total submission to the established order in existing liberal democracies, then acknowledging the efficaciousness of the private sphere enables Foucauldians and Marxists to say *more* nasty things about "actually existing liberalism," not fewer. It allows them, for instance, to add a new chapter to their stories of class rule or disciplinary practices, a long chapter that could be entitled "How the Private Sphere Enhances Domination by the Bourgeoisie."

I do not propose to write that chapter here. Rather, I want to scrutinize some of Rorty's objections to such an undertaking. In particular, I want to examine his disparagement, in *CIS* and subsequent works, of the very attempt to describe the private sphere and private selfhood in a political light. This requires turning our attention to his disparagement of the use of the word "ideology" and its cognates.

Rorty would like to convince his readers that "the" notion of ideology is useless.[67] In the following pages, however, it should become clear that his objections miss the mark when it comes to at least one conception of ideology, which I will recommend. Although we may grant that the proffered conception may be worse than useless for Rorty's apologetic purposes (to which we will return in chapter 5), it should become clear that others who are less prone to such apologetics may well find it useful not only for private purposes of "tracing the blind impresses our behavings bear,"[68] but also for redescribing personal behavings in a way that is conducive to quite different political purposes.

Let us review Rorty's objections to *Ideologiekritik*.[69] There are several related criticisms:

Speaking in the most general terms, he associates disquisitions about ideology with representationalist accounts of knowledge. He characterizes *Ideologiekritik* as an attempt to strip away systematically distorted representations of a thing, to unmask the one true description of it, its underlying dynamics.[70] Thus, if representationalism goes, so does *Ideologiekritik*.

As noted in chapter 1, Rorty has convincingly argued that representationalism should go. He congratulates Wittgenstein for diagnosing the urge to ask "...questions as to the *essence* of language, of propositions, of thought," and concluding that we must cure ourselves of the fixation that "the essence is hidden from us."[71]

Rorty also ascribes to some *Ideologiekritiker*, namely Marxists, "a fuzzy distinction between 'ideology' and a form of thought (the Marxists' own) which escapes being 'ideology.'"[72] With a little help, perhaps, from Kolakowski and Castoriadis, he interprets Marx, a man whose favorite motto was *De omnibus dubitandum*, to have held that, at long last having ascended to the heights of science, it is possible to cast all previous knowledge at once into doubt. By this account, Marx would appear to be one of those "committed to the construction of a permanent, neutral framework for inquiry, and thus for all of culture."[73]

Further on, Rorty provides an important clue as to what he means by "ideology" when he writes that the question of whether or not the critique of ideology is central to philosophy, as Habermas and others would have it, "turns on whether one thinks that one can give an interesting sense to the word 'ideology'—make it mean more than 'bad idea.'"[74] Rorty, of course, does not believe that one can make "ideology" mean anything more interesting than "bad idea." Presumably, a bad idea is an idea that one is warranted in declaring to be false, evil, unjust, or clumsy, because it has proven over time and in a variety of cases to be useless or detrimental for a particular purpose. To the extent that the false is the bad in the way of belief, then, Rorty's "deflated" notion of ideology is truth-functional.

Ideologiekritiker claim superscience status when they aspire to adjudicate beliefs in all vocabularies for all time and when they deny they are using a particular historically conditioned and temporary vocabulary. They have claimed to fulfill the latter role in at least one of at least two ways: (1) by permitting us to escape "class subjectivism," thus providing us with a putatively objective or scientific knowledge, something of a "view from nowhere"; or (2) by assuming the standpoint of the proletariat, thus allowing us to transcend the class subjectivism of those who, having a great deal more to lose than just their chains, have a vested interest in remaining blind to the sources of their wealth and privilege, the ignominious origins of the present regime, and the irrationality, contingency, and transitoriness of the status quo.

Both of these ways of claiming superscience status involve revealing the economic class determinants of beliefs, determinants that Marx described in a famous passage from his 1859 "Preface to *A Critique of Political Economy*" as the "real foundation" to which "definite forms of social consciousness" correspond. Lukacs's proletariat, for example, is in a position to gain scientific knowledge of its own debasement and the possibility of redemption because, as the objectified subject of history, it is the most thoroughly disillusioned subject heretofore. Rorty might have had some such formulation in mind when he wrote that *Ideologiekritik* is at the center of "the Marxist idea that a philosophical superscience can tell the working class their true situation."[75]

Against the view that those who remain prisoners of bourgeois class subjectivism remain blinded by ideology, Rorty protests that performing such tasks as sensitizing an audience to cases of suffering that they had not previously noticed is simply a matter of "redescription."[76] One way in which the notion of being blinded by ideology differs from "redescription" is that the latter term, unlike the former, is truth-neutral.

By Rorty's lights, then, "the" notion of ideology opposes false imaginings to the real. Accordingly, he criticizes a notion of ideology as:

(a) False consciousness; mystification (Condorcet); socially necessary illusion; Althusser's "imaginary version of a real relation"; "distorted discourse" (Habermas, Nielsen); Geuss' "ideology in the pejorative sense,"[77] or what Novosti literature sometimes used to refer to as "illusory ideology," in contrast to "scientific ideology."

The literary output of the vulgar economists exemplifies "ideology" in this sense of the word, as do (arguably) the fetishism of the commodity and the wage form.

This pejorative sense of *ideology*, however, is only one of several uses to which Marxists and others have put the word. Consider some other meanings of the word, to be found in the works of Marx and/or Marxist writers:

(b) Constellations of beliefs, attitudes, dispositions, and so on which serve to "mask social contradictions";[78]

FREEDOM AND LIBERALISM IN PRACTICE

(c) Juridical, philosophical and technical principles of state power, as in the phrases "official ideology" and "the ideology of the state," or as embodied in, say, Roman law, Shari'a, or the orthodoxy of Stalin's Russia;

(d) Conscious or unconscious rules, based on principles for morality and conduct;

(e)* Patterns of behavior (prominently including linguistic behavior), as in Althusser's formulation, "a lived relation to the world";

(f) Systematic ways of viewing things, in the broadest sense of the word; *Weltanschauungen*;[79] bodies of widely shared, important, and in some sense highly coherent perceptions or beliefs, as in "the German ideology";

(g) Ideals; Plekhanov's "ideology of the higher sort," consisting of science, philosophy, the arts, and so on;

(h)* Noncoercive practices, prominently including linguistic practices, which support the economic system or reproduce dominant relations of production;

(i) A social or collective practice distinct from but concerned with (nonlinguistic) action; a collective practice which is "more practical" than philosophy;[80]

(j)* A relatively noncoercive field of class conflict or competition for cultural and political hegemony (as in Gramsci);

(k)* A social determination which implies a *cause*, though not a *justification*.[81]

This list is not intended to be exhaustive. It is not clear to me, for instance, that it can accommodate a view Rorty ascribes to Marx and Habermas, according to which "ideology" is contrasted to "...a mode of thought which, because it represents 'human freedom' rather than any 'external constraints,' succeeds in being non-ideological."[82] The list should suffice, however, to bring home the point that various interpreters and different traditions or schools, Marxist and non-Marxist, have subscribed to different notions of ideology. Rorty is certainly right to observe that many writers have used "ideology" to mean "bad idea." Others, however, have provided accounts of ideology that are prefigured in the Marxist classics[83]—or for that matter in the works of, say, Karl Mannheim or Talcott Parsons—and that at the same time avoid the assumption that all contending vocabularies but their own are bad ideas. Consider, for example, the following variation on "functional" definition (h):

> (h$_2$) An attitude, ritual, or set of beliefs, dispositions, or linguistic practices viewed with an eye to its role in the reproduction of dominant relations of production, or alternatively, to its inhibition or subversion of those relations.

This definition appears at least prima facie to comport with the items in the list marked with an asterisk, and does not appear to conflict in any obvious way with any other item except (a). (The reason the recommended definition conflicts with (a) is that, in order to fulfill its role in the reproduction of dominant social relations, a belief would thereby serve the purposes of the dominant social group, and thus, at least from a pragmatist's perspective, the dominant group would not be warranted in asserting that it is false or illusory.) By contrast, Rorty's characterization of *Ideologiekritik* does not comport terribly well with any of the items on the list except (a), (b), and possibly (f).[84]

Ideology, according to definition (h$_2$), or in the sense of what Geuss called "ideology in a purely descriptive sense," could include both implicit and explicit discursive elements such as beliefs, concepts, and so on, as well as nondiscursive elements such as rituals, dispositions, attitudes, gestures, artifacts and what Dewey has referred to as "the habits of loyalty and obedience" that permit a government to rule.[85] Thus, ideology as (h$_2$) does not appear to be too far from Rorty's "forms of life," referred to above, that "...have been used to justify the systematic administration of pain and humiliation."[86] Ideological attitudes, rituals, beliefs, and so on, constitute and typically are embodied in institutions and institutional practices, both public and private.

It will be noted that this conception of ideology trivially proscribes what Nielsen refers to as *nonideological legitimating beliefs*: To view a belief as legitimizing an institution or political practice is to view it as ideology. And the same may be said of a belief that problematizes or challenges prevailing forms of exploitation and domination.

Even the most uncontroversially true, pragmatically confirmed axioms can be viewed with an eye to their function vis-à-vis the reproduction of relations of production. Thus, for example, both vulgar political economy and *Das Kapital* could be viewed as ideology, without prejudicing the claims of either to truth, scientificity, or usefulness for a given purpose. If the literary output of the vulgar economists or the fetishism of the commodity or the wage form are more obviously ideological than, say, Euclidean geometry or Boyle's Law, then this is because of their function vis-à-vis dominant social relations, not because of their alleged cognitive inferiority.

Moreover, as Nielsen has pointed out with reference to his own truth-functional conception of ideology, Davidson's observation about how the mass of mundane beliefs must be true does not impugn the claim that there are systems of legitimating beliefs or discourses that underwrite repressive social orders and reproduce existing relations of exploitation and political domination.[87] Gramsci's remarks on ideology are instructive here. The Italian Marxist viewed common sense as comprised of bits and pieces of the ideology of a ruling class at a given moment in its career. At the same time, he recognized that some—though certainly not all—widely held beliefs have been pragmatically confirmed by many agents over a long period of time. Gramsci referred to the latter sort of truisms as beliefs of *good sense*.[88] Clearly, there is an overlap of beliefs of good sense and common sense. Thus, we may readily admit that commonsense beliefs are often true, yet still be warranted in asserting that they underwrite existing relations of exploitation and political domination.

Ideology, viewed as a social practice along the lines of definition (h_2), looks like what a Foucauldian might call "a pluralism of power/discourse formations," plus nondiscursive attitudes, rituals, and dispositions. Thus conceived, the study of ideology would involve producing lots of what Rorty has called "detailed historical narratives of the sort Foucault offers us," without positing noncausal conditions of possibility, or constituting the sort of metanarrative Lyotard and Rorty profess to abhor.[89] To view ideology this way is not necessarily to subscribe to Rorty's picture of *Ideologiekritik* as "penetrating to the 'repressed' reality behind the 'ideological' appearances."[90] Nor need the examination of ideology depend in any obvious way—nor, as far as I can tell, in any unobvious way, for that matter—on the opposition between "true consensus" and "false consensus," or between "validity" and "power," either.[91] Rather, it could be described simply as a particular sort of first-order descriptive activity, one that consists of generating claims about the effects of discourse, rituals, and so on, as well as the purposes, and hence communities, that are served or frustrated by our ways of talking. Students of ideology so conceived would qualify as *naturalists*, in Rorty's sense of the word, as those who believe that all explanation is causal explanation of the actual, and that there is no such thing as a noncausal condition of possibility.[92]

Rorty has written that the genre of literature concerned with "unmasking bourgeois ideology" has long been overworked.[93] It is hard to disagree with his derogatory assessment of the impenetrable and pretentious jargon of many "cultural leftists," and he is probably right to doubt that they create so much as a ripple outside the increasingly rarefied and underfunded atmosphere of university humanities departments. Nevertheless, a great deal remains to be said about how, say, public school curricula, packaged news, or clinical psychology have either helped to reproduce prevailing social relations or have been appropriated by social forces in opposition to those relations. The same observation applies to religious and nationalist creeds, advertising and popular entertainment, a wide range of technical discourses, common-sense platitudes, and, yes, even Marvel Comics. So when in a rare moment Rorty describes "critique of ideology" as an "occasionally useful tactical weapon in social struggles, but as one among many others,"[94] we may dispute his use of the adverb *occasionally*, but otherwise agree with him.

※ ※ ※

In this chapter, I have sketched a picture in which both state and non-state institutions in the liberal North Atlantic, on the whole, function to reproduce prevailing economic and political relations by producing individuals as private, as well as public, persons or selves. In the course of sketching this picture, I have not invoked a picture of repressed potentialities, human essences, or universal autonomy. I have made my case, rather, by comparing the scope, scale, and forms of state power within the rich North Atlantic democracies to other cases, notably in Eastern Europe during the cold war. If this account is on target, then existing liberal democracies could hardly be said to embody one of Rorty's highest liberal ideals, namely, the ideal of leaving people alone to pursue their own idiosyncratic visions of personal perfection.

In the next chapter I will turn to Rorty's public ideal of ameliorating suffering. I will argue that if we give proper attention to the policies and practices of the richest North Atlantic democracies beyond their cartographic borders, they fare no better when it comes to this ideal than they did with reference to the ideal of individual freedom. I will also recommend an alternative political setup which, I believe, holds greater promise when it comes to ameliorating suffering.

NOTES

1. See n. 52 for chapter 2.

2. Richard Rorty, "Thugs and Theorists," *Political Theory* 15 no. 4 (November 1987): 567.

3. Rorty believes that "...it was images of freedom, conveyed through magazines and movies, that finally brought down the Berlin Wall." (L. S. Klepp, "Every Man a Philosopher-King: Richard Rorty of the University of Virginia," *New York Times Magazine*, December 2, 1990, p. 122.) He does not discern "any useful distinction between propaganda and the use of reason" (ibid., p. 122). Nevertheless, one still could raise lots of questions not only about how these images were received and interpreted, but how they were financed, framed, and transmitted.

4. Refer to Francis Fukayama, "The End of History?" *National Interest* 16 (Summer 1989): 3–18. "The End of History," of course, has been a regularly repeated theme of "futurists" and "culture critics" of various stripes. Not ten years earlier than Fukayama, for example, Jean Baudrillard announced that history had come to an end, thanks to the allegedly homeostatic coexistence of

"the Big Two"—that is, the United States and the Soviet Union (Jean Baudrillard, *Simultations* [New York: Semiotext(e), Inc., 1983], p. 66).

5. Although it has proven useful for Radio Liberty programmers, the term *free enterprise* is more than dubious as a description of leading contemporary economies, in view of (a) the crucial role of state fiscal and monetary policies and regulation in these economies, (b) the increasingly centralized private sector planning (cf. John R. Munkirs, *The Transformation of American Capitalism: From Competitive Market Structures to Centralized Private Sector Planning* [Armonk, N.Y.: M. E. Sharpe, Inc., 1985]), and (c) the increasingly close interaction and identification of state agencies and corporate capital. Recognizing this, David Bazelon has observed that "...the only existential meaning of *enterprise* is what businessmen generally happen to be doing at the moment, and *free* is merely the accompanying demand that they be left alone to do it" (quoted in ibid., p. 102).

6. The quote, from a passage in Kundera's *Art of the Novel*, appears as an epigraph to Richard Rorty, *Contingency, Irony, and Solidarity* (Cambridge: Cambridge University Press, 1989), p. vii (hereafter cited as *CIS*).

7. Reprinted in Martin Jacques, "Will 'End of Leninism' Bring a 'New Birth of Socialism'?" *Guardian Weekly*, December 10, 1989, p. 18.

8. All citations in this paragraph are from Vladimir Shlapentokh, *Public and Private Life of the Soviet People* (Oxford: Oxford University Press, 1989), pp. 4–6.

9. Ibid., p. 5. To his credit, Shlapentokh admits the inadequacy of his knowledge about "America and other countries" (ibid., p. 14).

10. Ibid., p. 7. As we shall see below, privatization may better be understood as a process of expansion of the private sphere at the expense of the public sphere—but not necessarily at the state's own expense, as Shlapentokh's picture would have it. For the time being, we might take *privatization* to refer merely to the economic, political, and ideological expansion of the private sphere, regardless of how this expansion takes place.

11. Many of Rorty's liberal colleagues, including Isaiah Berlin, Sidney Hook, and Leszek Kolakowski, have claimed to discern "totalitarian" bogeys lurking in every alternative creed. It is interesting to note in this regard that Dewey himself has been a recipient of the epithet "totalitarian" (refer to Corliss Lamont, ed., *Dialogue on John Dewey* [New York: Horizon Press, 1959], p. 113).

12. Alan Westin, "The Origins of Modern Claims to Privacy," in *Philosophical Dimensions of Privacy*, ed. Ferdinand D. Schoeman (Cambridge: Cambridge University Press, 1984), p. 56.

FREEDOM AND LIBERALISM IN PRACTICE

13. Karl Marx, *Karl Marx: Selected Writings*, ed. David McLellan (Oxford: Oxford University Press, 1977), p. 56.

14. Richard Rorty, "Review of Jacques Derrida's *Specters of Marx: The State of the Debt, the Work of Mourning, and the New International*" (unpublished, 1995), pp. 11–12.

15. Rorty, *CIS*, p. 177.

16. Rorty, "Thugs and Theorists," p. 567. Refer to John Rawls, *A Theory of Justice* (Cambridge, Mass.: Harvard University Press, 1971), pp. 60 ff. David Hall similarly has noted that there is a tension between Rorty's "radical separation of the public and private and his belief in a centerless self" (David L. Hall, *Richard Rorty: Prophet and Poet of the New Pragmatism* [Albany: SUNY Press, 1994], p. 167).

17. A *class* may be defined as a social group with a common relationship to the production and appropriation of surplus labor, a common relationship that differs greatly from or is opposed to one or more other such social groups (cf. Markar Melkonian, *Marxism: A Post–Cold War Primer* [Boulder: Westview Press, 1996], pp. 50–52). I am aware of alternative definitions of class, including a definition based on a relationship to ownership or control of the means of production (cf. Ralph Miliband, *The State in Capitalist Society* [New York: Basic Books, 1969], pp. 15–22; Erik Olin Wright, *Class, Crisis and the State* [London: New Left Books, 1978], pp. 96–97). These definitions, of course, are related in an obvious way: Ownership and control of the means of production permits appropriation of surplus labor or surplus value. Since one effect of class division is great inequalities of wealth and power, both of these class entry points are congenial to the present discussion.

18. With reference to slipping wages, refer, for example, to the Bureau of Labor statistics cited in the *Los Angeles Times* (September 4, 1995, pp. A1, A20, A22). The authors of the *New York Times* series (which appeared from Sunday, March 3, to Saturday, March 9, 1996) cite U.S. Department of Labor, Department of Commerce, and Datastream sources. Rorty cites the *New York Times* series in Richard Rorty, *Achieving Our Country* (Cambridge and London: Harvard University Press, 1998), p. 148 n. 4 (hereafter cited as *AOC*).

19. This and the next citation are from Richard Rorty, "Postmodernist Bourgeois Liberalism," *Journal of Philosophy* 80, no. 10 (October 1983): 585.

20. Refer, for example, to Jerry Kloby, "The Growing Divide: Class Polarization in the 1980s," *Monthly Review* 39, no. 4 (September 1987): 1–8.

21. Rorty, "Review of *Specters of Marx*," p. 18; Richard Rorty, "The End of Leninism and History as Comic Frame" (unpublished), p. 5. Rorty is not always

consistent, though. His recognition of the need to mitigate "class conflict, social division, patriarchy, racism" (Rorty, "Thugs and Theorists," p. 567) is, after all, a recognition of the reality of class division, among other evils. In response to a question from the audience at a lecture at Northwestern University, he even went so far as to endorse Marx and Engels's formulation, "The executive of the modern state is but a committee for managing the common affairs of the whole bourgeoisie" (Richard Rorty, "Intellectuals at the End of Socialism," lecture delivered at Northwestern University, January 17, 1992). A similar formulation appears in Rorty, *AOC*, p. 48.

22. Richard Rorty, "Movements and Campaigns" (unpublished), p. 4. More recently, it seems, Rorty has found it harder to ridicule talk about class conflict. By the time "Movements of Campaigns" was included as an appendix in *Achieving Our Country* (Cambridge and London: Harvard University Press, 1998), pp. 111–24, the facetious references to class struggle and *les rois fainéants* had disappeared.

23. Included in Louis Althusser, "Ideology and Ideological State Apparatuses," in *Lenin and Philosophy* (New York: Monthly Review Press, 1971), pp. 127–86. I do not want to give the impression that I endorse other well-known writings of Althusser, in particular some of his writings on epistemology and the philosophy of the sciences.

24. Ibid., p. 137. Note that I will use the word *state* to cover a narrower range of institutions than Althusser would have it cover.

25. The qualifier "as a whole" is important here. As the example of the Unidad Popular administration in Chile shows quite clearly, one class alliance can control much of the government and local administrations, while failing to control the political state as a whole. We will return to this point below.

26. A concise defense of the existence of class rule in the United States against the criticisms of pluralist sociologists appears in William Domhoff, "State and Ruling Class in Corporate America," *Insurgent Sociologist* 4, no. 3 (spring 1974): 3–16. More recent studies of class rule in the liberal democracies include Albert Szymanski, *The Capitalist State and the Politics of Class* (Cambridge, Mass.: Winthrop, 1978); Bob Jessup, *The Capitalist State* (New York: New York University Press, 1982); and Martin Carnoy, *State and Political Theory* (Princeton: Princeton University Press, 1984).

27. Cf. V. I. Lenin, *The State and Revolution* (New York: International Publishers, 1932), p. 96.

28. The passage, from a letter of September 7, 1931, to Tatiana Schucht,

appears in Antonio Gramsci, *Letters from Prison,* ed. Lynne Lawner (New York: Noonday Press, 1989), pp. 204–05.

29. Althusser, "Ideology and Ideological State Apparatuses," pp. 131–33.

30. Ibid., p. 144.

31. Cf. Nicos Poulantzas, *State, Power, Socialism* (London: NLB, 1978), p. 18.

32. Althusser, "Ideology and Ideological State Apparatuses," p. 144.

33. Gramsci observed that in his Italy no one was disorganized and without a party; individuals almost always belong to more than one private association. Indeed, he asked whether readers of a newspaper constitute an organization (Antonio Gramsci, *Selections from the Prison Notebooks* [New York: International Publishers, 1971], p. 265).

34. Weber famously acknowledged the importance of "political circumstances" vis-à-vis religious ideas (refer, for example, to Max Weber, *The Protestant Ethic and the Spirit of Capitalism* [London and New York: Routledge, 1992], pp. 277–78 n. 84).

35. Honi Fern Haber, *Beyond Postmodern Politics: Lyotard, Rorty, Foucault* (New York: Routledge, 1994), p. 61.

36. Gramsci, *Prison Notebooks,* p. 235, emphasis in the original. Gramsci did not succeed in finding a single, wholly satisfactory conception of civil society in relation to the state. On occasion, for example, he described the state as "political society + civil society," and as "hegemony protected by the armor of coercion" (ibid., p. 263); elsewhere, he wrote that "in concrete reality, civil society and State are one and the same" (ibid., p. 208 n). Gramsci sometimes used the term *civil society* "in the sense of political and cultural hegemony of a social group over the entire society, as ethical content of the State." Still elsewhere, he wrote: "Between the economic structure and the State with its legislation and its coercion stands civil society" (cf. ibid., pp. 207–08 n).

37. Ibid., p. 243.

38. Ibid., p. 236.

39. Rorty, *CIS,* p. 65.

40. Cf. Richard Rorty, "The Priority of Democracy to Philosophy," in *Reading Rorty,* ed. Alan Malachowski (Cambridge, Mass.: Basil Blackwell, 1990), p. 295.

41. Rorty, "Thugs and Theorists," p. 566.

42. Rorty, *CIS,* p. 171.

43. Citations in this sentence are from ibid., p. 182 and Richard Rorty, *Objectivity, Realism, and Truth* (Cambridge: Cambridge University Press, 1991), p. 221 (hereafter cited as *ORT*). Also refer to Rorty, "Thugs and Theorists," p. 566,

with reference to "... the steady extension of Moscow's empire throughout the Southern Hemisphere," a development that, in 1987, Rorty felt was likely to take place in the next century.

44. Richard Rorty, *Essays on Heidegger and Others* (Cambridge University Press, 1991), p. 26 n (hereafter cited as *EH*). One wonders, parenthetically, whether Lincoln was hated as thoroughly and unanimously by those he freed from slavery as Gorbachev is by the Russians he supposedly freed from totalitarianism. Still, Rorty's evaluation of Gorbachev compares favorably to the inane descant in Konstantin Kolenda, *Rorty's Humanistic Pragmatism: Philosophy Democratized* (Tampa: University of South Florida Press, 1990), pp. 65–84.

45. Refer to Rorty, *CIS*, p. 170, with reference to the grip of "Bolshevik propaganda" on the minds of French intellectuals.

46. To his credit, Rorty also describes the "shadowy millionaires manipulating Reagan" as a gang of thugs (Rorty, "Thugs and Theorists," pp. 566–67).

47. Shlapentokh, *Public and Private Life of the Soviet People*, p. 13. One can only imagine the howls of indignation from liberals in the West if Brezhnev, rather than Yeltsin, had asked Russian children to report their tax-dodging parents to the authorities.

48. Poulantzas, *State, Power, Socialism*, p. 247.

49. Shlapentokh, *Public and Private Life of the Soviet People*, p. 164.

50. Ibid., pp. 168–69.

51. Althusser, "Ideology and Ideological State Apparatuses," pp. 143–45. It should be noted, however, that many working class, poor, and black families in the United States today appear to lack the stability requisite for a well-functioning apparatus of class rule.

52. Jacques Donzelot has reported that, at the turn of the century in France, the state took steps in the areas of public assistance, juvenile law, medicine, public schooling, public housing, and psychiatry that reduced patriarchal authority, and hence the autonomy of the family among the "less-favored" classes (Jacques Donzelot, *The Policing of Families* [New York: Pantheon Books, 1979], p. 89). According to him, the family in its contemporary permutations is neither a guarantor against the encroachments of the state nor an ideological apparatus of the bourgeois state, as Althusser would have it (ibid., pp. 52–53).

53. Poulantzas, *State, Power, Socialism*, p. 72.

54. Munkirs, *Transformation of American Capitalism*, pp. 12–44.

55. Refer to Herbert I. Schiller, *Culture, Inc.: The Corporate Takeover of Public Expression* (New York: Oxford University Press, 1989).

56. Edward Said, *Culture and Imperialism* (New York: Alfred A. Knopf, 1993), p. 118.

57. Rorty, *EH,* p. 4.

58. Rorty, *CIS,* p. 176.

59. It is interesting to note that nowhere in volume 38 of Lenin's *Collected Works* will one find a conspectus of Hegel's *Philosophy of Right,* and a perusal of the index to the *Collected Works* reveals little evidence that the founder of the Bolshevik Party ever read the book. For Lenin, who in other respects was a great admirer of the German idealist, Hegel's philosophy of history was "obsolete and antiquated" (V. I. Lenin, *Collected Works,* vol. 38 [Moscow: Progress Publishers, 1976], p. 312).

60. Quoted in Goran Therborn, *What Does the Ruling Class Do When It Rules?* (London: New Left Books, 1978), p. 69.

61. On February 7, 1990, the Soviet Party's Central Committee voted to repudiate Article Six of the 1977 Constitution of the USSR. This article guaranteed that the Party would determine "...the general perspectives of the development of society and the course of the domestic and foreign policy of the USSR," as well as "the great constructive work of the Soviet people."

62. Gorbachev was correct at least in the view that this proposal—and for that matter, every other proposal on this list—is compatible with Leninist political practice. Referring to the Paris Commune, Lenin wrote: "We cannot imagine democracy, even proletarian democracy, without representative institutions, but we can and must imagine democracy without parliamentarianism" (quoted in Wright, *Class, Crisis and the State,* p. 201).

63. Cf. Mikhail S. Gorbachev, *Perestroika: New Thinking for Our Country and the World* (New York: Harper and Row, 1988).

64. It might be suggested that, rather than seeking to bring all subversive institutions within the compass of state sanction, democracy and workers' power would be better served by maintaining the existence of oppositional institutions in tension with state institutions. Holding state institutions accountable even to the most hostile criticism might actually strengthen them by enhancing their efficiency and stability. Paradoxically, however, once the ruling class is confident enough of its political power and in possession of sufficient resources to sanction the existence of oppositional institutions, this gesture itself has amounted to the cooptation and effective transformation of them into reformist institutions.

65. Hall, *Richard Rorty,* p. 156.

66. Ibid., p. 155.
67. Rorty, *CIS,* p. 59 n.
68. Rorty discusses Philip Larkin's trope in ibid., pp. 23 ff.
69. Geuss clearly has informed Rorty's discussion of *Ideologiekritik* (ibid., p. 59 n; Raymond Geuss, *The Idea of a Critical Theory: Habermas and the Frankfurt School* [Cambridge: Cambridge University Press, 1981], pp. x, 3). Geuss uses the word *Ideologiekritik* to designate "a reflective theory which gives agents a kind of knowledge inherently productive of enlightnenment and emancipation," where enlightenment involves attainment of knowledge of one's "*true interests*" (ibid., p. 2).
70. Rorty, "Thugs and Theorists," pp. 569–70; Rorty, *EH,* pp. 187–88.
71. Rorty, *EH,* p. 60, emphasis in the original. In the first section of chapter 1 I have glossed some key points in Rorty's case against searching for such essences.
72. Rorty, *CIS,* p. 59 n. This description, it will be noted, does not square easily with "...the idea Havel mocks when he says that a mark of the good communist is that he 'subscribes to an ideology and believes that anyone who doesn't subscribe to it must therefore subscribe to another ideology, because he can't imagine anyone's not subscribing to an ideology'" (Rorty, "The End of Leninism," p. 10; Rorty cites Havel's collection of interviews published under the title *Disturbing the Peace* [New York: Vintage, 1991], p. 80).
73. Richard Rorty, *Philosophy and the Mirror of Nature* (Princeton: Princeton University Press, 1979), p. 8 (hereafter cited as *PMN*). Like almost every opponent of Marxism, Rorty misinterprets it as an economic reductionism or determinism (Rorty, *AOC,* p. 93). Also see Cornelius Castoriadis, *The Imaginary Institution of Society* (Oxford: Polity Press, 1987), p. 29.
74. Rorty, *CIS,* p. 84 n.
75. The quote, from Rorty's "From Logic to Language Play," appears in Hall, *Richard Rorty,* p. 177.
76. Rorty, *CIS,* pp. 173–74. Also refer to Rorty, *AOC,* p. 11.
77. Geuss, *The Idea of a Critical Theory,* pp. 12 ff. This presumably would include Gustave Bergmann's definition of an ideological statement as " a value judgment disguised as or mistaken for a statement of fact" (cited in ibid., p. 14 n).
78. Cf. ibid., p. 18.
79. Refer to the discussion of ideology as worldview in ibid., pp. 9–11.
80. Cf. Geuss' "ideology in a programmatic sense" (ibid., p. 11).
81. Rorty himself comes close to this formulation when he approvingly

cites Davidson's view that "...new metaphors are causes but not reasons for changes of belief" (Rorty, *CIS*, p. 50), and when he notes that when metaphors die they cease to be merely causes and become reasons for beliefs (Rorty, *ORT,* p. 171).

82. Richard Rorty, "Habermas, Derrida, and the Functions of Philosophy" (unpublished), p. 20.

83. It will be noticed that Marx's treatment in *Das Kapital* of the fetishism of the commodity and the wage form is compatible not only with (a) and (b), but also with at least one of meanings (c) through (j).

84. With reference to (c) and (h): To the extent that principles of state power or economic practices are "efficacious," they likely would not be injurious to holders of state power or economically dominant groups. A similar remark would apply to (i). With reference to (d): To the extent that the rules in question are "efficacious," they likely would not be injurious to those like Rorty who wish to efface the morality-prudence distinction. With reference to (e): Unqualifiedly injurious behavior is not likely to be repeated by enough agents over a long enough period of time to constitute a pattern or lived relation to the world. With reference to (j) and (k): While neither of these formulations is obviously incompatible with Rorty's notion of ideology as "bad ideas," they do not appear to have any special relevance to it, either.

85. John Dewey, *John Dewey: The Later Works, 1925–1927*, vol. 2, ed. Jo Ann Boydston (Carbondale and Edwardsville: Southern Illinois University Press, 1984), p. 277.

86. Rorty, "Habermas, Derrida, and the Functions of Philosophy," p. 15.

87. Kai Nielsen, *After the Demise of the Tradition: Rorty, Critical Theory, and the Fate of Philosophy* (Boulder: Westview Press, 1991), p. 213. For the relevant views of Davidson, refer to Donald Davidson, "A Coherence Theory of Truth and Knowledge," in Malachowski, *Reading Rorty,* pp. 120–38.

88. Refer to Gramsci, *Prison Notebooks,* pp. 419–25. Also refer to the discussion in Nielsen, *After the Demise of the Tradition,* p. 174.

89. Cf. Rorty, *EH,* pp. 55, 166. With reference to Rorty's own "Grand Narrative" about the vicissitudes of Western philosophy, see Hall, *Richard Rorty,* pp. 8, 15, 245–46 n. 19. Charles Taylor hints that the result is a metanarrative of the sort Rorty claims to abjure (Charles Taylor, "Rorty in the Epistemological Tradition," in Malachowski, *Reading Rorty,* p. 257).

90. Rorty, *EH,* p. 185. Reviewing the list of definitions above, it will be noticed that in cases (c), (h), (j), (h_2), and possibly in (i) and (k), the study of ide-

ology need not pose or pretend to solve any heady epistemological problems about the appearance-reality distinction. After all, to cease opposing appearance to reality as mutually exclusive categories does not require us, absurdly, to deny the appearance/nonappearance distinction in first-order discourses. Since appearances presumably have causes, we could always think of them as part of a larger reality not limited to appearances.

91. Refer to ibid., p. 165.

92. Ibid., p. 55.

93. Rorty, "Thugs and Theorists," p. 569. Also refer to the discussion of the "Cultural Left" in Rorty, *AOC*, especially pp. 75–107.

94. Rorty, *EH,* p. 135. Also refer to Rorty, "Thugs and Theorists," p. 577 n. 16, with reference to feminism as "...the one area of *Ideologiekritik* where people are actually having some new ideas."

CHAPTER FOUR
DECENCY AND LIBERALISM IN PRACTICE

If we are to believe Rorty, America will go down in history as having done more than any of the great empires so far to promote what Sidney Hook called the cause of "enlarging human freedom in a precarious and tragic world by the arts of intelligent social control."[1] This prognostication, of course, is probably on target, at least in the medium run. As Rorty reminds us, "To say that *we* think we're heading in the right direction is just to say, with Kuhn, that we can, by hindsight, tell the story of the past as a story of progress."[2] Judging from more than ample evidence past and present, however, telling such a story is little more than a perfunctory gesture that may accompany indefinitely large volume displacements of the blood and tears of innocents. The historiographies to which most people are exposed, after all, are written *for*, if not entirely *by*, the victors: As a rule, the victors, their heirs and scribes are the "we" who spin stories of the past as histories of progress.

Judging from the context in which the passage quoted appears, however, Rorty intends it to be taken not as an observation about the politics of historiography, but as a congratulatory statement about the exemplary moral status of the United States of America and other "rich North Atlantic democracies." By his lights, these countries represent the best hope for propagating the ideals of freedom from the constraints of the state and amelioration of suffering. As we have seen, these are the highest private and public aims of strong poets and decent citizens, respectively. As ideals they figure prominently in Rorty's definitions of a liberal community as "one which has no purpose except freedom,"[3] and of a liberal as a person for whom cruelty is the worst thing we do.

In the previous chapter, by contrast, we saw that in existing liberal democracies such as the United States, freedom from the supervision and sway of state institutions is narrowly circumscribed. This consideration casts serious doubt on the claim that the United States has contributed notably to the cause of enlarging human freedom within its cartographic borders.

In this chapter, I will dispute Rorty's claim that the most powerful liberal democracies have done a notably good job of ameliorating suffering beyond their borders. This will complete the negative side of my indictment of his description of actually existing liberalism.

To make the case that the most powerful contemporary liberal democracies continually promote massive tyranny and suffering abroad, however, is not enough to compromise Rorty's paraphrase of Churchill, to the effect that the existing liberal democracies are the worst political setups imaginable, with the exception of all the other candidates.[4] Defenders of these liberal democracies could always claim, as they have done, that any realizable alternative to liberal democracy in its present form would result in even more tyranny and suffering.

As Rorty has emphasized, public criticism gains force by virtue of contrast effects. The effect may be achieved by comparing a past or present state of affairs invidiously with another actual state of affairs, or a past or present state of affairs invidiously with a particular utopian vision, or one utopia invidiously with another. The case of Foucault may serve as a negative illustration of this point. Rorty appreciates the late French author as an ironist theorist who is useful for tracing the

DECENCY AND LIBERALISM IN PRACTICE

blind impresses our individual behavings bear. However, he dismisses Foucault as a public thinker, in part because the author of *Surveiller et punir* (*Discipline and Punishment*) was unwilling or unable to offer an alternative vision to the pervasive disciplinary regimes he described.

Acknowledging Rorty's challenge, then, I will make the case toward the end of the first section of this chapter that it is possible to imagine a political setup that would be more conducive to the aim of ameliorating pain than mere preservation and piecemeal reform of existing liberal institutions and practices. In the second section, I will argue that, pace Rorty, existing liberal democracies do not contain the institutions necessary for improvement along these lines. If my account is on the mark, it will cast a bad light on Rorty's claim that existing liberal democracies are conducive to the liberal ideal of ameliorating suffering.

LIBERALISM AND SUFFERING

It is, of course, all too easy to compile a long, long list of atrocities committed by, for and in the name of liberalism. Basil Davidson, Noam Chomsky, Eduardo Galeano, and lots of other writers have described the emergence of the liberal democracies as a long litany of slavery, pillage, and genocide. And even if we purge from these accounts all depredations committed during the course of primitive accumulation and high colonialism, and concentrate only on the twentieth century, the list of horrors remains very lengthy indeed.

Rorty certainly does not emphasize the causal connections between these depredations and the existing liberal democracies. But he does not dispute the claim that genocide, pillage, and slavery were conditions of actuality of liberalism as it has come down to us today, either.[5] Nor does he provide any reason to doubt that claim. Moreover, he acknowledges that liberal ideals of universal freedom and equality continue to be betrayed in contemporary liberal democracies. He is even prepared to concede that they are *constantly* betrayed.[6]

He also acknowledges from time to time that the same liberal democratic governments that promote tolerance and liberty at home may promote tyranny abroad, and in fact have done so. He admits, for example, that poverty in Latin America is "partially due to the deals struck between local plutocracies and North American banks and governments."[7] Thus, he would not subscribe to the first premise in the following simplistic but familiar argument:

P[1]: Any political system which pursues a brutal and exploitative foreign policy cannot be liberal;

P[2]: The U.S. political system is liberal;

Therefore, by *modus tollens*, etc.

Yet he remains unflinchingly committed to both liberalism and existing liberal democracies.[8] In view of these observations, the question arises: How can Rorty remain a liberal, in Shklar's sense of the word as "one who believes that cruelty is the worst thing we do," while remaining unflinchingly committed to the institutions and practices of actually existing liberalism?

Rorty avers a response to this question: In addition to the horrors they have produced,

> the liberal societies of our century have produced more and more people who are able to recognize the contingency of the vocabulary in which they state their highest hopes—the contingency of their own consciences—and yet have remained faithful to those consciences.[9]

Such recognition, he adds on the same page, is the chief virtue of those who make up a liberal public. Over the past two centuries, these people have created institutions and practices—free presses, independent judiciaries, legal assemblies, representative political institutions, free universities, and so on—that have helped to abolish such practices as chattel slavery, child labor, direct colonial domination, and racial segregation. To advocate destroying or superseding these liberal institutions and practices would amount to condemning instruments that have proven to be effective in mitigating cruelty and humiliation. Because the liberal institutions that exist in some parts of the globe (preeminently, as it turns out, in the countries that benefited most from genocide,

DECENCY AND LIBERALISM IN PRACTICE 139

slavery, and pillage in the past) are a means of ensuring that ongoing horrors will be ameliorated, their continued existence may be viewed as a compensation for the horrors of the past. It may be small compensation in view of the magnitude of those horrors, but it is compensation nevertheless.

In *AOC*, Rorty builds a case along these lines for renewed hope for American liberalism. His case comports with the following two assumptions about liberal institutions:

(i) Free presses, independent judiciaries, and the other liberal institutions we have mentioned are compatible with any of a number of different political and economic setups. We can have these liberal institutions without the horrors committed by, for, and in their name. Furthermore, there is no "deep link between capitalism and democracy" or other liberal institutions, nor for that matter between "central economic planning and tyranny."[10]

(ii) Not only are these liberal institutions useful as a means of ameliorating horrors, but they are the best means at hand for doing so. Neither opponents of liberalism nor anyone else have provided alternatives to extant liberal institutions that realistically could be expected to do a better job of ameliorating these horrors. Again: Liberalism may be an unattractive political setup, but it is less unattractive than any other candidate.

If these two assumptions stand, Rorty has produced a compelling defense of actually existing liberalism against its detractors to his left. At best, "radical" opposition to liberalism would appear to be a pointless exercise in resentment. And at worst, it could, under some circumstances, come close to reckless endangerment of fragile but supremely precious institutions.

As one might have guessed from the discussion of socialism and privatization in the previous chapter, assumption (i) appears to be well-taken. Even if critics of liberalism were to succeed in showing the dependence of actually existing liberalism on betrayal of liberal ideals, they would not have succeeded in showing counterfactually that if this connection were broken liberal institutions could not be sustained. The observation that ex-colonial powers such as Great Britain, the Netherlands, and France managed to retain their liberal institutions in the postcolonial era might cast additional doubt on this.

With reference to the acknowledged evils of existing liberal democracies, Rorty writes: "Whereas liberals think of these evils as eventually reformable, radicals are concerned to show that they are somehow 'integral' to liberal society."[11] A radical, for Rorty, is a person who harbors no hope of improving existing liberal democracies in a piecemeal fashion. If such people turn out to be right, removing these evils will require things being changed utterly, including replacing or destroying—rather than reforming—some important institutions in the liberal West. Among these institutions we may count a corporate-dominated "free press," electoral systems that favor the candidates of big business, reformist unions with promanagement bureaucracies, and, of course, "the market economy"—that is, capitalism. These are the sorts of sweeping changes advocated by what Rorty refers to as *movements*, in contrast to *campaigns* focusing on piecemeal reform of specific institutions and practices.

The radicals hold that, as Richard Bernstein has put it,

> There are forces and tendencies at work, (e.g., class conflict, social division, patriarchy, racism) that are compatible with liberal political practices but nevertheless foster *real* inequality and limit effective political freedom.[12]

Rorty's likely response to this might be to agree with Bernstein's claim, but to point out that other forces and tendencies compatible with liberal practices are in place, too—forces and tendencies such as those already noted, which foster equality and expand political freedom.

For reasons already mentioned, this is a plausible response. Bernstein, however, has raised the stakes: It is not merely that the institutions and practices of actually existing liberalism are *compatible* with inequality and political unfreedom; nor is it merely that the former are results at least in part of past horrors. Rather, the former *continue to foster inequality and unfreedom as a condition of their actuality*. As Bernstein has put it, "the structural dynamics of bourgeois society systematically undermine and belie liberal ideals."[13]

With reference to the manner in which liberal ideals are betrayed, the difference between Bernstein's adverb *systematically* and Rorty's *constantly* is pivotal. Bernstein's adverb implies a logical, transcendental, or

DECENCY AND LIBERALISM IN PRACTICE 141

causal relationship of some sort, whereas Rorty's need imply little more than frequent occurrence.

Rorty evidently takes the adverb "systematically" to designate a relationship of final causality or transcendental conditionality. He might well view the "structural dynamics" allegedly responsible for the systematicity of the betrayal as synonymous with "essence," and as yet another example of the spurious discovery by theoreticians of "underlying structures" or "something deep down," a taproot to be eradicated. He is likely to dismiss the notion of any "dynamics of bourgeois society" as yet another "large theoretical construct" purporting to unmask what is *really* going on, a construct of the sort that *Ideologiekritik* is alleged to provide.[14] By inveighing against exploitation, class conflict, and imperialism as examples of "deep processes" that theoreticians like to invoke, but that allegedly make no discernible difference to the conduct of public affairs, he thereby preempts consideration of the hypothesis that there is a causal connection between exploitation or imperialism on the one hand and liberalism on the other. This makes it easier for him to acknowledge that "liberal ideals of universal freedom and equality are constantly betrayed in bourgeois capitalist societies," as Bernstein put it, while ignoring the question (which David Hall notes Rorty never raises) whether his goals of social justice and amelioration of suffering are at all likely to be attained under capitalism. Rorty can lament the shortsightedness of high officeholders in the rich North Atlantic and the greed of middle-class suburbanites, while never raising the question whether his utopian hope for capitalism with a human face is anything more than a will-o'-the-wisp.

For Rorty the historical nominalist, each individual instance of betrayal of liberal ideals has (efficient) causes. It is the task of the social engineer and the piecemeal reformer to identify these causes on a case-by-case basis and to eliminate or modify them one by one. A free press, free universities, and other liberal institutions play a crucial role in the performance of this task. In this way, liberal institutions gradually mitigate the betrayal of liberal ideals.

These considerations, even stated as sketchily as they are here, bolster the second assumption mentioned above, namely that liberal institutions are the best means at hand for ameliorating the horrors committed by and for existing liberal regimes. If this assumption stands, it serves as a strong support for Rorty's claim that "*Nothing* is more important than the preservation of these liberal institutions."[15]

There is a parallel here between the institutions and practices of liberalism on the one hand and "technology" on the other. In response to a correspondent's observation that much of the poverty of the Third World is caused by the West, Rorty impertinently writes: "My hunch is that more Western science and technology is about the only thing that can cope with the results of prior Western science and technology."[16] Only *more* modern technology, not less, will remedy environmental pollution, diminishing resources, toxic waste disposal, and other evils regularly laid at the door of the rich North Atlantic democracies. Rorty's techno-panacean views chime with maneuvers by protransnational corporate bodies such as the General Agreement on Tariffs and Trade (GATT), which tie access to the latest technologies to the production of "favorable investment climates" in the South. He hardly dispels this impression with such revealingly confused remarks as: "The reliance on Marxism on the part of the people trying to overthrow Third World oligarchies seems to me potentially as dangerous as their grandparents' reliance on the United Fruit Company or Anaconda Copper."[17]

Rorty acknowledges that liberal institutions often function as tools of local oligarchs. Nevertheless, he claims, if the conditions of actuality of liberalism have so far undermined and belied liberal ideals, then these conditions can and should be identified, one by one, and either reformed or replaced. This replacement, however, need not and should not involve the rejection or abandonment of liberal institutions already in place. As he puts it, "...the principal institutions of contemporary democratic societies do not require 'unmasking' but rather strenuous utilization, supplemented by luck."[18]

Unfortunately, liberal institutions are prey to a number of dangers, including the dangers of bureaucratization Weber discussed in *Economy and Society* (*Wirtschaft und Gesellschaft*), part 3. In addition, in times of sweeping social change liberal institutions have been among the first things to be swept away. Liberal institutions and practices have been easy targets for demagogues, who in times of crisis have focused on cases of abuse and inefficiency to transform these institutions and practices into targets of popular discontent. By inhibiting their operation, demagogues have removed obstacles to their own unchecked authoritarian rule.

These observations only underscore the preciousness of these "fragile, flawed institutions." Their fragility and preciousness only make it more imperative to take care to preserve them. Thus, nothing prohibits Rorty from recognizing that, like the public/private split, liberal institutions also are fortuitous accidents of time and chance, while at the same time he holds that nothing is more worthy of our unflinching allegiance.

Without wishing to dispute Rorty's characterization of liberal institutions as precious, I believe nevertheless that a liberal, as Judith Shklar defines one, could plausibly deny his unqualified assertion that nothing is more important than their preservation. In the course of making this point in the balance of this chapter, I will assume that no institution, liberal or otherwise, should be viewed in isolation from its larger social context. In order to evaluate whether or not contemporary liberal institutions in fact do ameliorate suffering, we should take special care to examine the larger context of state power and global capitalism.

THE SOLEMN COMPLEMENT OF RORTY'S IDEALS

Another reason Rorty cannot accommodate the suggestion that liberal institutions be recast within the context of working-class state power is that, as he has made clear in more recent writings, he is committed not merely to the several liberal institutions mentioned above, but also to "the institutions of large market economies." "Large market economies," he believes, constitute the "economic determinants" of liberal democracies: The North Atlantic has achieved its measure of decency and equality by relying on "a free market in capital and on compromises between pressure groups."[19] In this respect, he is once again backing away from Dewey's New Liberalism to a position closer to that of the English classical liberals who associated liberty with laissez-faire economic policies.

Rorty sidesteps questions about exploitation, class domination, and managerial despotism at the work site. Nor has he much to say about the enormous concentration of capital in fewer and fewer hands in his "large market economies," or the merging of corporate and state power, or the repercussions of what I have referred to as *globalism* on the notion of government by consent. And even after *Achieving Our Country*, he does not seem particularly cognizant of the impact, on cities and on the planet as a whole, of what Hall has called the capitalist celebration of "the multiplication of desires and their transmogrification into needs."[20]

Although he has little to say, even in passing, about these defects of "large market economies," he does identify one or two of its drawbacks: Capitalism, notably, breeds greed and inequality. Still, he can think of no better way to mitigate the greed and inequality that capitalism spawns than liberal institutions and the welfare state, together with good will and the patience to muddle through campaigns for piecemeal reform.

As luck would have it, the liberal democracies themselves have produced decent public citizens with the requisite patience, toleration, and good will.[21] The allegedly greater ability of members of liberal democracies to enlarge their conception of "us" is itself the result of institutions internal to liberal democracies. The greater freedom and decreased pain for which liberal institutions and practices deserve credit compensates for the greed and inequality they spawn, as well as the constraints Foucault associated with them.[22] Indeed, the existence of these institutions is reason enough to hope that the rich North Atlantic democracies may prefigure "the utopian world community envisaged by the Charter of the United Nations and the Helsinki Declaration of Human Rights."[23]

Lamentably, bourgeois capitalist society is "irrelevant to most of the problems for most of the population of the planet."[24] Rorty decries

> the impossibility of feeding countries like Haiti and Chad except by massive charity which the rich nations are too selfish to provide, and the unbreakable grip of the rich or the military on the governments of most of the Third World.[25]

Continuing in this vein, he invokes Robert Kaplan's "memorable" image of "people like ourselves—middle-class American and European readers of magazines like [*Dissent*]" riding in "a stretch limousine, making its way through a mob of ragged and desperate people moving in the opposite direction." "Kaplan's way of describing our situation," Rorty goes on to explain,

> amounts to saying that while Europe and America have been worrying about how to go forward from capitalism, a lot of the rest of the world has been hoping to advance to feudalism.[26]

With a bit of nominalism at this point, one might conclude that there are plenty of ragged and desperate people in Europe and America, too. Surely it is significant, moreover, that among the most ragged and desperate people outside of Europe and America are those subjected not to some prefeudal regime, but to Europe and America's neocolonial surrogates, IMF conditionalities, and superexploiting megalopolies. Kaplan's image, conjuring up as it does a homogeneously affluent "us" and a homogeneously ragged and desperate "other," does little to advance Rorty's professed aim to de-essentialize the West, "to break up the lump."[27]

Rorty's (rather selective) disparagement of those who, he says, are constantly on the lookout for "something 'deep down'—something ahistorical and international,"[28] together with Kaplan's image of limousines and ragged mobs passing each other in opposite directions, complement the claim that bourgeois capitalism is irrelevant to most of the globe. It would be easy to challenge this view, of course. One might point out, for example, that the IMF, the World Bank, and the World Trade Organization—G-7-dominated institutions that advertise themselves as advancing the ideals of liberal democracy—explicitly have "planetary projects" of their own, including most recently the General Agreement on Tariffs and Trade and the Multilateral Agreement on Investments. These projects—under which top executive officers of the largest oligopolies and strategic planners in the leading capitalist centers most assuredly subsume *their* hopes[29]—are instances of centralized economic planning on a global scale.[30] Rorty's insouciance on this point has prompted one commentator to score his "skepticism concerning 'metanarratives' that disavows the movement of world spirit but that seems willfully ignorant of the movement of world capital."[31]

In *AOC*, Rorty has managed, at long last, to acknowledge "the globalization of the labor market—a trend which can reasonably be expected to accelerate indefinitely."[32] A century and a half earlier, however, Marx and Engels described with astonishing accuracy trends that Rorty would only get around to registering in the late 1990s. The twenty-odd pages of the *Communist Manifesto* bristle with descriptions of "a cosmopolitan character [of] production and consumption in every country"; of "new wants, requiring for their satisfaction the products of distant lands and climes"; of "intercourse in every direction, universal interdependence of nations"; of "immensely facilitated means of communication"; of "an epidemic that, in all earlier epochs would have seemed an absurdity—the epidemic of overproduction"; and of "that single unconscionable freedom—Free Trade." These phrases from section 1 of the *Manifesto* could be headlines from tomorrow morning's *Wall Street Journal*. Other passages read like clippings from the latest "postie" journals: Capitalist development, according to Marx and Engels, brings with it a "constant revolutionizing of production, uninterrupted disturbance of all social conditions, everlasting uncertainty and agitation." "All fixed, fast-frozen relations, with their train of ancient and venerable prejudices and opinions, are swept away," Marx and Engels wrote, "all new-formed ones become antiquated before they can ossify. All that is solid melts into air, all that is holy is profaned." "Modern bourgeois society," according to the *Manifesto*, "is like the sorcerer, who is no longer able to control the power of the nether world which he has called up by his spells." As a result, we end up with "too much civilization, too much means of subsistence, too much industry, too much commerce." According to Rorty, "What industrialization was to America at the end of the nineteenth century, globalization is at the end of the twentieth."[33] Marx and Engels, by contrast, drew a vivid picture of how, at the *beginning* of the modern age, capitalism set into motion both "modern industry" and "the world market." Their account in 1848 could hardly be further from Rorty's contention that bourgeois capitalism is irrelevant to "the rest of the world," which, at the end of the twentieth century, is still hoping to advance feudalism.

These considerations notwithstanding, and inadequate "foreign assistance" aside, Rorty praises the liberal West for its readiness to embrace an ever more inclusive conception of community. By his lights, as we have seen, "contemporary democratic societies are *already* organized around the need for continual exposure of suffering and injustice."[34] As he explains it,

> the liberal culture of recent times has found a strategy for avoiding the disadvantage of ethnocentrism. This is to be open to encounters with actual and possible cultures, and to make this openness central to its self-image.[35]

By fostering an ever broader recognition of suffering and injustice, liberal institutions make possible the kind of dialogue with foreigners that helps extend solidarity beyond the borders of existing liberal democracies.[36] This ever more inclusive conception of a public "we" increases with education, just as the number of communities with which an inhabitant of a rich North Atlantic democracy may identify increases with civilization.

Unfortunately, liberal intellectuals do not always manifest a concern to make sure that their fellow citizens notice suffering when it occurs. Far from it. Edward Said has observed that the amazing thing about the fact that the United States continues to try through force and threats to dictate its views about law and peace all over the globe, "is not that it is attempted, but that it is done with so much consensus and near unanimity in a public sphere constructed as a kind of cultural space expressly to represent and explain it."[37] Rorty himself does not exactly disrupt this consensus, as anyone may confirm by reading "Thugs and Theorists," "The Priority of Democracy to Philosophy," "The End of Leninism," much of *EH*, part 3 of *CIS*, and *AOC*. Even when Balslev, Bernstein, and others have directly challenged him to take measure of the demonstrable connection between the domestic political stability of the liberal democracies and the violence they engender abroad, he has demurred.

Referring to his colleagues in university humanities departments, Said has written:

> There is, I believe, a quite serious split in our critical consciousness today, which allows us to spend a great deal of time elaborating Car-

lyle and Ruskin's aesthetic theories, for example, without giving attention to the authority that their ideas simultaneously bestowed on the subjugation of inferior peoples and colonial territories.[38]

Rorty has enjoined us to stop worrying about "which theorists to pair off with which thugs."[39] When it comes to the Suslovs of the cold war East, however, he appears willing to accept that some theorists are thugs, not merely *contingently*, in the manner perhaps of Heidegger at the University of Heidelberg, but in their very capacity as theorists.[40] It should be noted, however, that if we substitute "moral and political" for "aesthetic" in the passage just cited, Said's observation applies equally well to Carlyle and Ruskin's contemporary, J. S. Mill, and Mill's admirer Isaiah Berlin. According to Berlin, the younger Mill opposed the dissolution of the East India Company because "he feared the dead hand of Government more than the paternalist and not inhuman rule of the Company's officials."[41] A number of writers have presented a rather different picture of East India Company rule.[42] If the latter writers are even close to the mark, Berlin and Rorty have spent time elaborating Mill and Berlin's political views while overlooking the authority that their ideas simultaneously have bestowed on the subjugation of inferior peoples and colonial territories.[43] This is not exactly a resounding testimony in favor of Rorty's claim that contemporary liberal democracies are already organized around the need for continual exposure of suffering and injustice.

Instances of liberal institutions (including "free presses" and "free universities") concealing massive suffering and injustice could be cited indefinitely. One further example, however, should suffice to cast serious doubt on Rorty's claim just mentioned: In consideration of their usefulness in the war against Communism, U.S. officials and more than one administration for decades protected from prosecution high-ranking Japanese military and political leaders, up to and including Emperor Hirohito himself. These leaders were responsible for the deaths of more than twenty million people in China between the years 1931 and 1945. Thus, a leading liberal democracy played an important role in helping to whitewash one of the most horrendous holocausts in recorded history, measured in absolute numbers of victims.[44] True, this holocaust eventually has come to the attention of an American audience larger than a

DECENCY AND LIBERALISM IN PRACTICE

handful of scholars. However, in view of the fact that it took five decades—and a shift in U.S.–Chinese relations—for this to happen, the belated recognition could hardly be said to redeem Rorty's picture of liberal institutions continually exposing suffering and injustice.

This example highlights a problem with Rorty's "thin" notion of community as a voluntary association, "one more of Nature's 'experiments.'"[45] This problem has less to do with its alleged thinness or thickness than with its broadness or narrowness. In one respect, Rorty's notion of community is too broad: As we have already noted with reference to class divisions within the North Atlantic democracies, he runs roughshod over existing conflicts, predatory relationships, and political domination within the formations he defines as communities. He assumes not only that the diverse impulses that animate the liberal democracies can be harmonized into common purposes, but that they can be identified as "our European purposes."[46]

Noting this, Fraser asks why we should assume, as Rorty does, "a quasi-Durkheimian view according to which society is integrated by way of a single monolithic and all-encompassing solidarity?"[47] Why, she asks, should we not assume instead "a quasi-Marxian view according to which modern capitalist societies contain a plurality of overlapping and competing solidarities"? As a good pluralist, of course, Rorty would agree that the liberal democracies contain a plurality of overlapping and competing solidarities. Clearly, however, Fraser is referring to competing solidarities that are distinguishable on the basis of a predatory relationship, such as that between exploiter and exploited, or perpetrator of violence and target of violence.

Perhaps the most obvious response to Fraser's question is tied up with Rorty's "we's," discussed above. The reason "we" should not assume Fraser's "quasi-Marxian view" is that such a view makes it more difficult to mount apologetics for bourgeois liberal democracy. As Said has noted, with reference to the all-important "we,"

> this pronoun, almost more than any other word, fortifies the somewhat illusory sense that all Americans, as co-owners of the public space, participate in the decisions to commit America to its far-flung foreign interventions.[48]

When, in *AOC*, Rorty writes of the need to foster of new sense of American national pride, rather than identity-group pride—and, one might add, *as opposed to* working-class pride—he runs the risk of feeding into the illusion Said has described.

In another respect, Rorty's notion of community is too narrow: Communities in the rich North Atlantic that establish ties of solidarity abroad have not always done so by first expanding their sense of solidarity to all or even most of their fellow citizens. Often, a community will demonstrate greater solidarity with "foreigners" than with their fellow citizens. In part 1 of his book *Solidarity in the Conversation of Humankind*, for example, Norman Geras cites many instances of "the righteous of the nations" in central and eastern Europe risking their lives to save supposed foreigners from Nazi persecution. But solidarity with "foreigners" in the face of the apathy or resistance of one's fellow citizens is not just a matter of noteworthy individuals or small solidarity groups within the rich North Atlantic joining hands with the wretched of the earth, in opposition to "our European purposes." On the other side of the fence, corporate officers and top managements of G-7-based transnational corporations continue to join with their brokers in the South to move production facilities to cheaper labor markets, in the face of working-class opposition at home, and foreign policy officers in the North collaborate with their counterparts in the South to create "favorable climates for investment" that result in higher unemployment and lower wages in the North and deeper burdens of debt, urban poverty, and pollution in the South. These examples might suffice to make the point that Rorty's "quasi-Durkheimian view" is not well suited for describing the reality of transnational capitalist class solidarity at the close of the American Century.

Maurice Merleau-Ponty noted that "It is not just a question of knowing what the liberals have in mind but what in reality is done by the liberal state within and beyond its frontiers."[49] Rorty the pragmatist might well have endorsed Merleau-Ponty's statement if the words "Marxists" and "socialist" were substituted for "liberals" and "liberal." As one critic has noted, however, when it comes to evaluating liberalism, Rorty "...tends to downplay what has become a major problem for liberals, viz.

'the disparity between the "ideals" of liberty and equality that liberals profess and the actual state of affairs in so-called liberal societies.'"[50]

As we have already noted, Rorty concedes that the existing liberal democracies constantly fall short of their ideals. One important reason for this is that, as he writes in a paper published in the waning years of Gorbachev's tenure,

> the social democratic scenario of steady reform along increasingly egalitarian lines...has been stalled for decades, largely because the political right within the First World (made up of the people who have no interest in increasing equality) diverted public attention, money, and energy to combating Soviet imperialism.[51]

"Soviet imperialism," Rorty hastens to add in the next sentence, "is indeed a threat."

If this account is at all in the ballpark, then with the disappearance of the Soviet threat, and all other things being equal, one would have expected to see "moderates" or "the political center" within the victorious First World seize the initiative: One would have expected at minimum to see signs of the resurrection of Rorty's social democratic scenario, of the expansion of the so-called welfare state, of "steady reform along increasingly egalitarian lines." In view of Reagan's enormous military buildup in the 1980s (a buildup that Reagan promoted by conjuring the image of the Evil Empire), for example, one might have expected in the post–cold war era to have seen deep cuts in military spending, and perhaps the reallocation of tax revenue from "defense" to education, health care, environmental protection, and so on. One might have expected at least to have seen some sort of more or less substantial "peace dividend." One certainly would not have expected to see hundred-billion-dollar contracts for a new generation of weapons systems, even greater spending on the CIA, cuts in nonmilitary "foreign aid," and the sweeping dismantlement of domestic social programs in the United States, England, Italy, France, and other leading liberal democracies.

What we have witnessed, however, is the latter scenario, not the former. In the wake of the cold war, there has been not a decrease but an *increase* of inequalities of wealth and opportunity within the United

States and other liberal democracies, along with exacerbated inequalities between North and South. More recently, Rorty has registered the calamity—at least judging from his description in *AOC* of a supernational dystopia run by a conspiratorial Orwellian Inner Party, with the support of a bribed and privileged "overclass."[52] Strangely, however, at a time of almost undisputed U.S. "world leadership," hundred-billion-dollar weapons systems, and U.S. military interventions on four continents, Rorty has lamented "the postwar failure of American nerve," and "the loss of America's hope to lead the nations."[53] True, U.S. "economic aid" to foreign countries has dropped 40 percent in real terms since the end of the cold war (one should keep in mind that during the cold war the United States devoted one of the smallest percentages of GDP of any highly industrialized country to such "aid"). U.S. arms exports, however, rose to over 60 percent of total arms exports globally—even before the announcement in the summer of 1997 of new sales of warplanes and high-tech weapons systems in Latin America. It has long been conceded even by observers in the West that the prospect of Soviet retaliation served to chasten U.S. leaders when it came to decisions whether or not to launch nuclear strikes against Korea, China, and North Vietnam. And it is hardly less controversial that the fear of expanding Soviet influence spurred the Marshall Plan and a host of other ambitious foreign aid projects in Asia, the Middle East, and Latin America, and helped to accelerate the postwar decolonization of Africa and much of Asia. As soon as the Soviet bogey dematerialized, however, Uncle Sam's posture of magnanimity abroad gave way to pious sermonizing about the salutary effects of entrepreneurship, "free markets," and "tough love." America, "the nuclear superpower which halted the spread of an Evil Empire," has never less resembled "the leader of an international movement to replace oligarchy with social democracy around the world."[54]

Turning to the domestic scene, a convincing case could be made that some of the most consequential initiatives benefiting the most disadvantaged at home were, at least in large part, responses to the threat of militancy on the home front, as well as fear of the expanding influence of Bolshevism.[55] These initiatives included the New Deal, social security, corporate income tax, civil rights legislation, and the revealingly entitled National Defense Education and National Defense

DECENCY AND LIBERALISM IN PRACTICE 153

Highway Acts. As soon as the struggle against Communism at home and abroad abated, however, many of the most celebrated achievements of the so-called welfare state were revoked. A host of social programs have been slashed at home, from healthcare to welfare, unions have been decimated, and the tax burden has shifted ever more squarely onto the shoulders of the working class.

These developments, moreover, have taken place despite propitious circumstances for Rorty's social democratic scenario, including a liberal Democratic administration in Washington, D.C., quiescent leaders in the South, and an abjectly subservient regime in the Kremlin. These trends, then, do not appear to have been caused because the institutions of liberal democracy are fragile or vulnerable. On the contrary, liberal democracy in practice has been *least* amenable to self-improvement along the lines Rorty suggests and has diverged most sharply from his liberal ideals precisely when it has found itself without threats from either the Evil Empire abroad or the Militant Tendency at home. There is strong empirical evidence, then, to doubt Rorty's claim that "... contemporary liberal society already contains the institutions for its own improvement."[56] Indeed, if the lessons of the past are any guide, the case could be made that the best hope for the resurrection of the so-called welfare state in the rich North Atlantic is the renewed threat of popular insurrection at home or abroad.

Rorty advises us to concede Fukayama's point that,

> if you still long for total revolution, for the Radically Other on a world-historical scale, the events of 1989 show that you are out of luck. Fukayama suggested, and I should agree, that no more romantic prospect stretches before the left than an attempt to create bourgeois democratic welfare states, and to equalize life-chances among the citizens of those states by redistributing the surplus produced by market economies.[57]

Leaving romance aside, events *since* 1989 have shown that, if you still long for "capitalism with a human face," you would appear to be out of luck, too. As we have seen, the "social democratic scenario" has, to a large extent, consisted not of self-reforming liberal institutions but of forced concessions in the face of foreign and domestic opposition. And as the perceived threat to capitalism has disappeared in the final years of the American Century, so have the liberal concessions. Thus, post–cold war developments have vindicated Marxists on yet another point upon which just a few years earlier there had been a near unanimous consensus that they were wrong.

Of course, these observations, taken singly or in combination, do not prove that existing liberal democracies systematically undermine and belie liberal ideals. If this claim is to be corroborated, then the burden of proof still lies with the critics of liberalism. They must identify the dynamics that belie liberal ideals, explain how they work, and argue that they make a big difference. Moreover, by the very nature of the question, they must do this on a case-by-case basis, building up enough of a body of evidence to justify a generalization about bourgeois society as a whole. If they fail to do this, then we are justified, at most, in withholding judgment.

It may not be an easy task to meet this burden of proof. But it is not necessarily a transcendental task, either. Surely it is possible to determine—in a first-order, nontranscendental sense of the verb—whether or not, say, capitalist class rule and imperialism are compatible with liberal political practices but nevertheless foster inequality and cruelty and limit effective political freedom. Rorty's public vocabulary may not be particularly well suited to this task.[58] Fortunately, however, alternative vocabularies are available, and at least one of these alternative vocabularies, namely the one introduced in chapter 3, does not involve specifying transcendental conditions of anything at all.

Describing the international scene in this vocabulary, it becomes apparent that massive violence and exploitation have constituted not only causal conditions for the appearance of the liberal democracies, but conditions of their ongoing actuality. Merleau-Ponty's observation continues to be as poignant in the final years of the American Century as it was in 1947:

> Judging from history and by everyday events, liberal ideals belong to a system of violence which, as Marx said, are the "spiritual *point d'honneur*," the "solemn complement" and the "general basis of consolation and justification."[59]

DECENCY BEYOND LIBERALISM

We have already granted that, at least to some extent and in some cases, liberal institutions have as a matter of fact mitigated the ongoing depredations committed by, for, or in the name of liberalism. Nevertheless, in view of the sheer scale, persistence, and frequency of these depredations, it should not be surprising that some parties—especially the targets and victims themselves—have come to suspect that there must be more efficacious means of ameliorating suffering than those of the rich North Atlantic democracies.

Rorty, however, claims that neither the "radical" opponents of liberalism nor anyone else has offered a workable alternative to liberalism that would be better at ameliorating pain and making the scene safe for strong poets. For one thing, few of these left-wing opponents, except the Marxists among them, have registered any notable success at even tabling a sustainable program for sweeping social change in the twentieth century. Moreover, the alleged attempt of Marxists to abolish private property—a proposal that Rorty describes as "just about the only constructive suggestion Marx made"[60]—did not work. This record of failure has led him to conclude that,

> Though I was brought up to be a socialist, I no longer want to nationalize the means of production (because the experience of Central and Eastern Europe suggests that nationalization is, to put it mildly, no help in redistributing wealth and power). I suspect we are stuck with market economies—which means with private property—for the foreseeable future.[61]

On those occasions when Rorty acknowledges that the word "socialism" has a use—and as we have seen, he sometimes advocates abandoning the term—he uses it to mean something like "attempts to foster institutions conducive to liberal aims." He contrasts this with what he (perhaps under the influence of Kolakowski) apparently takes to be a Marxist use of the word, to designate "nationalization of industry" or abolition of private property.[62]

It is worth noting that the experience of the 1990s has, "to put it mildly," cast suspicion on Rorty's suspicion about nationalization and redistribution of wealth: At the date of this writing, one would be hard pressed to cite even one case in eastern Europe or the former Soviet Union in which *de*-nationalization of the means of production has not coincided with ever wider disparities of wealth and deeper poverty for the majority. Setting these doubts aside, however, Rorty prefers Alan Ryan's suggestion that the best we can hope for is "a kind of welfare-capitalism-with-a-human-face, not easy to distinguish from a 'socialism' with a big role for private capital and individual entrepreneurs."[63]

It should be pointed out, however, that the two "isms" that Ryan's hope invokes would not be hard to distinguish if one were to define socialism *as state power of workers rather than capitalists*. As we have seen, however, Rorty does not wish to draw sharp distinctions along class lines or to emphasize political domination. To do so would clash with his Deweyan vision of the Great Community as a voluntary association of publics united by shared interests. It might even raise the question of the legitimacy of capitalist class rule in the rich North Atlantic. As we have seen, however, Rorty associates sweeping schemes for reordering the political landscape with, at best, pointless resentment. He expresses the hope that our successors in the next century will agree that "history is an endless network of changing relationships, without any great big climactic ruptures or peripities."[64]

Rorty gives the impression that, by dismissing the Marxist competition, he has dispensed with all programs for abrupt, sweeping change that need to be taken seriously. Foucault, who is sometimes described as an anarchist, offers little or nothing in the way of an alternative to liberalism. Various brands of "progressive nationalism" have either felicitously resolved themselves into liberalism (as in, say, India, the Philippines, or Tanzania) or—more typically—have been commandeered by thugs (or both, as in, say, Mexico, Algeria, or Egypt). Unger might represent a more attractive option, but he is working within the liberal tradition.

Whether or not Rorty is right on this point, there is reason to believe that he has not in fact dispatched Marxism, in at least one of its forms. In addition to the abolition of private ownership of the means of production, of course, Marx made at least one other suggestion which many people have considered to be constructive: From the *Communist*

Manifesto (1848) to the *Critique of the Gotha Program* (1875), he insisted that the first step in working class revolution is, as he and Engels put it in the *Manifesto*, "to raise the proletariat to the position of ruling class, to win the battle of democracy."

With this in mind, an obvious response to Rorty's defense of liberal institutions could be: All right, let us accept that the many betrayals of liberal ideals are only contingently related to such institutions and practices as an uncensored press, free universities, an independent judiciary, multiparty elections, and so on. And let us assume, furthermore, that these institutions and practices are effective instruments for ameliorating suffering. Let us have them, then—*but let us have them within the context of working-class state power, rather than corporate capitalist rule.* Since workers far outnumber capitalists in the rich North Atlantic democracies, this would appear to be a recommendation for a more democratic setup than exists under even the most liberal capitalist regimes. It also comports with a long-standing Marxist emphasis on democracy and republicanism as the most appropriate forms of political rule under the dictatorship of the proletariat.

If indeed liberal institutions are not a priori incompatible with noncapitalist alternatives, then it is natural to ask why such institutions could not be combined with, say, working-class state power or armed defiance of U.S. domination. In a paper published in 1987, Rorty came as close as he has ever come to posing this question: "There is one question I wish Marxists would discuss more than they do: Why can we not yet point with pride to a noncapitalist democracy?"[65] Without pausing for a response from Guatemalans, Chileans, or Nicaraguans, he immediately adds, apparently with a straight face,

> Is the only answer that you cannot, in the present situation, be a Marxist government without becoming a client of Moscow, and that Moscow will not let its clients encourage a free press, free universities, and so on? Does this entirely explain the absence of such institutions in, for example, Cuba?[66]

Escalating U.S. aggression against the Republic of Cuba in the post-Soviet era suggests a rather different answer to these questions: U.S.

leaders and their agencies have resorted to sponsorship of massive terrorism, unilateral acts of war, and economic blackmail—frequently in violation of international law and numerous agreements of which the U.S. is itself a signatory—to destabilize dozens of countries and impoverish their people, precisely in order to foment political instability, thereby obstructing the development of "a free press, free universities, and so on." Sometimes this aim has been surprisingly explicit. For example, Edward Korry, the Kennedy-liberal U.S. ambassador to Chile during the *Unidad Popular* years (1970–1973), stated that the U.S. would "do all within our power to condemn Chile and the Chileans to utmost deprivation and poverty, a policy designed for a long time to come to accelerate the hard features of a Communist society in Chile."[67] For three decades—until pliant leaders in Moscow bowed to Washington's demands that Russia abrogate mutually beneficial trade agreements with Cuba—Washington has viewed socialism in Cuba not as a failure but as an *alarmingly workable* example to others. When it has come to health care, nutrition, infant mortality, literacy, worker self-management, and other important components of social welfare, Cuba has demonstrated its clear superiority over the so-called democratic regimes Uncle Sam and the graduates of the School of the Americas have foisted onto people elsewhere in Latin America and the Caribbean. Indeed, in a number of important respects, such as infant mortality and public healthcare, Cuba has ranked higher than the United States itself. Moreover, as Uncle Sam's eventually successful campaign of enforced impoverishment of the island reminds us, Cuba's thirty-year record of achievement was won in the face of vicious and unrelenting foreign aggression.

Rorty has written that, "Only if one refuses to divide the public from the private realm will one dream of a society which has 'gone beyond mere social democracy,' or dream of 'total revolution.'"[68] The foregoing discussion, by contrast, should at the very least have indicated that one can indeed imagine going beyond social democracy, while also retaining many of the liberal institutions that Rorty is concerned with preserving. Having said this, however, it should be acknowledged that the struggle to achieve and build workers' power might well involve sweeping or convulsive social change, including perhaps the overthrow of one or another reigning liberal regime, or the dismantlement of

DECENCY AND LIBERALISM IN PRACTICE

some of the existing liberal institutions which, according to Rorty, are supremely precious.

Of course, this goal, if achieved, is bound to fall short of what Bernard Yack has dubbed "total revolution," or "a world without social sources of dissatisfaction."[69] This, however, would hardly have bothered Marx or Engels. The founders of Marxism, after all, were at least as thoroughly critical of utopianism in the perjorative sense of the word as is Yack.

※ ※ ※

In chapter 2 we saw that Rorty envisions a liberal utopia that serves the highest purposes of two paradigmatic figures, the strong poet and the decent citizen. These figures personify two liberal ideals: leaving people's private lives alone and minimizing suffering, respectively. Rorty believes there should be no aims higher than these.

In chapter 3, I suggested that Rorty seriously underestimates the role social institutions, including political institutions, play in defining the private sphere and private selfhood. Taking this into account, the rich North Atlantic democracies do not appear to exemplify Rorty's ideal of leaving people's private lives alone.

In the present chapter, I have suggested that Rorty likewise has failed to take full measure of the extent to which his favorite liberal democracies project power beyond their cartographic borders. Once we do so, however, it becomes clear that he has not provided convincing evidence that liberal institutions are the best means at hand for ameliorating the suffering liberal regimes continue to cause. In view of these considerations, actually existing liberalism could hardly be said to exemplify Rorty's ideal of public decency.

As I have emphasized, however, one would not be warranted in concluding from this that "a free press, free universities, and so on" are incompatible with a vision of the future in which minorities of exploiters no longer wield state power. Indeed, a vision of these institutions *within the context of workers' power* might well satisfy Rorty's pragmatic requirement for an alternative vision that more closely approximates his public ideal than either the status quo or his liberal utopia.

As the title of one of Rorty's better-known papers would indicate, he advocates placing politics before philosophical considerations. Before bringing this discussion to a close, then, it would be wise to take a look at his public and private vocabularies from the perspective of his explicit political commitments.

NOTES

1. The quotation appears in Richard Rorty, *Consequences of Pragmatism* (Minneapolis: University of Minnesota, 1982), pp. 69–70 (hereafter cited as *CP*).

2. Richard Rorty, *Objectivity, Realism, and Truth* (Cambridge: Cambridge University Press, 1991), p. 27 (hereafter cited as *ORT*).

3. Richard Rorty, *Contingency, Irony, and Solidarity* (Cambridge: Cambridge University Press, 1989), pp. 60–61 (hereafter cited as *CIS*).

4. Richard Rorty, "Objectivity or Solidarity, in *Post-Analytic Philosophy*, ed. John Rajchman and Cornel West (New York: Columbia University Press, 1985), p. 11.

5. He acknowledges, for instance, that "the desire for gold on the part of bigoted and fanatical sixteenth-century monarchs...in fact contributed to an admirable result," namely the United States of America (Richard Rorty, "Dewey between Hegel and Darwin," in *Modernism and the Human Sciences*, ed. Dorothy Ross [Baltimore: Johns Hopkins Press, 1994], p. 65).

6. Richard Rorty, letter to author, August 29, 1995.

7. Richard Rorty, *Essays on Heidegger and Others* (Cambridge: Cambridge University Press, 1991), p. 135 (hereafter cited as *EH*). Also refer to Richard Rorty, "Thugs and Theorists," *Political Theory* 15 no. 4 (November 1987): 566, and numerous passages in Richard Rorty, *Achieving Our Country* (Cambridge and London: Harvard University Press, 1998; hereafter cited as *AOC*).

8. Rorty, *CIS*, p. 46.

9. Ibid.

10. Rorty, "Thugs and Theorists," p. 576 n. 7.

11. Ibid., p. 568.

12. Richard J. Bernstein, "One Step Forward, Two Steps Backward: Richard Rorty on Liberal Democracy and Philosophy," *Political Theory* 15 no. 4 (November 1987): 553.

13. Ibid., p. 552.

14. Rorty, "Thugs and Theorists," p. 568 ff.
15. Ibid., p. 567, emphasis in the original.
16. Richard Rorty, in *Cultural Otherness: Correspondence with Richard Rorty*, ed. Anindita Niyogi Balslev (New Delhi: Indian Institute of Advanced Study Shimla, in collaboration with Munshiram Manoharlal, 1991), p. 78.
17. Rorty, "Thugs and Theorists," p. 577 n. 18. In the course of bolstering his contention that one cvan be both a fervent anti-Communist and a good leftist, Rorty provides an interesting insight into what counts, for him, as a good leftist: During the cold war, he recalls, "It seemed to me perfectly predictable that the CIA should contain both rightist hirelings of the United Fruit Company... and leftist good guys who used the taxpayers' money to finance what Christopher Lasch was to describe disdainfully as the 'Cultural Cold War' " (Rorty, *AOC*, p. 63).
18. Richard Rorty, "Habermas, Derrida, and the Functions of Philosophy" (unpublished), p. 21.
19. Rorty, *EH*, p. 180. These views are consistent with a pluralist approach to political sociology, represented by, say, Arnold Rose, Seymour Martin Lipset, or Robert Dahl. According to pluralist theory, the state arbitrates the interests of a multitude of competing pressure groups that vie for limited resources on a more or less level playing field. C. Wright Mills, Grant McConnell, William Domhoff, and Michael Parenti, among others, have raised serious objections to pluralist theory.
20. David L. Hall, *Richard Rorty: Prophet and Poet of the New Pragmatism* (Albany: SUNY Press, 1994), p. 45. With reference to the latter consideration, for example, the "market-driven" processes of automobilization in countries such as India and China promise to significantly boost per capita consumption of steel, glass, concrete, plastics, oil, and other petroleum products, and to redraw urban landscapes along the lines of the most congested and wasteful models in the West.
21. Rorty, *ORT*, p. 213.
22. Rorty, *CIS*, p. 63.
23. Richard Rorty, "Relativism: Finding and Making," in *Debating the State of Philosophy: Habermas, Rorty, and Kolakowski*, ed. Józef Niznik and John T. Sanders (Westport, Conn. and London: Praeger, 1996), p. 47.
24. Rorty, *CP*, p. 210 n. 16.
25. Rorty, *EH*, p. 26.
26. Richard Rorty, "Movements and Campaigns" (unpublished), p. 4.

27. Rorty, in Balslev, *Cultural Otherness*, p. 90.

28. Rorty, *EH*, p. 182.

29. Cf. Richard Rorty, "The End of Leninism and History as Comic Frame" (unpublished), p. 9.

30. And, to a large and increasing degree, centrally planned domestic economies, too. After taking care to distinguish his centralized private sector planning model from the Soviet-style centralized public sector planning model, John Munkirs claims that 55 to 60 percent of the U.S. economy is centrally planned and controlled, with administered prices (see John R. Munkirs, *The Transformation of American Capitalism: From Competitive Market Structures to Centralized Private Sector Planning* [Armonk, N.Y.: M. E. Sharpe, Inc., 1985]). Munkirs's thesis that the richest economies in the West are characterized by centralized private sector planning may be simplistic, largely ignoring as it does the inextricable interconnectedness of corporate and state institutions; nevertheless, it casts serious doubt on the supposed lesson of 1989 that "complex societies cannot reproduce themselves, if they do not leave intact the logic of self-regulation of a market economy" (Rorty, "The End of Leninism," p. 6; Rorty is quoting Habermas).

31. Bill Martin, "Toward Post-Eurocentric Social Theory," abstract in *Proceedings and Addresses of the American Philosophical Association* 67, no. 5 (February 1994): 65–66. Cold war liberals loudly and continually denounced the Soviet Party as an imperious, self-elected elite. An innocent observer might wonder why these vociferous "democrats" have had so little to say about the imperious, self-elected IMF and World Bank.

32. Rorty, *AOC*, p. 84.

33. Ibid.

34. Rorty, *EH*, p. 25, emphasis in the original.

35. Rorty, *ORT*, p. 2.

36. It is not clear why "conversation with foreigners" necessarily excludes conquest of them, as Rorty appears to assume (ibid., p. 25).

37. Edward Said, *Culture and Imperialism* (New York: Alfred A. Knopf, 1993), p. 286.

38. Ibid., p. 12.

39. Rorty, "Thugs and Theorists," pp. 574.

40. Ibid., p. 576 n. 13. At least one author has disputed Rorty's assertion that (the philosopher) Heidegger's link to the Nazis was merely contingent (cf. Victor Farías, *Heidegger and Nazism* [Philadelphia: Temple University Press, 1989]).

41. Isaiah Berlin, *Four Essays on Liberty* (Oxford: Oxford University Press, 1969), p. 180.

42. Refer, for example, to Ramkrishna Mukherjee, *The Rise and Fall of the East India Company: A Sociological Appraisal* (New York: Monthly Review Press, 1974); and John Keay, *The Honorable Company: A History of the English East India Company* (New York: HarperCollins, 1991).

43. As Rorty recognizes with reference to Jefferson (refer to Norman Geras, *Solidarity in the Conversation of Humankind: The Ungroundable Liberalism of Richard Rorty* [London and New York: Verso, 1995], p. 97), other liberal luminaries have bestowed authority on the subjugation of inferior peoples closer to home. Similar criticisms could be leveled against some of Rorty's more contemporary liberal luminaries. To cite one instance from a multitude that rush to mind, the same Sidney Hook who Rorty praises for having "kept political morality alive among the intellectuals" during the Depression (Rorty, *CP,* p. 63) lent his authority not only to a U.S. war in Southeast Asia that claimed over two million lives, but also to the persecution of "conspirators" in academia during the McCarthy years (George Novack, *Pragmatism versus Marxism: An Appraisal of John Dewey's Philosophy* [New York: Pathfinder Press, 1975], p. 276). By allowing such episodes to taint one's appraisal of Hook, admittedly, one might thereby have committed the sin of demanding from our heroes "complete freedom from sin," as Rorty imagines "Lenin, like Savonarola" to have done (Rorty, *AOC,* p. 46). Still, Hook compares unfavorably to his mentor, Dewey, who in the immediate postwar years opposed the exclusion of so-called subversives from public teaching positions.

44. Cf. Sheldon H. Harris, *Factories of Death: Japanese Biological Warfare, 1932–45, and the American Cover-Up* (London and New York: Routledge, 1997). I wish to thank Mr. Kuo-Hou Chang, of the Alliance for Preserving the Truth of the Sino-Japanese War, and Ms. Iris Chang for helping me to identify English-language sources dealing with these events.

45. Rorty, *CIS,* p. 60.

46. Rorty's phrase is quoted in William E. Connolly, "Mirror of America," *Raritan Review* (summer 1983): 129.

47. This and the passage quoted in the next sentence are from Nancy Fraser, "Solidarity or Singularity?" in *Reading Rorty,* ed. Alan Malachowski (Cambridge, Mass.: Basil Blackwell, 1990), p. 308.

48. Said, *Culture and Imperialism,* p. 293.

49. Maurice Merleau-Ponty, *Humanism and Terror* (Boston: Beacon Press, 1969), p. xiv.

50. Roy Bhaskar, *Philosophy and the Idea of Freedom* (Oxford and Cambridge, Mass.: Blackwell, 1991), p. 104. The passage quoted within the citation is from Bernstein, "One Step Forward," p. 552.

51. Rorty, "Thugs and Theorists," pp. 565–66.

52. Rorty, *AOC*, pp. 87–88.

53. Rorty, *ORT*, p. 77.

54. Rorty, *AOC*, p. 63.

55. It will be recalled that Dewey ascribed salary hikes for high-school and college instructors after the Great War to "a fear that poorly paid 'intellectuals' would be attracted toward Bolshevism" ("What Is the Matter with Teaching?" in John Dewey, *John Dewey, The Later Works, 1925–1927*, vol. 2, ed. Jo Ann Boydston [Carbondale and Edwardsville: Southern Illinois University Press, 1984], p. 117).

56. Rorty, *CIS*, p. 63.

57. Rorty, "The End of Leninism," p. 2. A more consistent nominalist might have described the social surplus as having been produced by *workers* rather than "market economies."

58. It would require a clock shop full of epicycles, for example, to pretend that, say, the forty cases of CIA subversion of democracy that William Blum examines in his book *Killing Hope: U.S. Military and CIA Intervention since World War II* (Monroe, Maine: Common Courage Press, 1995) were merely the contingent results of moral failure or shortsightedness on the part of a succession of greedy individuals who, time and again over the course of decades, just happen to have ensconced themselves in high office.

59. Merleau-Ponty, *Humanism and Terror*, pp. xiii–xiv. He cites passages from Marx's Introduction to *A Contribution to the Critique of Hegel's Philosophy of Right*.

60. Richard Rorty, "Review of Jacques Derrida's *Specters of Marx: The State of the Debt, the Work of Mourning, and the New International*" (unpublished, 1995), p. 8. The claim just cited underscores what some commentators have observed, namely, that Rorty does not display much familiarity with Marxist literature (Bhaskar, *Philosophy and the Idea of Freedom*, p. ix; Fraser, "Solidarity or Singularity?" p. 320 n. 5). This should have been apparent long before his unapologetic admission of the fact (Rorty, "Review of *Specters of Marx*," p. 2). He has confirmed this impression, for example, when he has written that "Nobody [on 'the left'] bothers to criticize the 'ideology' of communist countries" (Rorty, "Thugs and Theorists," p. 576 n. 13), or when he poses what he apparently takes

to be the rhetorical question: "Has the left any positive suggestions about some actions for the American government to take, or some middle-range policy goals?" (ibid., p. 577 n. 15), or when he blithely states, "*Dissent* remains pretty much the only leftist organ in the U.S. which is more concerned with spelling out tactics for fighting injustice that with maneuvering for strategic position in intellectual or political circles" (Rorty, "Movements and Campaigns," p. 8).

61. Rorty, in Balslev, *Cultural Otherness*, p. 89. With reference to Rorty's upbringing as a socialist, it is interesting to note that one of the "six liberals" to whom he dedicated *CIS* is his maternal grandfather, the social gospel advocate Walter Rauschenbusch. Rauschenbusch attended conferences at Oberlin Theological Seminary at about the time George Herbert Mead was an undergraduate there, in the 1880s. Another person to whom Rorty dedicated *CIS*, his father, James, was a contributor to *The Nation* and had been active with Sidney Hook in "Communist front organizations" until they publicly broke with the Communists in 1933—two years after the younger Rorty, a red-diaper anti-Communist baby, was born (L. S. Klepp, "Every Man a Philosopher-King: Richard Rorty of the University of Virginia," *New York Times Magazine*, December 2, 1990, p. 117; Rorty, *AOC*, p. 58). With reference to an instance of James Rorty's subsequent political writings, refer to Geras, *Solidarity*, p. 43.

62. Citations in this paragraph are from Rorty, "Review of *Specters of Marx*," p. 8.

63. Rorty, "The End of Leninism," p. 1. Rorty notes that he is quoting from Alan Ryan, "Socialism for the Nineties," *Dissent* (fall 1990): 442.

64. Rorty, "Movements and Campaigns," p. 11.

65. Rorty, "Thugs and Theorists," p. 576 n. 7.

66. Ibid.

67. Quoted in Noam Chomsky, *Deterring Democracy* (New York: Hill and Wang, 1992), p. 395.

68. Rorty, *EH*, p. 196.

69. Bernard Yack, *The Longing for Total Revolution: Philosophic Sources of Social Discontent from Rousseau to Marx and Nietzsche* (Princeton: Princeton University Press, 1986), p. 365.

CHAPTER FIVE
OF LIGHT MINDS AND HEAVY HANDS

We have already noted that existing liberal institutions and practices are incompatible in important or systematic ways with Rorty's two highest liberal ideals. In the balance of this discussion, we will contrast his public role as an apologist for actually existing liberalism to his private role as a lighthearted ironist. It should become clear that Rorty the ironist is similarly at cross-purposes with Rorty the apologist.

A CIRCLE WITHOUT CIRCUMFERENCE

Increasingly, Rorty has written as though pragmatism is not and should not be merely "an anti-representationalist account of experience and an anti-essentialist account of nature," but also, as Dewey has put it, "a project for a social-democratic utopia."[1] In a footnote, he avers that

Dewey would have endorsed Unger's slogan, "everything is politics." Unger's slogan, he says, follows from Dewey's admonition that we "start with our social hopes and work down from there to theories about standard philosophical topics."

"Working down from there" does not involve the futile exercise of trying to provide philosophical justifications or foundations for one's social hopes. Rather, as Rorty indicates in "The Priority of Democracy to Philosophy," among other places, it involves redescribing things, past, present, and future, in terms that will make one's social hopes appear attractive and convince others to embrace them. This being the case, says Rorty, "it would be well for us to debate political topics explicitly, rather than using Aesopian philosophical language."[2] With reference to the suggestion that he ought to have some theoretical justification for the claim that freedom and equality are "the West's most important legacy," for instance, Rorty has written:

> I do not have any philosophical backup for this claim, and do not feel the need of any. The claim is little more than a hunch that the way in which the recent West differs most interestingly from other cultures that have existed is in the utopian social aspirations which it has developed.[3]

Theory is useful for public purposes when it comes to thinking through these utopian visions. Accordingly, "the philosopher of liberal democracy may wish to develop a theory of the human self that comports with the institutions he or she admires."[4] Rorty stresses, however, that "such a philosopher is not thereby justifying these institutions by reference to more fundamental premises, but the reverse: He or she is putting politics first and tailoring a philosophy to suit."

In keeping with this view, he acknowledges promoting a particular account of selfhood, namely the Davidsonian-Freud account glossed in chapter 1, primarily because it suits the political purposes of "us social democrats."[5] As the reader will recall from chapter 1, Rorty refers to this sort of tailoring operation as philosophical *articulation* of a political vision. Liberal democracy does not require philosophical justification or backup, though it does stand to gain from philosophical articulation. In this context, "apologetics"—a word we have already encountered above, and to which we will return in the final section—could be used interchangeably with "articulation." Both words have been put to paradigmatically *ideological* use, as I defined this word in the final section of chapter 3.

At times, Rorty has identified himself as a "leftist intellectual" addressing what he supposes to be a left-wing audience. This is apparent, for example, when he has recommended Roberto Unger to Third World leaders, or advised a future generation of leftist university students to adopt Vaclav Havel as a hero, or lamented the overtheoretical obsessions of left-wing Americans, or collegially chastised "the Cultural Left" for worrying so much about such topics as the Meaning of Modernity that it has failed to help get liberal Democrats elected to office (as if this goal were uncontroversially acceptable to "leftists"!).[6]

Although he expresses impatience with what, following Harold Bloom, he dubs "the School of Resentment," he betrays a somewhat bemused sympathy for "the Cultural Left" and a more sober sympathy for some feminists.[7] Perhaps in part because of the last two considerations, some commentators have claimed that his occasionally alleged cultural conservatism is not backed up by political conservatism.[8] Key terms in Rorty's cultural conservatism that would be easy to confuse with political conservatism are *elitism, aestheticism, ethnocentrism*, and *Eurocentrism*. Indeed, he has made it so easy for "third-rate critics" to conflate his own cultural use of these words with prevalent political uses that one suspects that, in lightminded ironic style, he is inviting them to score quick but illusory points.

There is, of course, no hard-and-fast factual connection between the two conservatisms: Lots of political "radicals" have been cultural conservatives, and at least as many cultural radicals have been political conservatives. As Rorty's social and political views have become more explicit, however, his 1987 statement that "fortunately" he has received "as much flak from the right as from the left"[9] has become increasingly doubtful. Witness not only the generally hostile reception he has received from his fellow social democrats,[10] but also the increasing sympathy with which he is viewed by such neoconservative luminaries as Dinesh D'Souza.

One reason he has been receiving more sympathy from the Right might well be his escalating expressions of antipathy to "radical" critics of existing liberal democracies. In such recent writings as "The Priority of Democracy," "Thugs and Theorists," "Postmodernist Bourgeois Liberalism," "The End of Leninism," "Movements and Campaigns," *AOC*, and "Review of *Specters of Marx*," Rorty increasingly sounds like a proponent of what Roy Bhaskar has described as "old-fashioned cold war liberalism." Indeed, he has come close to describing himself as such.[11]

It should not come as a surprise, therefore, that Rorty has targeted Marxists for special consideration. According to him, Marxists "see political theory and philosophy as foundational because they see it as penetrating to a social reality behind contemporary appearances."[12] He associates the attempt to penetrate to the true, natural, ahistorical matrix of all possible language and knowledge with what he describes (with the unselfconsciousness of the vanquishing missionary) as the "state religion" of Marxism. Taking another cue from Kolakowski, perhaps, he lumps Marxists together with Hegel and the nineteenth-century liberal historian, Lord Acton, as votaries of History with a capital *H*. Writers of History present us with a long story of the realization of a latent potentiality—the return of Spirit to itself in its plenary fullness, the realization of freedom, or increasing technological command over nature. In other words, such writers present us with teleological sagas of maturation. The twists and turns in these sagas, their main phases or chapter structure, reveal the "shape and movement of History."[13] As we have seen, Rorty advocates turning away from this sort of "radical critique" and the movement politics associated with it. As he describes it,

> The turn away from movements to campaigns which I am suggesting is, in philosophical terms, a turn away from Kant, Hegel, and Marx and toward Bacon, Hume, and Mill—considered not as empiricists but as proto-pragmatists. It is a turn away from the transcendental question "what are the conditions of possibility of this historical movement?" to the pragmatic question "what are the causal conditions of replacing this present actuality with a better future actuality?"[14]

Rorty, then, associates programs for sweeping political change, or as he puts it, "movement politics," with the transcendental project, and reformist politics with pragmatism. Upon a little reflection, however, this association is both undermotivated and implausible. Although one would not guess it from Rorty, the larger part of Marx's writings consists of thousands of pages of detailed narratives about what certain contemporary communities have done in the past and what they might do in the future.[15] Clearly, the preconditions for the appearance of capitalism that Marx discussed in, say, part 8 of *Das Kapital*, vol. 1, are straightforward, nontranscendental historical causes. So are the preconditions for the emergence of private property, precapitalist economic formations, modern political institutions, and so on. These constitute the sort of first-order "historical narratives" of which Rorty the historical nominalist should approve. So when he writes that Marxism involves "metaphilosophical scientism," or that it is "a perfect example of the metaphysics of presence,"[16] he appears merely to have scored yet another direct hit on a large, slow-moving straw man bearing the placard: "Karl Marx: Transcendental Philosopher."

In the final years of the cold war—but before the wave of strikes that swept over France in the mid-1990s—Rorty announced, with perhaps a touch of wishful thinking, that "Marxism no longer looks plausible even in Paris."[17] At times his opposition to Marxism, and especially to what he describes as "the more blood-thirsty side of Marxism, the specifically Leninist side,"[18] has bordered on caricature. This is apparent, for instance, when he writes: "But now that we leftist intellectuals can no longer be Leninists, we have to face up to some questions which Leninism helped us evade."[19] To read such passages, one might never guess that the greater part of Rorty's audience resides in the rich North Atlantic, where Lenin has been almost universally vilified. In any case, one of the questions that Leninism allegedly has helped "us" to evade has to do with the importance of theory to politics. According to Rorty, Leninism has held an appeal within academia(!) precisely because, enthralled as academics are with deep theories about deep causes, they have reserved a place of honor for philosophers to play within the proletarian movement.[20] By encouraging academics to imagine themselves as occupying this place of honor, Leninism allows them to pretend they can play an important public role, while at the same time gratifying their blood lust by letting them picture themselves as "swept up by the aroused masses—borne along toward the slaughter-bench of history, the altar where the bourgeoisie will be redemptively sacrificed."[21]

In order to avert this gruesome scenario, and in recognition of the futility of the attempt to combine sublimity and decency in one overarching theory, he advocates abandoning not only "Leninism" but the very attempt to get underlying realities right before proceeding to political visions. To eschew such political theorizing, he argues, would not require giving up very much that is useful for the public purposes of a liberal. The concerns of public morality, after all, are adequately handled by the greatest happiness principle and the principles of procedural justice already built into current liberal democratic political structures. Thus, when it comes to Western social and political thought,

> J. S. Mill's suggestion that governments devote themselves to optimizing the balance between leaving people's private lives alone and preventing suffering seems to me pretty much the last word.[22]

Rorty's Dickensesque references to "poor inner-city children" and a desperate Third World victimized by "greedy white suburbanites," "greedy, short-sighted democracies," "greedy and stupid conservatives," and so on appear to be self-conscious reaffirmations of the futility of political theory. If leftists would stop trying so hard to penetrate to a social reality underlying contemporary appearances, they would have more time and energy to devote to getting on with the hard work of ameliorating suffering and extending freedom. Thus, not only do leftists not need deep theories about deep causes, but the obsession with such theories is an impediment to getting on with the main event. To avoid this distraction, Rorty advises leftists to transvalue banality in public discourse. As he puts it,

> I hope we can banalize the entire vocabulary of leftist political deliberation. I suggest that we start talking about greed and selfishness rather than about bourgeois ideology, about starvation wages and layoffs rather than about the commodification of labor, and about differ-

ential per-pupil expenditure on schools and differential access to health care rather than about the division of society into classes.[23]

One striking feature about this passage, and about Rorty's advice to those to his left in general, is how poorly motivated they are. In the passage just cited, he writes as though talk about class divisions on the one hand, and differential per-pupil expenditure on schools on the other, were an "either-or" proposition: Either you do one or you do the other, but you cannot do both.[24] Clearly, however, this is not the case at all: One could perfectly well talk about expenditure on schools or access to health care—and much else besides—as these mark out class divisions. Indeed, lots of Marxists have done exactly this.

It may be worthwhile to illustrate this point by turning, however briefly, to the liberal institutions Rorty praises. As we have already noted, the more carefully we attend to the details that Ben Bagdikian, Michael Parenti, Herbert Schiller, and others have provided, the clearer it becomes that the print and electronic media are increasingly corporate owned, the corporations that own them are ever fewer and larger in number, the range of opinions presented approximates ever more narrowly the opinions of corporate owners and advertisers, and there is a seamless connection between state institutions and what the corporate media itself refers to as "the business community." In view of these observations, liberal democracies today can hardly be said to promote domination-free communication, as Rorty claims they do.[25]

It would be easy to make similar remarks with reference to the alleged inviolability of the private sphere, the "independence" of judiciaries, the "representative" character of political institutions, the "freedom" of universities, the "vigilance" and "enlightenment" of public opinion, and so on down Rorty's list of liberal institutions in the rich North Atlantic. In each of these cases, the more details one attends to, the less precious the actual institutions and practices under scrutiny might well come to appear when measured against the very ideals of which they are the solemn complement. More importantly, perhaps, such an exercise might well cast additional doubt on Rorty's claim that "the rich democracies of the present day already contain the sorts of institutions necessary to their own reform."[26]

Rorty, Dewey, and Weber may be correct in pointing out that, once ends are decided upon, it is often a straightforward pragmatic exercise to determine what means are at hand to meet those ends. This may amount to little more than simply looking steadily and carefully. *Once ends are set*, it may well be true that "...no 'radical critique' is required, but just attention to detail."[27] Rorty's invocation of attention to detail—together with his *inattention* to the question "Which detail?"—is instructive, however, coming from one who has reminded us more than once that nature has no preferred self-description. By reminding us also that alternative descriptions of the same causal process are useful for different purposes,[28] he acknowledges what in any case is commonly conceded on all sides, namely, that different observers will attend to different details, depending on their purposes, among other things.

Before one can identify the most efficient means, one must of course first identify one's ends. The latter task, however, involves a familiar difficulty: Just as surely as one cannot get outside one's skin, one cannot describe a problem from no perspective at all, or from all at once. And the problems we identify—not just the ways we conclude how to ameliorate "avoidable suffering," for example, but the very evaluation from case to case of what *constitutes* avoidable suffering—themselves depend on our political ends: They depend on who we are. Even the words used to describe a problem—"freedom fighter" as opposed to "terrorist," for example, or "riot" as opposed to "uprising"—often cannot be settled empirically, without reference to political ends.

Rorty, presumably, would not dispute this point. When it comes to particular cases, however, it is not always clear that he accepts it in practice. To take one particularly relevant example, the standard vocabulary of public discourse portrays a central theme of political philosophy as an age-old trade-off between the rights of "the individual" and the rights of "the community." Whatever the latter term is assumed to be, it typically is viewed as a more or less homogeneous given that exists in contrast to individuals. Rightists are champions of the rights of individuals, while leftists are champions of community welfare. Thus, the hallowed dilemma "Higher taxes or fewer social programs?" is portrayed as a litmus test, to distinguish Left from Right: Leftists want higher taxes and more social programs; rightists want lower taxes and less government. In either case, "government" is assumed to be something neutral and devoid of class character or hegemonic function. As we have seen, Rorty's vocabulary, and his account of the public/private split in particular, is consistent with this usage.

After reading a book by, say, William Domhoff, Victor Perlo, or Michael Parenti, however, one might come to the conclusion that this supposedly intractable dilemma is arbitrary and unperspicacious. One might then pose the alternatives: "Higher taxes for corporations and capitalists or higher taxes for workers?" or "More social programs for the working class and the poor, or more social programs, subsidies, and bailouts for monopolies and the superrich?" Here we have one example, among dozens that could be drawn from daily headlines, of how an alternative public vocabulary may enable one to pose very different questions from the conventional, banal questions Rorty wishes exclusively to focus on.

These observations are significant when it comes to Rorty's claim that,

> We [liberals closer to Daniel Bell's end of the political spectrum than to "radicals" like Althusser and Jameson—MM] think that Dewey and Weber absorbed everything useful Marx had to teach, just as they absorbed everything useful Plato and Aristotle had to teach, and got rid of the residue.[29]

The judgment of what is useful, to repeat, follows from one's purposes. In this case, it follows from Rorty's prior commitment to apologetics on behalf of existing liberalism. If, indeed, "everything is politics"—and Rorty agrees with Jameson on this point—then as we already have noted, it is not surprising, in view of the prior political commitments of Bell and Rorty, that they would consider what Marx has to say about, say, exploitation, class struggle, and the dictatorship of the bourgeoisie to be a useless residue, at best. Nor is it surprising that Rorty would give his readers permission to write off any description of capitalist exploitation, class rule, and imperialism as an instance of resentment, "Hegelian romance," the yearning for "total revolution" or the "Radically Other," the satisfaction of blood lust, or some other similarly pernicious trait of those to his left with whom he disagrees.

One further illustration might reinforce the connection between the discussion in the preceding paragraphs and the discussion of ideology in the last section of chapter 3: Rorty, the advocate of "anti-ideological liberalism," has written that:

> Whether soviet imperialism is a threat is a paradigm of a non-"ideological," unphilosophical, straightforwardly empirical, question. It is a question about what will happen if such and such other things happen (if NATO collapses, if South America goes Communist, and so on).[30]

In order to resolve such questions in a suitably nonideological way, he recommends in the next sentence that one consult such sources as "intelligence reports on what the Politburo and the Soviet Generals have been saying to one another lately." Presumably, neither the opinions just quoted nor the intelligence reports would qualify as ideological because none of them is "a bad idea"—at least with reference to the purposes their authors have set themselves.

As we have seen, Rorty would like "us" to start talking about greed, selfishness, and short-sightedness, rather than bourgeois ideology, the commodification of labor power, and class divisions. It is worth noting, however, that technocrats, official speechifiers, and editors of corporate-owned newspapers do not need to *start* talking this way. Despite obvious problems with using psychological terms to describe institutional policies, they have long preferred Rorty's prescribed ways of talking. This, after all, is in large part what makes these ways of talking *banal* in the first place. Indeed, talking the way Rorty advises his readers to talk is arguably just part of what it is to be a *non*leftist intellectual. When Rorty advises "us" to start talking this way, then, he would appear to be referring to (though not necessarily addressing) the small number of embattled dissenters from hegemonic public vocabularies. By thus exercising his right not to take all vocabularies seriously, he abets those who would limit "responsible" political discourse to the narrow parameters of conservation versus reform, "big" versus "small" government, and incumbent leadership versus loyal opposition. Under the circumstances, then, Rorty's "real leftist politics"[31] would appear to be coterminous with reform within the framework of corporate capitalist state power. Within the context of liberalism in practice, then, his advice once again amounts to the promotion of conformity to a political vocabulary, which already exercises a near-total monopoly on public discourse. This is a strange view, coming from a professed advocate of "keeping the conversation going," a person who hopes that the crust of convention will be as superficial as possible,[32] or one who nurtures a "deep wish for everything to be wonderfully, utterly changed."[33]

As we have seen, Rorty's vocabulary is poorly suited to the task of describing such contemporary trends and states of affairs as the enormous and rapid concentration of capital, gaping distributive inequalities, overproduction, booming arms sales in the absence of a Soviet threat, and unilateral militarism on a global scale. Noting this, David Hall has identified "the strand of modernity" Rorty effectively omits from his Grand Narrative as "...the interweaving of the capitalist/Marxist dialectic in the origin and development of the modern age." "In modern society," Hall writes, with reference to one side of the aforementioned dialectic, "the capitalist celebrates the multiplication of desires and their transmogrification into needs." He concludes:

> It seems to me that if, as Rorty contends, pragmatism "helps us get what we want," then we should certainly be worried about the manner in which a capitalist liberal democratic society helps us to shape the character of wants and needs.[34]

Rorty, like Dewey, would like to maintain a consensus on the question of wants and needs to be met. Solidarity consists in arriving at a consensus as to the problems to be solved and how to go about solving them. However, if establishing such a consensus across national, regional, and class lines has always been problematic, then surely it is more so today, in view of the extreme inequalities and national oppression that have characterized this century. And even if within a particular country one could speak of a rough consensus on the question of wants and needs to be met, meeting those wants and needs has increasingly involved denying the wants and needs of people south of the border or in other parts of the globe. Moreover, in view of considerations noted above with reference to class rule and the corporate media, such a consensus, pace pluralist claims, is likely to continue to reflect the priorities of "the business community." This community, however, accounts for a rather small proportion of the total population of the rich North Atlantic, and it is not a foregone conclusion that its perceived interests are the interests of everyone else.

Rorty is aware of the obstacles to consensus, of course. Nevertheless, he remains optimistic. The public Rorty approximates Nancy Fraser's "cartoon version" of the technocratic impulse which sees history as "a succession of social problems posed and social problems solved, a succession that is in fact a progression," thanks to good luck, increasing technical competence, and public-spiritedness.[35]

It will be noticed that we have come full circle: Confronted with the charge that existing liberal institutions systematically betray liberal ideals, Rorty acknowledges constant betrayal but claims that, thanks to those very same institutions, it is possible to approximate the ideals ever more closely. In so doing, however, he assumes the point originally in question, namely, the efficaciousness of existing liberal institutions when it comes to realizing liberal ideals. He acknowledges the circularity of this sort of justification, but can see no way around it. With reference to "we pragmatists," he writes:

> We should say that we must, in practice, privilege our own group, even though there can be no noncircular justification for doing so. We must insist that the fact that nothing is immune from criticism does not mean that we have a duty to justify everything. We Western liberal intellectuals should accept the fact that we have to start from where we are, and that this means that there are lots of views which we simply cannot take seriously.[36]

One thing that makes "Western liberal intellectuals" what they are, presumably, is that they already do not take certain views seriously. Thus, we may rephrase Rorty's position as follows: *People who do not take certain views seriously should not take those views seriously.* This amounts to a circular justification so tight that it has no circumference. The question Rorty raises here is not the innocuous: "Can we start from anywhere but where we already are?" The question, rather, is: "Can or should we *go* anywhere from where we already are?" And his answer appears to be "No."

Returning to the discussion at the end of chapter 3, then, one might agree with the commentator's observation that: "Just because sophisticated liberalism professes to be non-ideological, does not mean that it *is* non-ideological."[37] Indeed, as the same commentator has added, Rorty's claims that he is beyond ideology just *are* what liberal ideology comes down to. As an admitted apologist for bourgeois liberalism and a missionary of the American Dream, Rorty would not be doing his job if he failed to disclaim the ideological character of his ideology.

Before bringing this section to a close, it should be noted that Rorty cites at least one additional reason for rejecting the vocabularies of opponents to his left. As he has put it:

> One reason why all of us in the international left are going to have to weed terms like "capitalism," "bourgeois culture" (and, alas, even "socialism") out of our vocabulary is that our friends in Central and Eastern Europe will look at us incredulously if we continue to employ them.[38]

This passage, published as late as 1992, is fully in keeping with an author who "reinterprets objectivity as intersubjectivity, or as solidarity."[39]

Less than one year after these lines were published, however, it had become clear that the *consensus gentium* in Eastern Europe had shifted dramatically. By that time, Polish workers had pretty much abandoned the Solidarity union in favor of the former Workers' Party union, and Polish voters had returned self-described socialists to national office, where they came to dominate the government and the parliament. A year later, in Hungary—a country free-marketeers frequently pointed to as their exemplary post-Soviet success story—voters overwhelmingly elected self-described socialists to local and national office. In the years 1994 and 1995, election officials in Ukraine, Slovakia, Slovenia, and Bulgaria reported similar results, while in Poland, self-described socialists also won the presidency. In a 1995 radio interview, pro-Western journalist Vladimir Pozner reported that anti-American sentiment among his fellow Russians was higher then than it had been at the height of the cold war. And by 1996, the largest of several self-titled Communist parties in Russia had rebuilt a burgeoning membership of over half a million, handily defeating all "proreform" parties in elections to the Duma. Even in Albania—one of the poorest, most isolated, and repressive Stalinist regimes in the postwar era (and thus, one would think, one of the easiest of the regimes in eastern Europe to redeem for liberalism), pro-capitalist forces rapidly discredited themselves, prompting a popular insurrection led by the former ruling party.

Thinktank pundits have interpreted Yeltsin's victory in the July 3, 1996, presidential runoff as proof positive that Russians have embraced Western-style liberalism. In a broadcast interview shortly after announcement of election results, one such pundit confidently predicted that the Communist Party of the Russian Federation would disappear in a couple of months. Subsequent events have not borne out this prognosis. Indeed, more recent revelations about Yeltsin's deceit, bribery, censorship, graft, and acquiescence to foreign manipulation have expunged any residual enthusiasm for Western-style "democracy" on the part of large numbers of Russians, just as his privatization and "market reform" programs have disgusted the overwhelming majority of Russian adults.

Rorty wrote of the label *socialist* that, "The quarter of the world which has worn that label the longest never wants to hear the word again."[40] As we can see, however, his statement, only a few years old, has already been outrun by events. Nevertheless, he has repeated similar statements as late as 1995: "If one reminds Czech or Ukrainian intellectuals that Marx was a remarkably original thinker...and that he may haunt European thought for centuries," he wrote, "they are likely to shrug their shoulders."[41] In view of the fact that so many of these intellectuals' compatriots have come to prefer self-identified socialist candidates and parties to their self-identified liberal counterparts, the last-mentioned reason for rejecting anticapitalist vocabularies is itself defunct. To paraphrase Mark Twain, the reports of Marxism's death are exaggerated. And they are likely to remain so, as it becomes clear to more and more people in eastern Europe and elsewhere that the liberals, the self-proclaimed democrats, and the "free-market reformers" have failed miserably to live up to their promises.

Of course, it would be easy to challenge the credentials of the self-described socialist candidates: There is no more reason to believe that Gennady Zyuganov is a genuine Communist than that Vladimir Zhirinovsky is a genuine liberal democrat. Moreover, other self-styled socialist leaders in eastern Europe, exemplified by "reformed Communist" Aleksander Kwasniewski, clearly qualify as what Rorty would call "social democrats," rather than Marxists. And, of course, there is not much chance that the self-described socialist candidates will be able to deliver on their campaign promises, once elected. None of these considerations, however, mitigate the fact that, Rorty's claims notwithstanding, such labels as *capitalism* and *socialism* remain current in eastern Europe.

RORTY'S INCOMPATIBLE ROLES

Rorty and his sympathizers have used the adjectives *de-divinized, historicized, nominalist, deflationary,* and *relaxed* to describe his views on a broad range of topics, including social science, culture, liberalism, and community. All or some of these adjectives, presumably, are roughly synonymous with "thin"—another adjective commentators have used to describe his views. Instances of his celebrated thinness might include: his pragmatist definitions of such words as *truth* and *rationality*; his abandonment of the search for foundations of knowledge, justice, and culture; his disparagement of Philosophy with a capital *P*; his deflationary conception of the sciences; his disparagement of "methodolatry" and preference for narrative over theory; his dismissal of theories of reference in favor of a notion of "talking about"; his definition of rationality as "the way things are done around here"; the light he makes of attempts by critical theorists to do deep thinking and to discern deep processes at work; his nonessentialist conception of selfhood; his identification of autonomy with self-enlargement and restriction of autonomy to the private sphere; and his emphasis on the contingency of human affairs.

A variety of critics have taken Rorty to task for presenting *too* thin a picture of our predicament.[42] Early in this discussion, by contrast, I registered my substantial agreement with him when it comes to such topics as his "anti-isms," his views on selfhood and rationality, and his substitute for a theory of reference. I might also have revealed a mild sympathy when it comes to his prognostications and recommendations regarding philosophy as a *Fach*, a distinct field of intellectual activity.

I want to emphasize, however, that I do not agree across the board with all of Rorty's nonsociopolitical views. I have already mentioned my misgivings about his undervaluation of causal depth in scientific explanation. I have also suggested here and there in the preceding pages that his accounts of intellectual and cultural change exaggerate the efficacy of discourse in human affairs, at the expense of biology, work, power, and other predominantly nondiscursive processes and practices.[43]

On the whole, however, I have not taken Rorty to task for excessive historicism, nominalism, or thinness. Indeed, turning to several of his preferred topics, I am of the opinion that his views could stand to be *further* deflated, *less* divinized, *more* historicized, more consistently nominalist, and thinner. These topics include his insistence on viewing human affairs as more than "just more nature," his account of liberal community as essentially integrated and homogeneous, his invocation of "our European purposes," and his picture of the inviolable private sphere neatly insulated from political power.

Rorty's thinness is selective, and this selectivity works in favor of his explicit forensic aim of making bourgeois liberal democracy look good. The terms he uses to describe existing liberal democracies help advance this aim. As we have seen, for example, Rorty has adopted Roberto Unger's term *rich North Atlantic democracies* to describe what others have called "bourgeois democracies,"[44] "advanced capitalist countries," or "imperialist states." Rorty claims that Unger's awkward and misleading circumlocution is "more neutral" than other terms intended to cover the same semantic field, presumably in the sense that it is less laden with value or emotive connotations. Here as elsewhere, Rorty—the advocate of abandoning the fact-value, scheme-content, and science-culture distinctions—has advanced a claim that is incompatible in both tone and implication with other points he has labored to establish.[45] In any case, he abruptly drops his preference for "more neutral" terms when it comes to adopting expressions such as *Soviet imperialism*. Once again, Rorty's conservative instincts work against the grain of his theses.

The unevenness of Rorty's thinness is also obvious when, for example, he ignores his own advice to abandon the attempt "to find a successor to 'capitalism' or 'bourgeois ideology' as the name of The Great Bad Thing."[46] After all, "Leninism," "Stalinism," and "Soviet imperialism" seem to have done the same work for Rorty that other scare words designating evil essences have done for the Marxists he has castigated, and that "logocentrism" allegedly has done for Derrida.[47] Keeping in mind that a devil is a fallen angel, it is hard to see how Rorty's diabolifications advance his avowed aim of de-divinizing culture.

Reviewing these inconsistencies, it is possible to distinguish between Rorty's apologetics for the institutions and practices of existing bourgeois liberal democracies on the one hand and at least two other recurring themes of his. These two themes are (a) his highest liberal ideals, and (b) other related historicist and ironist formulations he wishes to defend. The latter category would include his admonition that when it comes to discourse every metaphor should have its chance for self-sacrifice,[48] or that the crust of convention should be as thin as it can be.

I have taken up point (a) in chapters 3 and 4. In the remaining pages I will add a few words about (b).

In the course of this discussion, I have highlighted Rorty's blind spots—points where his conversation abruptly fades to silence, irony lapses into apologetics, and lightmindedness becomes heavy-handedness. This happens most notably when it comes to his inattention to the political character of the private sphere. It also happens when it comes to his inability or unwillingness to break up the lump of the West, and in particular to his lack of recognition of the state on the one hand and the public sphere on the other as distinct analytical categories. It happens when it comes to his dismissal of exploitation, class conflict, and class rule as constraints on the possibility of informed consensus within liberal democratic communities, and of imperialism as a constraint on the extension of solidarity abroad. And it happens when it comes to his lack of recognition that his "we's" do not encompass the entire range of tolerant, cruelty-averse intellectuals in the north Atlantic.

A recurring pattern is discernible among these lapses, omissions, and "unconscious presuppositions":[49] Time and again Rorty the ironist appears to lose nerve when he encounters Rorty the apologist for bourgeois liberalism. This pattern constitutes the background of a certain silence that, once attended to, simultaneously compromises his credentials as an ironist and confirms what he acknowledges to be his role as an apologist for bourgeois liberalism.

If liberal ironists of the past have escaped this conflict—if their roles as apologists did not get too much in the way of (and at times perhaps even complemented) their roles as ironists—this was because they were invidiously comparing liberal ideals or utopias yet unsullied by repeated betrayal with incumbent institutions that repudiated these ideals and openly stood against them. In Enlightenment France, for example, where the bourgeoisie had yet to settle final accounts with the ancien regime, it was easier for ironists to be apologists for the bourgeoisie. Rabelais, Montaigne, Molière, Bayle, and Voltaire contributed to the self-image of an increasingly confident bourgeoisie facing down the reaction. Their public enemies, namely the church and the political reaction, corresponded more or less neatly to their private enemies, the hidebound defenders of tradition and the enemies of free expression.

In Jefferson's day, public office and diplomacy seemed to be exciting and attractive fields of self-assertion, along with scientific and technical innovation. The second U.S. ambassador to France, like the first one, hurled himself headlong into both public affairs and natural philosophy. However, over the course of the next century and a half, as the natural sciences attracted fewer and fewer of Jefferson's "natural *aristoi*," the marriage of ironic self-creation and apologetics for bourgeois liberal democracy became increasingly problematic, too. Liberal ideas came to be less "infused with passion," to use Daniel Bell's expression. When Rorty notes ruefully that "most American intellectuals in Dewey's day still thought their country was a shining historical example,"[50] we might lay special emphasis on the word *still*. During President Woodrow Wilson's tenure it was still possible for a conscientious young opponent of the Spanish-American War to read Whitman without giggles. *Song of America*, not yet overwhelmed by Twain's *War Prayer*, found a diminished echo in Carl Sandburg.

Yet Dewey had a problematic and sometimes inconsistent reaction to U.S. imperialism. Although he courageously defended war resisters, he eventually threw his support behind the "war to end all wars," even to the point of allowing chauvinist-sounding writings to be published, implicating Hegel as a prop for the kaiser.[51]

Dewey appeared on the scene at a time of rapid urbanization, industrialization, the changing demographic character that resulted from waves of immigration, and the growth of a laissez-faire ideology, in the face of a newly emerging monopoly capitalism. As a leading figure of the Chicago School, he personified progressivism as a political movement. "If radicalism be defined as perception of the need for radical change," he famously wrote, "then today any liberalism which is not also radicalism is irrelevant and doomed."[52] This oft-quoted passage—so different in tone from what one finds in Rorty—should, however, be read in light of the fact that many of Dewey's contemporaries were convinced that the conservation of U.S. capitalism required sweeping change. The thirty-second president of the United States summarized this conviction when he declared: "Liberalism becomes the protection of the far-sighted conservative."[53]

Stalin's depredations lent life to the increasingly dysfunctional marriage of liberal apologetics and ironism in the West. Both the Orwells and the Nabokovs adopted and promoted the official vocabularies of the free world. During the cold war years, and especially after the Twentieth Congress of the Soviet Communist Party, the *samizdat* sustained a burgeoning readership in Eastern Europe, while dissidents there found a sympathetic liberal audience in the West, confirming the officially promoted metaphors of iron curtains, captive nations, dominos, and gulags.

As the Soviet Union's influence waned in Eastern Europe and elsewhere, however, it became increasingly difficult for some liberals to sustain their monodemonological metaphors, especially in the face of unrelenting U.S. interventions abroad and revelations of covert alliances between agencies such as the CIA, on the one hand, and a large assortment of unsavory confederates, including dictators, mafiosos, death-squad leaders, nationalist fanatics, and narcotraffikers, on the other. By 1987, Rorty could write that, "There is no way to consolidate our enemies in an interesting 'theoretical' way." These enemies by then had come to include "the shadowy millionaires manipulating Reagan," as well as "the nomenklatura in Moscow, the Broederbond in South Africa, and the ayatollahs in Iran."[54] Among the rogues in this gallery, however, Rorty still counted the Soviet leadership as the worst by far.

With the disappearance of the Evil Empire in the final years of the American Century, however, the liberal imagination had been deprived of a suitably threatening Great Bad Thing with which to invidiously contrast actually existing liberalism. In the meantime, class divisions have deepened in the North Atlantic, "market reforms" have pauperized much of eastern Europe, and the gap between North and South gapes ever wider. Despite these developments, however, Rorty has concluded that Marxist analyses are dispensable today, because they allegedly do not illuminate the prevailing *Bandenkriegen*, "between, for example, the Cali and Medellin cartels, or between a cutthroat Azeri general and a bloodstained Armenian colonel."[55]

One reason it is difficult for Rorty to consolidate his enemies in an interesting theoretical way might be that his public allies are his private enemies: Among the legions that collaborate to bring the "light of American democracy" unto the nations may be counted the shadowy millionaires behind Reagan—and Clinton, too. And among these may be counted some of the most enthusiastic opponents of free expression in U.S. public schools, universities, libraries, public radio and television, and the Internet. Today's abridgers of personal freedoms in eastern Europe are also advocates of NATO expansion (of which Rorty seems to approve). Some of the worst enemies of freedom in Latin America and elsewhere are some of the staunchest opponents of "totalitarianism."[56] Illustrations of the following point could be multiplied almost at will: Conspicuously many of the functionaries and apologists for existing liberal democracies—conspicuously many of those who defend in word and deed the public institutions than which, according to Rorty, nothing is more precious—happen also to oppose not only self-determination and the mitigation of suffering abroad, but also such private desiderata as an inviolable private sphere and a thin crust of convention at home.

As Nancy Rosenblum has noted, privatization, detachment, and self-absorption are typical responses to powerlessness. Rorty's message of privatized theory, ironic detachment, and duty to self as distinct from others is a message of diminished expectations for the powerless (though of course it is not a message addressed *to* the powerless). By virtue of their poverty and vulnerability, those who stand to benefit most from Alan Ryan's "welfare-capitalism-with-a-human-face" have little chance of achieving it by relying on their own resources and efforts. If Ryan's hope is to be realized, then, it must be achieved for the poor and vulnerable by others in positions of influence and with access to the right resources.

Nancy Fraser has described Rorty as vacillating between *technocratism*, or the view that solutions to public problems are best left to technical experts, and *romanticism*, characterized as the belief that self-creation is the highest aim in life. Within this context, as we can see, politics is not a field for the self-emancipation of the working class or any other underdog community. Rather, it becomes a field for philanthropists, noblesse oblige, and "well-intentioned, confused, university-trained young crypto-leftists."[57] These civic-minded individuals mark their time in the public sphere not by trying to come up with new political vocabularies and theories or by listening to the language of the oppressed, but by patiently improving technical means to ameliorate the suffering of the less fortunate, whose fates are describable in the inherited vocabulary of social democracy that Weber and Dewey helped cobble together.

Social experimentation, stripped of pompous theoretical dissertations and reduced to little more than the piecemeal tinkering of earnest technocrats, is hardly an inspiring career choice for the best and the brightest youth, the natural *aristoi*. At times, Rorty appears to acknowledge the uninspiring state of liberal affairs, at least with reference to "we rich, fat, tired North Americans." Nevertheless, he defends liberal democracy as much preferable to all competitors: The fact that liberal democracies produce so many petty, greedy, narrow-minded people is offset by the freedom such political setups provide.

At other times, however, it seems Rorty would like his fellow citizens to rekindle Dewey's sense of national mission. It is not hard to discern the promotional tone of passages such as the following:

> We Deweyans have a story to tell about the progress of our species, a story whose later episodes emphasize how things have been getting better in the West during the last few centuries, and which concludes with some suggestions about how they might become better still in the next few.[58]

Aside from the occasional expression of enthusiasm, however, he provides little in the way of inspiration to nudge the natural *aristoi* of a coming generation in the direction of public-spirited community service. Rorty probably would not deny that he has produced precious little in the way of new ideas for the public sphere: When it comes to his conceptions of democracy, autonomy, and resolution of the opposition between public and private spheres, as we have seen, he has backed away from Dewey and reverted to formulations of the classical liberalism of Locke, Bentham, and the Mills—the professed spring of inspiration of contemporary neoliberals. With reference to Marxism, Rorty has written: "We see no more point in trying to rework a political vocabulary developed in the middle of the nineteenth century than in trying to rework one developed in the middle of the fourth century."[59] Nowhere does he explain, however, why he prefers trying to rework a liberal vocabulary developed in the seventeenth and eighteenth centuries. The observation is as true of Karl Marx as it is of Charles Darwin: Those who claim to have "gone beyond" either of these "obsolete nineteenth-century thinkers" have merely resurrected much older views, which Marx and Darwin scoffed at when they still had hair on their heads.

Dewey could still convince himself and others that his public role as advocate of the ideals of the French Revolution did not conflict with his public role as defender of the institutions and practices of existing liberal democracies. As I have attempted to point out, however, it has become more difficult to believe Rorty when he makes the same claim. His interventions in sociopolitical discourse, appearing as they do in a context of slipping wages and living standards in the rich North Atlantic, a growing gap between rich and poor both at home and abroad, and the dismantling of the so-called welfare state, have a very different political thrust from Dewey's interventions in an era of optimistic social engineering.[60]

Rorty has described himself as a happy-go-lucky pragmatist.[61] As an ironist who, like Nietzsche, manages to be ironic about theory, the private Rorty does appear to qualify as such. When it comes to what Rorty and Jefferson considered to be the properly private themes that allegedly give meaning and purpose to our lives—those religious and metaphysical themes of ultimate purposes—Rorty encourages good-natured public indifference:

OF LIGHT MINDS AND HEAVY HANDS

> If one's moral identity consists in being a citizen of a liberal polity, then to encourage light-mindedness will serve one's moral purposes. Moral commitment, after all, does not require taking seriously all the matters that are, for moral reasons, taken seriously by one's fellow citizens. It may require just the opposite. It may require trying to josh them out of the habit of taking those topics so seriously.[62]

Playfulness and moral commitment coexist peacefully when promoting lightminded aestheticism as a way of promoting the Jeffersonian compromise.

It should be noted, however, that when it comes to his social hopes, Rorty's happy-go-lucky persona abruptly exits stage right. For instance, he cannot conceal his irritation with what he calls the "loose, resentful Heideggerian talk about Russia and America being 'metaphysically speaking, the same,'" and "all the loose, resentful analogies between the Gulag and the 'carceral archipelagoes' of the democracies."[63] He himself, however, has produced loose, resentful analogies of his own, as in his statement that the difference between Lenin, Stalin, and Hitler is merely one of facial hair,[64] and his rhetorical association of guards in Auschwitz with guards in the Russian gulags.[65] Echoing Daniel Bell, he even asseverates, offhandedly, that by the time Orwell wrote *Animal Farm*,

> efforts to see important differences between Stalin and Hitler, and to continue analyzing recent political history with the help of terms like "socialism," "capitalism," and "fascism," had become unwieldy and impracticable.[66]

—as if this preposterous pronouncement were becoming common knowledge.

During the cold war, news correspondents and expatriate Russian comedians enjoyed reporting the most recent jokes circulating on the streets in Moscow. Their appreciation for popular wit has noticeably diminished in the post–cold war era; in any case, one joke that circulated among Muscovites in the mid-1990s poses the question: "What have five years of capitalism achieved that seventy years of socialism failed to accomplish?" The punch line: "It's made socialism look good."

According to a joke circulating in the city of Yerevan in 1996: "Everything the commissars told us about socialism turned out to be a lie. But everything they told us about capitalism turned out to be true."

These, of course, are just anecdotes. Yet it is hard to dispute the claim that in eastern Europe and Russia today the sharp edge of irony has flipped around, and is now menacing the pro-Western, procapitalist liberal democrats. In the early 1990s, Slavenka Drakulic was feted on the radio talk-show circuit in the United States. Her widely reviewed book, *How We Survived Communism and Even Laughed*, was billed as a lighthearted celebration of newfound freedom in eastern Europe. In interviews, Drakulic poked fun at Tito and his drab, straitlaced cohorts. During the nearly fifty years of their leadership, it seems, they never got around to producing a feminine napkin. This epitomized the irrationality of the Tito regime and the hypocrisy of its profeminist declarations. In the few years since the full restoration of capitalism, women in the former Yugoslavia who can afford feminine napkins presumably now have easy access to them. Thus, the feminine napkin takes its place next to the rape camp as notable achievements of the post-Tito era. Drakulic's former compatriots, it seems, have had a harder time surviving capitalism. After tens of thousands of victims of ethnic cleansing, three million refugees, and billions of dollars worth of property damage, the laughter appears to have subsided in the former Yugoslavia.[67]

In recent years, Rorty has lamented that "Americans are suffering the consequences of the globalization of the labor market, without having established a welfare state."[68] He has failed to acknowledge, however, that the same process is taking place, though at a slower pace, in Sweden, Denmark, the Netherlands, and other erstwhile exemplary welfare states. It is hard to be happy-go-lucky, even in the camp of the cold war victors, when one is surrounded by evidence that the institutions and practices one considers to be most precious are in the process of being hauled out the back door to the dumpster. In the final years of the American Century, the liberal democracies have achieved virtually undisputed global hegemony. Yet liberal hopes for equality, justice, amelioration of suffering, and a realm of negative freedom beyond the pale of state institutions appear to be ever more wistful exercises in nostalgia, the stuff of sappy inaugural addresses that nobody takes seriously anymore. (Or *almost* nobody. One can imagine Rorty's amusement in the company of fawning friends in eastern Europe—among them, self-styled Roman Catholic defenders of free thought!—who, in the late-1990s, have managed to remain unembarrassed by gushy effusions about the American Dream.[69] One should not expect the same reaction, however, from a less gullible audience "closer to the United States and further from God.")

Of course, one could describe the practice of liberalism in the American Century differently, as I have done in chapters 3 and 4. One might then be able to evaluate it from the perspective of a "we" that has no great investment in the health or continued existence of bourgeois liberalism, because it envisions the possibility of a future that—though still ridden with social sources of dissatisfaction—is nevertheless far better than the present. This might be one way to josh oneself out of the habit of taking seriously, say, Uncle Sam's pretensions as the disinterested arbiter of global conflicts, or the increasingly grotesque spectacle of Yankee electoral politics, or the importance of good citizenship in the age of the corporate-government nexus, or any of dozens of other idols on very high—and by now very shaky—pedestals. By thus relinquishing the view that bourgeois democracy is exceedingly precious, one might well be in a position to be more happy-go-lucky and more consistently or persistently ironic than Rorty can be. There are, after all, people to the left of Rorty who view the evaporation of the so-called welfare state, and rising popular scorn toward "free-market reformers," with a sort of bemused, I-told-you-so detachment unavailable to Rorty's dutiful citizen. Rorty is free to label such detachment "resentment," "spectatorship," "self-protective knowingness," or anything else he wishes. Others, however, might feel no need to describe it in terms any fancier than simply the satisfaction one gets from having been proven right, after all.

It should be pointed out that this brand of ironism does not necessarily earn one membership in the silly fraternity of "the Cultural Left." Such ironism need not be any less useful for purposes of, say, building revolutionary working-class organizations or anti-imperialist movements than Havel's brand of ironism was for purposes of expanding Czech chauvinism, Western markets, and NATO. Ironism and direct participation in freedom struggles may be a rare combination, but I suspect that it is not as rare as some people would like to think.

Honi Fern Haber has noted that Rorty's aesthetic and political impulses, essentially private and public concerns respectively, "seem to be at odds with each other."[70] Viewed in the light of the preceding remarks, this observation is well-taken, as far as it goes. The mere drawing of a distinction between public and private spheres, however, does not necessarily set public and private concerns against each other. As I indicated earlier in this section, public and private impulses have not always been at odds in the manner Rorty's are: His impulses are at odds in a way that liberal impulses were not at odds with ironism in Enlightenment France, Tocqueville's northern states, Whitman's America, Dewey's Chicago, or behind the Iron Curtain. Ironic self-creation and civic-spirited decency do not *necessarily* conflict. Nor do ironism and apologetics for bourgeois liberalism. *At the end of the American Century*, however, ironism and apologetics for bourgeois liberalism do indeed appear to conflict. Rorty's public vocabulary, the vocabulary he uses to defend the liberal democracies, is at odds with the ironic, de-divinized, antiessentialist vocabulary he uses to satisfy his duty to himself. In order for him to fulfill his role as apologist for contemporary liberalism in practice, he must become not merely a nonironist, but an *anti*-ironist.

This point may be illustrated with reference to Rorty's comments about "thoughtlessness," in Heidegger's sense of the word, as meaning "inability to imagine alternatives to the particular beings that have been opened up by the languages we are speaking."[71] In his role as apologist, he must be thoughtless with reference to the distinction between public and private persons, the political character of the private sphere, relations of exploitation, and so on. This sort of thoughtlessness is a far cry from the lightmindedness or insouciance that he prescribes for theory in the private sphere.

Rorty can, of course, switch back and forth between his public and private roles. In this sense, his public and private selves can and do coexist. They coexist, however, at each other's expense, conflictually, like two enemy armies of metaphors locked in mutual siege (to mix metaphors borrowed from Nietzsche and Gramsci, respectively). As we saw in chapter 3, it is literally self-defeating—that is, it defeats purposes defining a public or a private self—to commit oneself, as Rorty does, to the inviolability of the private sphere on the one hand, while defending existing liberalism on the other. Where bourgeois liberalism reigns supreme today, there the private sphere has tended to be *least* inviolable vis-à-vis institutions of the state and other public institutions. Moreover, as we saw in chapter 4, Rorty's public role as apologist for the liberal democracies is incompatible with his public role as mitigator of suffering, particularly with reference to the massive suffering these countries continue to engender beyond their cartographic borders.

The problem, then, is not that Rorty's public and private roles are *incommensurable in principle;* rather, they are *incompatible in fact.* On the one hand, the better he fulfills his role as ironist-theorist, as defender of the inviolability of the private sphere, or as mitigator of suffering, the more explicitly he will have to abrogate his role as apologist for the bourgeois liberal democracies. On the other hand, the better he is at defending the institutions and practices of existing liberal democracies, the more he contributes to "thoughtlessness," the concealment of cruelty, the "freezing over of culture," and the constriction of permissible discourse. This might be an example of what David Hall has referred to as Rorty's "dichotomy of the intellectual and the moral virtues," and it helps explain why, in the words of another commentator, his project "refuses to give birth to the offspring it conceives," or why, in the words of yet another commentator, his argument "loses its grip whenever reassurance is being dispensed."[72]

This dichotomy has become more pronounced in more recent writings, as time and again Rorty has conceded a point to his Marxist opponents, only to ignore that point a few pages latter. Throughout *AOC*, for example, he condemns individuals and parties that have worked outside the same political system that he has already described on page 6 as a "false front," and on page 48 as "often little more than the executive committee of the rich and powerful." On page 83 he laments that "America is now proletarianizing its bourgeoisie," and a few pages later he draws a bleak picture of class polarization in the last quarter of the century. Yet he begins the book by insisting that there is still a point to hoping that America will become the first cooperative commonwealth, the first classless society.[73] On page 85, he laments that "This world economy will soon be owned by a cosmopolitan upper class." Then, for the next several pages, he describes a process underway in America, leading to the formation of hereditary classes and a dystopic future analogue of Orwell's Inner Party—"namely, the international, cosmopolitan super-rich."[74] Yet, toward the end of the chapter, he writes that "the Left should get back into the business of piecemeal reform within the framework of a market economy"—within the framework, that is, of the very same market economy that is largely to blame for having deposited us at this nightmare scenario, in the first place. These examples might lead one to suspect that Rorty's dismissal of Marxism has less to do with an aversion to theorizing than to his inability or unwillingness to allow his own conclusions to *add up*, or to register on his story about America.

As I have indicated, Rorty's lapses of critical acumen conspicuously benefit his apologetic aims. When his apologetics conflict with ironism, as they frequently do, the apologetics more often than not come out on top. As Haber has noted with reference to Rorty, "In the wedding of liberalism and ironism, one of the partners is dominated by the other."[75] These observations lend credibility to another critic's conclusion that,

> despite occasional protests to the contrary, it begins to look as if Rorty's defense of liberalism is little more than an *apologia* for the status quo—the very type of liberalism that Dewey judged to be "irrelevant and doomed."[76]

❦ ❦ ❦

In the preceding pages, we have encountered instance after instance in which Rorty's descriptions of bourgeois liberalism and the American Century are poles apart from mine. He thinks that Orwell's problem of remaining free inside was primarily a problem of the erstwhile East: I view it as primarily a problem of the "rich North Atlantic democracies." He has described innovations in information technologies as a prop for the cold war regimes of Eastern Europe; I have viewed them as threats to those regimes. He views privatization as an extension of negative freedom; I view it as an extension of bourgeois political power. Where he sees the proliferation of discourses, I see the constriction of discourse and the monopolization of the means of production and distribution of words and ideas by an ever-smaller minority. Rorty viewed the existence of the Soviet threat as a brake on decolonization and social reform in the West; I saw it as a spur to decolonization and social reform. Where Rorty sees the defeat of centralized planning in the collapse of the Soviet model, I see the apotheosis of centralized economic planning on a global scale, in the form of unrestrained international monetary fundamentalism. Rorty sees little relationship between misery in the South and freedom and prosperity in the North Atlantic; I see the former as one (but not the only) condition of actuality of the latter. Rorty views the leaders of the velvet revolutions in Eastern Europe as venerable figures, for the most part; I view the best of them as naïfs or buffoons, and the worst of them as power-hungry demagogues, chauvinists, and ethnic cleansers. Rorty views reforms in the rich North Atlantic as episodes in the steady expansion of community; I view these reforms as revocable concessions in the face of militancy at the bottom. Rorty views the end of the "Soviet threat" as holding a promise of the fulfillment of the welfare state; I see it as undermining the need to maintain the welfare-state charade, at least until militancy rises again from the bottom.

What have emerged in these pages, then, are two very different sets of descriptions of liberalism in practice, sets of descriptions that are serviceable for very different political purposes. Future generations may or may not adopt Rorty's preferred descriptions. By the same token, no iron laws of economic or technological development guarantee that the future will remain the private preserve of technocrats and free marketeers. The future is open—much more open than the Fukayamas and the Rortys are willing to admit. In the meantime, a large part of Rorty's audience is likely to find his pragmatist defenses of the existing liberal democracies convincing, despite the defects I have registered in this discussion. In the class struggle, after all, there is no argument like success.

NOTES

1. Richard Rorty, *Essays on Heidegger and Others* (Cambridge: Cambridge University Press, 1991), p. 47 (hereafter cited as *EH*). The next two citations in this paragraph are from Richard Rorty, "Thugs and Theorists," *Political Theory* 15, no. 4 (November 1987): 578 n. 20.

2. Rorty, *EH,* p. 25.

3. Richard Rorty, in *Cultural Otherness: Correspondence with Richard Rorty,* ed. Anindita Niyogi Balslev (New Delhi: Indian Institute of Advanced Study Shimla, in collaboration with Munshiram Manoharlal, 1991), p. 20.

4. All citations in this paragraph are from Richard Rorty, *Objectivity, Relativism, and Truth* (Cambridge: Cambridge University Press, 1991), p. 178 (hereafter cited as *ORT*).

5. Rorty, "Thugs and Theorists," p. 577 n. 20.

6. See: Rorty, *EH,* pp. 177–92, with reference to Unger; Richard Rorty, "The End of Leninism and History as Comic Frame" (unpublished), pp. 7–8, with reference to Havel; Rorty, "Thugs and Theorists," p. 570, with reference to overtheoretical obsessions; and Rorty, *EH,* p. 137, with reference to the "Cultural Left." The remark about electing democrats was part of a reply to a question from the audience at Richard Rorty, "Intellectuals at the End of Socialism," lecture delivered at Northwestern University, January 17, 1992. Also refer to Rorty, "The End of Leninism," pp. 3–4, 9, and Richard Rorty, "Review of Jacques Derrida's *Specters of Marx: The State of the Debt, the Work of Mourning, and the New International*" (unpublished, 1995), p. 2.

7. See Rorty, *EH,* pp. 179, 184, and Richard Rorty, *Achieving Our Country* (Cambridge and London: Harvard University Press, 1998), pp. 73–107 (hereafter cited as *AOC*), with reference to the School of Resentment. Rorty speculates that the reason feminist *Ideologiekritiker* "are actually having some new ideas" is "…in part, because the patriarchy-nonpatriarchy distinction swings free of the capitalism-socialism distinction" (Rorty, "Thugs and Theorists," p. 577 n. 16).

8. David L. Hall, *Richard Rorty: Prophet and Poet of the New Pragmatism* (Albany: SUNY Press, 1994), p. 176. Presumably, allegations of cultural conservatism are a consequence of his conception of social change as largely cultural change, the dependence of cultural change on changing vocabularies, and the parasitic dependence of abnormal discourse on normal discourse.

9. Rorty, "Thugs and Theorists," p. 575 n. 5.

10. Ibid., pp. 564, 574–75 n. 2, 3.

11. Cf. Roy Bhaskar, *Philosophy and the Idea of Freedom* (Oxford and Cambridge, Mass.: Blackwell, 1991), pp. 99–100. With reference to Rorty's self-implication as a cold war liberal, refer to Rorty, "Thugs and Theorists," p. 576 n. 11, and Rorty, *AOC,* p. 58.

12. Rorty, *EH,* p. 25. See Rorty, "Thugs and Theorists," pp. 568–69, with reference to the role of philosophers in achieving socialism.

13. Rorty, "The End of Leninism," p. 1; cf. Józef Niznik and John T. Sanders, eds., *Debating the State of Philosophy: Habermas, Rorty, and Kolakowski* (Westport, Conn. and London: Praeger, 1996), p. 121. With reference to teleologies, see Richard Rorty, "Movements and Campaigns" (unpublished), pp. 5–6, 14.

14. Rorty, "Movements and Campaigns," p. 16.

15. Cf. Richard Rorty, "Postmodernist Bourgeois Liberalism," *Journal of Philosophy* 80, no. 10 (October 1983): 585.

16. Rorty, "Thugs and Theorists," p. 578 n. 21. Rorty ascribes to Marxists a notion of "History" as an inspiring blur (Rorty, "The End of Leninism, p. 4). It should be pointed out, however, that some Marxists could without difficulty restrict themselves to talking about the constitution of modes of production at given times and places, and dispense entirely with "history," whether capitalized or not, except as an abbreviation for "social transformations."

17. Rorty, *EH*, p. 137.

18. Rorty, "The End of Leninism," p. 2.

19. Ibid., p. 3. I have not encountered evidence that would suggest that Rorty ever considered himself to be a Leninist in any familiar sense of the term.

20. With reference to deep theories about deep causes, see ibid., p. 3. With reference to the role of philosophers within the proletarian movement, see Rorty, "Thugs and Theorists," p. 570. The latter view does not square well with Rorty's more recent observation that left-wing intellectuals in the United States typically have not ascribed much importance to philosophy (Rorty, "Movements and Campaigns," p. 6).

21. Rorty, "The End of Leninism," pp. 4–5. Elsewhere, Rorty disparages "Lenin's blood-curdling sense of 'objective'" (Richard Rorty, *Consequences of Pragmatism* [Minneapolis: University of Minnesota Press, 1982], p. 173 [hereafter cited as *CP*]). Not only does this sound silly, but it is unfair, in view of the regularity with which Western academics, editors, and opinion-makers for decades have wielded the word "objective" and its cognates as a handy stick with which to indiscriminately beat their Marxist opponents.

22. Richard Rorty, *Contingency, Irony, and Solidarity* (Cambridge: Cambridge University Press, 1989), p. 63 (hereafter cited as *CIS*).

23. Rorty, "The End of Leninism," p. 1.

24. This presumably is an instance of what Roy Bhaskar has dubbed Rorty's "disjunctivitis" (Bhaskar, *Philosophy and the Idea of Freedom*, p. 133). By presenting the matter in this manner, it will be noticed, Rorty casts doubt on his claim that, "There are no facts about economic oppression or class struggle,

or modern technology, which that vocabulary [that is, the vocabulary of social democratic politics that Dewey and Weber helped cobble together—MM] cannot describe and a more 'radical' metaphoric can" (Rorty, *EH*, p. 26).

25. Rorty, *CIS*, p. 68. Rorty acknowledges "such things as the control of mass-circulation magazines by people who want to safeguard their own wealth and power at the expense of the poor and weak" (Richard Rorty, "Habermas, Derrida, and the Functions of Philosophy" [unpublished], p. 3). In the course of doing this, however, he avoidably mystifies these instances of exploitation by describing them as mere variations on the "old, old" story of the rich "continuing to steal from the poor," as he puts it in Rorty, "Review of *Specters of Marx*," p. 8. This raises a number of questions: One is tempted to ask, for starters, how exactly it is that he knows the character traits of the people who own mass-circulation magazines. What if the major shareholders of, say, Time Warner or Gannett are not especially greedy or power-hungry personalities? And even if they were, as seems unlikely, why should one assume that corporate policy would be appreciably different if those individuals happened to be more attractive personalities?

26. Rorty, "Habermas, Derrida, and the Functions of Philosophy, "p. 21.

27. Rorty, *EH*, p. 25.

28. Rorty, *ORT*, p. 60.

29. Rorty, "Thugs and Theorists," p. 571. It is not clear, however, that John Dewey had enough of an exposure to Marx to absorb very much at all (refer to Jim Cork, "John Dewey and Karl Marx," in *John Dewey, Philosopher of Science and Freedom* [New York: Dial Press, 1950], p. 335).

30. Rorty, "Thugs and Theorists," pp. 578–79 n. 25.

31. The author contributes to our appreciation of banality in public discourse by defining "real leftist politics" as "initiatives for the reduction of human misery" (Rorty, "The End of Leninism," p. 4).

32. Rorty, *EH*, p. 18.

33. Richard Rorty, "On Moral Obligation, Truth, and Common Sense," in Niznik and Sanders, *Debating the State of Philosophy*, p. 51.

34. Hall, *Richard Rorty*, p. 46. Previous citations in this paragraph appear in ibid., pp. 41, 45.

35. Nancy Fraser, "Solidarity or Singularity?" in *Reading Rorty*, ed. Alan Malachowski (Cambridge, Mass.: Basil Blackwell, 1990), p. 304.

36. Richard Rorty, "Solidarity or Objectivity," in *Post-Analytic Philosophy*, ed. John Rajchman and Cornel West (New York: Columbia University Press, 1985), p. 12.

37. Jo Burrows, "Conversational Politics: Rorty's Pragmatist Apology for Liberalism," in Malachowski, *Reading Rorty,* p. 327, emphasis in original.

38. Rorty, "The End of Leninism," p. 9.

39. Rorty, *ORT,* p. 13.

40. Rorty, "The End of Leninism," p. 15 n. 13.

41. Rorty, "Review of *Specters of Marx,*" p. 1. The saving grace of this statement is that, thanks in large measure to the operation of Rorty's "large free market economies" (Rorty, *ORT,* p. 209), it has become much more difficult for a Czech or Ukrainian dissident to make herself heard. The erosion of state subsidies for intellectuals, the evaporation of academies of science and writers' unions, a newly acquired popular disinterest in books and ideas, and the brain drain from impoverished central and eastern Europe—all of these developments have relieved the current rulers of much of the annoyance of a new generation of influential dissident writers.

42. See, for example: Norman Geras, *Solidarity in the Conversation of Humankind: The Ungroundable Liberalism of Richard Rorty* (London and New York: Verso, 1995), p. 85, with reference to Rorty's "nothing deeper" account of the basis of solidarity; C. G. Prado, *The Limits of Pragmatism* (Atlantic Highlands, Humanities Press, 1987), p. 137, with reference to his "perhaps excessive historicism"; Kai Nielsen, *After the Demise of the Tradition: Rorty, Critical Theory, and the Fate of Philosophy* (Boulder: Westview Press, 1991), pp. 29–31, with reference to Alastair MacIntyre's reported inability to stomach Rorty's thin analysis of truth, and p. 31, with reference to MacIntyre's criticism of Rorty for telling too thin a story of the history of analytic philosophy; Ibid., pp. 39 ff, with reference to Jaegwon Kim, Ian Hacking, and Alan Goldman's defenses of putatively central tenets of analytic philosophy against Rorty; Konstantin Kolenda, *Rorty's Humanistic Pragmatism: Philosophy Democratized* (Tampa: University of South Florida Press, 1990), p. 91, with reference to David Hiley and Michael Sandels's objections to Rorty's Humean notion of the self as a web of beliefs and desires; Sabina Lovibond, "Feminism and Pragmatism: A Reply to Richard Rorty," *New Left Review* 193 (May/June 1992): 56–74, for critical comments on Rorty's antiuniversalism and antiessentialism; Habermas's criticisms of Rorty on truth and other topics, as Rorty reports them in "Habermas and Lyotard on Postmodernity" (Rorty, *EH,* pp. 164–76) and elsewhere; Tom Sorell's claim that Rorty's account of intellectual change is "too deflationary" (Malachowski, *Reading Rorty,* p. 20); Bernard Williams' criticisms or Rorty for having seriously underdescribed the sciences (ibid., pp. 26–37); Frank Farrell's disparagement of Rorty's "extremely thin world" emptied of the given, and so on.

43. With reference to Rorty's undervaluation of causal depth in scientific explanation, see note 19 for chapter 1. For criticisms of Rorty's exaggerated account of the efficacy of discourse in human affairs, see: Rebecca Comay, "Interrupting the Conversation: Notes on Rorty," *Telos* 69 (fall 1986): 123; Frank B. Farrell, *Subjectivity, Realism, and Postmodernism—The Recovery of the World* (Cambridge: Cambridge University Press, 1994), pp. 122–25; and relevant sections in Bhaskar.

44. Rorty, *ORT,* p. 15.

45. Refer, for example, to relevant remarks in: Rorty, *CP,* pp. 37, 74, 195–96; Rorty, *CIS,* pp. 54–55; and Rorty, *ORT,* pp. 25, 62 n.

46. Rorty, "The End of Leninism," p. 12.

47. Refer to Rorty, *EH,* p. 112 n.

48. Ibid., p. 18.

49. The term is from ibid., p. 87.

50. Rorty, *ORT,* p. 201.

51. Rorty gives the impression that Dewey's Marxist critics unanimously write him off as "the philosopher of American imperialism" (Rorty, *EH,* p. 133). Some Marxists have indeed denounced Dewey's version of pragmatism as "the main-line philosophy of U.S. imperialism," and members of the Frankfurt School have associated pragmatism with U.S. business values. Other Marxists, however, have provided more nuanced characterizations. One, for example, has argued that Dewey's pragmatism was not the outlook of rising finance capital and the monopolies, but of "...the educated petty bourgeoisie in the epoch of the climb of American capitalism to world domination and the transformation of bourgeois democracy into imperialist reaction" (George Novack, *Pragmatism versus Marxism: An Appraisal of John Dewey's Philosophy* [New York: Pathfinder Press, 1975], p. 41). According to this account, Dewey's pragmatism is "...the conciliatory philosophical instrument of the middle classes on the downgrade, trying to clutch at any means for salvation" (ibid., p. 278).

52. The quote, from "Liberalism and Social Action" in John Dewey, *The Later Works of John Dewey*, vol. 11 (Carbondale: Southern Illinois University Press, 1987), p. 45, appears in Richard J. Bernstein, "One Step Forward, Two Steps Backward: Richard Rorty on Liberal Democracy and Philosophy," *Political Theory* 15, no. 4 (November 1987): 540, and Bhaskar, *Philosophy and the Idea of Freedom,* p. 108 n. 4. Refer to Rorty's comments on this passage in Rorty, "The End of Leninism," pp. 15–17 n.15.

53. Quoted in Novack, *Pragmatism versus Marxism,* p. 16.

54. Citations in this paragraph are from Rorty, "Thugs and Theorists," p. 566.

55. Rorty, "Review of *Specters of Marx*," p. 10.

56. Rorty has decried "graduates of Patrice Lumumba University" (now defunct) who, he feared, are likely to head up "ruthless oligarchies" in the Third World (Rorty, "Thugs and Theorists," p. 566). As far as I am aware, however, he has never gone on record to discomment the School of the Americas, located just down the road from Charlottesville, Virginia. In the name of the democracy and freedom Rorty so regularly invokes, and with his tax money, this institution has so far graduated some fifty thousand alumni, among whom may be counted some of the most prodigiously murderous tyrants since Cortez and de Soto.

57. Rorty applauds Unger's assertion that hope for the victimized masses lies not in the workers and peasants of Brazil (that is, not in the victimized masses themselves) but rather in the hands of well-intentioned petty-bourgeois technocrats (Rorty, *EH*, p. 182). It would seem, then, that Rorty and Unger have opened themselves to the charges of elitism and condescension that Kolakowski, Castoriadis, and others have repeatedly leveled against Leninists.

58. Rorty, *ORT*, p. 212.

59. Rorty, "Thugs and Theorists," p. 571.

60. See John Dewey, *Reconstruction in Philosophy* (Boston: Beacon Press, 1957), p. vi. Compare to: "Unger, Castoriadis and the Romance of a National Future," in Rorty, *EH*, pp. 177–92; Richard Rorty, "The Priority of Democracy to Philosophy," in Malachowski, *Reading Rorty*, pp. 279–302; Rorty, "Postmodernist Bourgeois Liberalism," Rorty, "Thugs and Theorists," and relevant sections of Rorty, *CIS* and *AOC*.

61. Rorty, "Review of *Specters of Marx*," p. 3.

62. Rorty, "The Priority of Democracy to Philosophy," p. 293.

63. Rorty, *EH*, p. 192 n.

64. Rorty, "Intellectuals at the End of Socialism." Rorty associates Lenin with Stalin (as, for example, at Rorty, *EH*, p. 25), Stalin with Hitler (ibid., p. 189; Rorty, *CIS*, p. 174), and Lenin directly with Hitler, too (ibid., p. 157; Rorty, "Review of *Specters of Marx*," p. 1), while at the same time excluding from the mix monstrous butchers like Henry Kissinger, who have ordered their exterminations in the name of democracy and freedom.

65. Rorty doubts that Marxist movements will survive the opening of the Lubyanka Prison (Rorty, *AOC*, p. 146 n. 19). It is interesting to note that it was

not until Yeltsin's tenure that Russia's per capita prison population began to exceed that of the United States. Moreover, prison conditions in Russia have deteriorated significantly in the post-Soviet era—although one would not guess it, judging from the lack of concern about *post*-Soviet gulags on the part of liberals in the West.

66. Rorty, *CIS,* p. 174. When Rorty writes that Marxism has done nothing to clarify "the struggle for power between those who currently possess it ... and those who are starving or terrorized because they lack it" (Rorty, *EH,* pp. 25–26), one is tempted to ask just what it would take to "clarify" such struggles. This question is especially acute in view of Rorty's claim, cited above, that contemporary liberal democracies are "*already* organized around the need for continual exposure of suffering and injustice." It should also be noted that, in more recent writings, Rorty has resorted to using the "unwieldy and impracticable" word *fascism* to describe a possible American future (Niznik and Sanders, *Debating the State of Philosophy,* p. 29).

67. Refer to Rorty's conspicuously somber discussion of events in the former Yugoslavia, "Human Rights, Rationality and Sentimentality," in *On Human Rights: The Oxford Amnesty Lectures,* ed. Stephen Shute and Susan Hurley (Boston: Basic Books, 1993), which appears in translation as "Droits de l'homme, rationalité et sentimentalité," in *Richard Rorty: Ambiguïtés et limites du postmodernisme,* ed. Gilbert Hottois and Maurice Weyembergh (Paris: Librarie Philosophique J. Vrin, 1994), pp. 13–36. This lecture goes some distance to recuperate Rorty as an honest liberal, in Shklar's special sense of the word.

68. Rorty, "Emancipating Our Culture," in Niznik and Sanders, *Debating the State of Philosophy,* p. 29.

69. Refer, for example, to Niznik and Sanders, *Debating the State of Philosophy,* pp. 117–25.

70. Honi Fern Haber, *Beyond Postmodern Politics: Lyotard, Rorty, Foucault* (New York: Routledge, 1994), p. 49.

71. Rorty, *EH,* pp. 43, 46.

72. The three commentaries cited in this sentence are: Hall, *Richard Rorty,* p. 167; John Rajchman and Cornel West, eds., *Post-Analytic Philosophy* (New York: Columbia University Press, 1985), p. 268; and Joe McCarney, "Edifying Discourses," *Radical Philosophy* 32 (autumn 1982): 6, respectively.

73. Rorty, *AOC,* pp. 8, 30.

74. Ibid., p. 87.

75. Haber, *Beyond Postmodern Politics,* p. 64.

76. Bernstein, "One Step Forward," p. 541.

BIBLIOGRAPHY

Aboulafia, Mitchell. "George Herbert Mead and the Many Voices of Universality." In *Recovering Pragmatism's Voice: The Classical Tradition, Rorty, and the Philosophy of Communication*, edited by Lenore Langsdorf and Andrew R. Smith. Albany: SUNY Press, 1995.

Althusser, Louis. "Ideology and Ideological State Apparatuses." In *Lenin and Philosophy*. New York: Monthly Review Press, 1971.

Bagdikian, Ben H. *The Media Monopoly*. 3d ed. Boston: Beacon Press, 1990.

Balslev, Anindita Niyogi. *Cultural Otherness:Correspondence with Richard Rorty*. New Delhi: Indian Institute of Advanced Study Shimla, in collaboration with Munshiram Manoharlal, 1991.

Baudrillard, Jean. *Simulations*. New York: Semiotext(e), Inc., 1983.

Berlin, Isaiah. *Four Essays on Liberty*. Oxford: Oxford University Press, 1969.

Bernstein, Richard J. "One Step Forward, Two Steps Backward: Richard Rorty on Liberal Democracy and Philosophy." *Political Theory* 15, no. 4 (1987): 538–63.

Bernstein, Richard J., ed. *Habermas and Modernity*. Cambridge, Mass.: MIT Press, 1985.

BIBLIOGRAPHY

Bhaskar, Roy. *Philosophy and the Idea of Freedom.* Oxford and Cambridge, Mass.: Blackwell, 1991.

Blum, William. *Killing Hope: U.S. Military and CIA Intervention since World War II.* Monroe, Maine: Common Courage Press, 1995.

Burrows, Jo. "Conversational Politics: Rorty's Pragmatist Apology for Liberalism." In *Reading Rorty,* edited by Alan Malachowski. Cambridge, Mass.: Basil Blackwell, 1990.

Carnoy, Martin. *State and Political Theory.* Princeton: Princeton University Press, 1984.

Cornelius Castoriadis. *The Imaginary Institution of Society.* Oxford: Polity Press, 1987.

Chomsky, Noam. *Deterring Democracy.* New York: Hill and Wang, 1992.

Colby, Gerard, and Charlotte Dennet. *Thy Will Be Done: The Conquest of the Amazon: Nelson rockefeller and Evangelism in the Age of Oil.* New York: HarperCollins, 1995.

Comay, Rebecca. "Interrupting the Conversation: Notes on Rorty." *Telos* 69 (fall 1986): 119–30.

Connolly, William E. "Mirror of America." *Raritan Review* (summer 1983): 124–35.

Cork, Jim. "John Dewey and Karl Marx." In *John Dewey: Philosopher of Science and Freedom,* edited by Sidney Hook. New York: Dial Press, 1950.

Davidson, Donald. "A Coherence Theory of Truth and Knowledge." In *Reading Rorty,* edited by Alan Malachowski. Cambridge, Mass.: Basil Blackwell, 1990.

Derrida, Jacques. *Specters of Marx: The State of the Debt, the Work of Mourning, and the New International.* New York and London: Routledge, 1994.

Dewey, John. *Intelligence in the Modern World: John Dewey's Philosophy.* Edited by Joseph Ratner. New York: Random House, 1939.

———. *Reconstruction in Philosophy.* Boston: Beacon Press, 1957.

———. *John Dewey: The Later Works, 1925–1927.* Vol. 2. Edited by Jo Ann Boydston. Carbondale and Edwardsville: Southern Illinois University Press, 1984.

———. *The Later Works of John Dewey.* Vol. 11. Carbondale: Southern Illinois University Press, 1987.

Domhoff, William. "State and Ruling Class in Corporate America." *The Insurgent Sociologist* 4, no. 3 (1974): 3–16.

Donzelot, Jacques. *The Policing of Families.* New York: Pantheon Books, 1979.

D'Souza, Dinesh. "Pied Pipers of Relativism Reverse Course: Richard Rorty, Stanley Fish, and Jacques Derrida Reassert to a Degree the Validity of a

Canonical Curriculum for a Liberal Education." *Wall Street Journal,* July 27, 1993, p. A18.

Farías, Victor. *Heidegger and Nazism.* Philadelphia: Temple University Press, 1989.

Farrell, Frank B. *Subjectivity, Realism, and Postmodernism—The Recovery of the World.* Cambridge: Cambridge University Press, 1994.

Filmer, Sir Robert. "Patriarcha." In *John Locke: Two Treatises of Government.* New York: Hafner, 1947.

Foucault, Michel. *Discipline and Punish: The Birth of the Prison.* New York: Vintage, 1979.

———. *The History of Sexuality.* Vol. 1. New York: Vintage, 1980.

Fraser, Nancy. "Solidarity or Singularity?" In *Reading Rorty,* edited by Alan Malachowski. Cambridge, Mass.: Basil Blackwell, 1990.

Fukayama, Francis. "The End of History?" *National Interest* 16 (summer 1989): 3–18.

Geras, Norman. *Solidarity in the Conversation of Humankind: The Ungroundable Liberalism of Richard Rorty.* London and New York: Verso, 1995.

Geuss, Raymond. *The Idea of a Critical Theory: Habermas and the Frankfurt School.* Cambridge: Cambridge University Press, 1981.

Gorbachev, Mikhail S. *Perestroika: New Thinking for Our Country and the World.* New York: Harper and Row, 1988.

Gramsci, Antonio. *Selections from the Prison Notebooks.* New York: International Publishers, 1971.

———. *Letters from Prison.* Edited by Lynne Lawler. New York: Noonday Press, 1989.

Haber, Honi Fern. *Beyond Postmodern Politics: Lyotard, Rorty, Foucault.* New York: Routledge, 1994.

Hall, David L. *Richard Rorty: Prophet and Poet of the New Pragmatism.* Albany: SUNY Press, 1994.

Harris, Sheldon H. *Factories of Death: Japanese Biological Warfare, 1932–45, and the American Cover-Up.* London and New York: Routledge, 1997.

Heal, Jane. "Pragmatism and Choosing to Believe." In *Reading Rorty,* edited by Alan Malachowski. Cambridge, Mass.: Basil Blackwell, 1990.

Hegel, G. W. F. *Hegel's Philosophy of Right.* Translated by T. M. Knox. Oxford: Oxford University Press, 1967.

Hobbes, Thomas. *Leviathan.* London and New York: Penguin, 1985.

Hollis, Martin. "The Poetics of Personhood." In *Reading Rorty,* edited by Alan Malachowski. Cambridge, Mass.: Basil Blackwell, 1990.

Hottois, Gilbert, and Maurice Weyembergh, eds. *Richard Rorty: Ambiguïtés et limites du postmodernisme*. Paris: Librairie Philosophique J. Vrin, 1994.

Jacques, Martin. "Will 'End of Leninism' Bring a 'New Birth of Socialism'?" *Guardian Weekly*, December 10, 1989, p. 18.

James, William. *Pragmatism: A New Name for Some Old Ways of Thinking*. New York: Longman, Green, and Co., 1914.

Jefferson, Thomas. *The Life and Selected Writings of Thomas Jefferson*. Edited by Adrienne Koch and William Peder. New York: Modern Library, 1944.

Jessup, Bob. *The Capitalist State*. New York: New York University Press, 1982.

Kant, Immanuel. *Critique of Pure Reason*. Translated by Norman Kemp Smith. New York: St. Martin's Press, 1965.

Keay, John. *The Honorable Company: A History of the English East India Company*. New York: HarperCollins, 1991.

Klepp, L. S. "Every Man a Philosopher-King: Richard Rorty of the University of Virginia." *New York Times Magazine*, December 2, 1990, pp. 56–TK.

Kloby, Jerry. "The Growing Divide: Class Polarization in the 1980s." *Monthly Review* 39, no. 4 (1987): 1–8.

Kolakowski, Leszek. *Main Currents of Marxism: Its Rise, Growth, and Dissolution*. Vol. 2. Translated by P. S. Falla. Oxford: Clarendon Press, 1978.

Kolenda, Konstantin. *Rorty's Humanistic Pragmatism: Philosophy Democratized*. Tampa: University of South Florida Press, 1990.

Krauthammer, Charles. "Decade Marks the Triumph of Western Democracy." *Washington Post*, September 15, 1988, p. A31.

Lamont, Corliss, ed. *Dialogue on John Dewey*. New York: Horizon Press, 1959.

Langsdorf, Lenore, and Andrew R. Smith, eds. *Recovering Pragmatism's Voice: The Classical Tradition, Rorty, and the Philosophy of Communication*. Albany: SUNY Press, 1995.

Larson, Eric. *The Naked Consumer: How Our Private Lives Become Public Commodities*. New York: Henry Holt, 1992.

Lenin, V. I. *The State and Revolution*. New York: International Publishers, 1932.

———. *Collected Works*. Vol. 38. Moscow: Progress Publishers, 1976.

Locke, John. *Treatise of Civil Government and a Letter Concerning Toleration*. New York: Irvington Publishers, Inc., 1979.

Lovibond, Sabina. "Feminism and Postmodernism." *New Left Review* 178 (November/December 1989): 5–28.

———. "Feminism and Pragmatism: A Reply to Richard Rorty." *New Left Review* 193 (May/June 1992): 56–74.

BIBLIOGRAPHY

Lyotard, Jean-François. *The Post Modern Condition: A Report on Knowledge.* Minneapolis: University of Minnesota Press, 1984.
McCarney, Joe. "Edifying Discourses." *Radical Philosophy* 32 (autumn 1982): 4–7.
Macpherson, C. B. *The Life and Times of Liberal Democracy.* Oxford and New York: Oxford University Press, 1977.
Malachowski, Alan, ed. *Reading Rorty.* Cambridge, Mass.: Basil Blackwell, 1990.
Martin, Bill. "Toward Post-Eurocentric Social Theory." Abstract in *Proceedings and Addresses of the American Philosophical Association* 67, no. 5 (1994): 65–66.
Marx, Karl. "On the Jewish Question." In *Karl Marx: Selected Writings*, edited by David McLellan. Oxford: Oxford University Press, 1977.
Mead, George Herbert. *Mind, Self, and Society.* Chicago: University of Chicago Press, 1934.
Melkonian, Markar. *Marxism: A Post-Cold War Primer.* Boulder: Westview Press, 1996.
Merleau-Ponty, Maurice. *Humanism and Terror.* Boston: Beacon Press, 1969.
Miliband, Ralph. *The State in Capitalist Society.* New York: Basic Books, 1969.
Mill, John Stuart. *On Liberty.* New York: Penguin, 1987.
Mukherjee, Ramkrishna. *The Rise and Fall of the East India Company: A Sociological Appraisal.* New York: Monthly Review Press, 1974.
Munkirs, John R. *The Transformation of American Capitalism: From Competitive Market Structures to Centralized Private Sector Planning.* Armonk, N.Y.: M. E. Sharpe, Inc., 1985.
Murphy, John D. *Pragmatism: From Peirce to Davidson.* Boulder: Westview Press, 1990.
Nielsen, Kai. *After the Demise of the Tradition: Rorty, Critical Theory, and the Fate of Philosophy.* Boulder: Westview Press, 1991.
Niznik, Józef, and John T. Sanders, eds. *Debating the State of Philosophy: Habermas, Rorty, and Kolakowski.* Westport, Conn. and London: Praeger, 1996.
Novack, George. *Pragmatism versus Marxism: An Appraisal of John Dewey's Philosophy.* New York: Pathfinder Press, 1975.
Parenti, Michael. *Make-Believe Media: Politics of Film and Television.* New York: St. Martin's Press, 1994.
Popper, Karl. *The Open Society and Its Enemies.* Vol. 1. Princeton: Princeton University Press, 1963.
Poulantzas, Nicos. *State, Power, Socialism.* London: NLB, 1978.
Prado, C. G. *The Limits of Pragmatism.* Atlantic Highlands: Humanities Press, 1987.

Rajchman, John, and Cornel West, eds. *Post-Analytic Philosophy.* New York: Columbia University Press, 1985.
Ratner, Joseph, ed. *Intelligence in the Modern World: John Dewey's Philosophy.* New York: Random House, 1939.
Rawls, John. *A Theory of Justice.* Cambridge, Mass.: Harvard University Press, 1971.
Rorty, Richard. *Philosophy and the Mirror of Nature.* Princeton: Princeton University Press, 1979.
———. *Consequences of Pragmatism.* Minneapolis: University of Minnesota Press, 1982.
———. "Postmodernist Bourgeois Liberalism." *Journal of Philosophy* 80, no. 10 (1983): 583–89.
———. "Pragmatism without Method." In *Sidney Hook: Philosopher of Democracy and Humanism,* edited by Paul Kurtz. Amherst, N.Y.: Prometheus Books, 1983.
———. "Signposts along the Way that Reason Went." *London Review of Books,* February 16, 1984, pp. 5–6.
———. "Habermas and Lyotard on Postmodernity." In *Habermas and Modernity,* ed. Richard Bernstein. Cambridge, Mass.: MIT Press, 1985.
———. "Solidarity or Objectivity." In *Post-Analytic Philosophy,* edited by John Rajchman and Cornel West. New York: Columbia University Press, 1985.
———. "Posties." *London Review of Books,* September 3, 1987, pp. 11–12.
———. "Thugs and Theorists." *Political Theory* 15, no. 4 (1987): 564–80.
———. *Contingency, Irony, and Solidarity.* Cambridge: Cambridge University Press, 1989.
———. Introduction to *Pragmatism: From Peirce to Davidson,* by John D. Murphy. Boulder: Westview Press, 1990.
———. "The Priority of Democracy to Philosophy." In *Reading Rorty,* ed. Alan Malachowski. Cambridge, Mass.: Basil Blackwell, 1990.
———. *Essays on Heidegger and Others.* Cambridge: Cambridge University Press, 1991.
———. "Feminism and Pragmatism." *Radical Philosophy* 59 (autumn 1991): 3–14.
———. *Objectivity, Relativism, and Truth.* Cambridge: Cambridge University Press, 1991.
———. "Intellectuals at the End of Socialism." Lecture delivered at Northwestern University, January 17, 1992.

———. "Trotsky and the Wild Orchids." *Common Knowledge* (winter 1992): 140–53.

———. "Human Rights, Rationality and Sentimentality." In *On Human Rights: The Oxford Amnesty Lectures*, edited by Stephen Shute and Susan Hurley. Boston: Basic Books, 1993.

———. "Dewey between Hegel and Darwin." In *Modernism and the Human Sciences*, edited by Dorothy Ross. Baltimore: Johns Hopkins Press, 1994.

———. "Review of Jacques Derrida's *Specters of Marx: The State of the Debt, the Work of Mourning, and the New International*." (Unpublished, 1995): 1–18.

———. "On Moral Obligation, Truth, and Common Sense." In *Debating the State of Philosophy: Habermas, Rorty, and Kolakowski*, edited by Józef Niznik and John T. Sanders. Westport, Conn. and London: Praeger, 1996.

———. "Relativism: Finding and Making." In *Debating the State of Philosophy: Habermas, Rorty, and Kolakowski*, edited by Józef Niznik and John T. Sanders. Westport, Conn. and London: Praeger, 1996.

———. *Achieving Our Country*. Cambridge and London: Harvard University Press, 1998.

———. "The End of Leninism and History as Comic Frame." (Unpublished manuscript).

———. "Habermas, Derrida, and the Functions of Philosophy." (Unpublished manuscript).

———. "Movements and Campaigns." (Unpublished manuscript. A later version was included as an appendix in Richard Rorty, *Achieving Our Country* [pp. 111–24]).

Rosenblum, Nancy L. *Another Liberalism: Romanticism and the Reconstruction of Liberal Thought*. Cambridge, Mass., and London: Harvard University Press, 1987.

Saatkamp, Herman J., Jr., ed. *Rorty and Pragmatism: The Philosopher Responds to His Critics*. Nashville and London: Vanderbilt University Press, 1995.

Said, Edward. *Culture and Imperialism*. New York: Alfred A. Knopf, 1993.

Schiller, Herbert I. *Culture, Inc.: The Corporate Takeover of Public Expression*. New York: Oxford University Press, 1989.

Shlapentokh, Vladimir. *Public and Private Life of the Soviet People*. Oxford: Oxford University Press, 1989.

Sorell, Tom. "The World from Its Own Point of View." In *Reading Rorty*, edited by Alan Malachowski. Cambridge, Mass.: Basil Blackwell, 1990.

Sosa, Ernest. "Nature Unmirrored, Epistemology Naturalized." *Synthese* 55, no. 1 (1983): 49–72.

Szymanski, Albert. *The Capitalist State and the Politics of Class.* Cambridge, Mass.: Winthrop, 1978.
Therborn, Goran. *What Does the Ruling Class Do When It Rules?* London: New Left Books, 1978.
Tiles, J. E. *Dewey.* London and New York: Routledge, 1988.
Tocqueville, Alexis de. *Democracy in America.* Vol. 2. New York: Alfred A. Knopf, 1948.
Weber, Max. *The Protestant Ethic and the Spirit of Capitalism.* London and New York: Routledge, 1992.
Westbrook, Robert. *John Dewey and American Democracy.* Ithaca, N.Y.: Cornell University Press, 1991.
Westin, Alan. "The Origins of Modern Claims to Privacy." In *Philosophical Dimensions of Privacy,* edited by Ferdinand D. Schoeman. Cambridge: Cambridge University Press, 1984.
Wright, Erik Olin. *Class, Crisis and the State.* London: New Left Books, 1978.
Yack, Bernard. *The Longing for Total Revolution: Philosophic Sources of Social Discontent from Rousseau to Marx and Nietzsche.* Princeton: Princeton University Press, 1986.

INDEX

Acton, Lord, 170
adaptive preferences, 30
AFL-CIO, 11
Africa, 152
Albania, 180
Algeria, 156
Alliance for Progress, 38
Althusser, Louis, 24, 175
   on the family, 109, 130n
   on ideology, 120, 121
   on the state, 96, 99–100, 101, 128n
altruism
   Dewey on, 61–62
   Rorty on, 68–69, 72–73, 75, 92
American Dream, 31, 179, 191
American Philosophical Association, 11
Anaconda Copper, 142

analytic philosophy. *See* philosophy: analytic
anarchists, 56, 96, 156
antiessentialism, 22, 41n, 192
   and Jefferson's compromise, 69
   Rorty on, 27–30, 71, 73
   See also essentialism
antifoundationalism, 22–25, 80n. *See also* foundationalism
antirepresentationalism, 22, 25–27. *See also* representationalism
Arendt, Hannah, 58
Aristotle, 37, 175
Ashbery, John, 12
Asia, 152
   Central, 67
   Southeast, 163n

INDEX

autonomy, 58, 59, 89, 104, 117–18, 125
  Dewey on, 60, 62, 76, 77
  Rorty on, 17, 76–78, 79, 181, 188

Bacon, Francis, 170
Bagdikian, Ben, 112, 173
Baltic republics, 67
banality, 172, 175–76, 198n
Baudrillard, Jean, 125–26n
Bayle, Pierre, 184
Bazelon, David, 126n
Bell, Daniel, 175, 184, 189
Bentham, Jeremy, 57, 63, 188
Bergmann, Gustave, 132n
Berlin, Isaiah, 55, 64, 92, 126n, 148
Berlin Wall, 12, 67, 125n
Bernstein, Richard, 140–41, 147
Bhaskar, Roy, 170, 197n
Bill of Rights, 110, 111
Black Power movement, 84n
Blake, William, 37
Bloom, Harold, 169
Bolsheviks, 113, 131n
"bourgeois capitalist societies," 31, 140, 141, 144, 146, 154. *See also* capitalism; capitalists
bourgeois state, 91, 130n. *See also* capitalists; class rule
Boyle's law, 123
Brandeis, Louis, 91
Brazil, 98, 201n
Brezhnev, Leonid, 130n
Broederbond, 185
Bulgaria, 179
Bureau of Alcohol, Tobacco and Firearms, 110

Cali drug cartel, 186
capitalism, 12, 86, 101, 112, 139, 140–41, 144, 145, 146, 154, 171, 179, 181, 183, 189–90, 196n
  advanced, 87, 108, 109, 112, 149, 182
  "free enterprise," 126n
  global, 112, 143, 150, 200n
  with a human face, 141, 153, 156, 187
  monopoly 53, 95, 185
  private enterprise, 99, 100
  See also bourgeois capitalist societies; capitalists
capitalists, 95, 97, 175, 180
  class rule, 103, 112, 117, 154, 156–57, 176
  exploitation, 95, 96–97, 114, 116, 117, 123, 141, 144, 145, 154, 175, 183, 192, 198n
  and needs, 144, 177
  propaganda, 87
  See also capitalism; dictatorship of the bourgeoisie
Carlyle, Thomas, 148–49
Castoriadis, Cornelius, 119, 132n, 210n
Central Asia. *See* Asia, Central
centralism, bureaucratic or democratic, 102
Chad, 144
Chicago School, the, 185
Chile, 90, 128n, 157, 158
China, 65, 87, 148, 152, 161n
Chomsky, Noam, 137
Churchill, Winston, 136
CIA (Central Intelligence Agency), 151, 161n, 164n, 185

INDEX

civil society, 80n, 89, 111
  burgerlich Gesellschaft, 93
  Gramsci on, 99, 103, 129n
  Hegel on, 92–93
  Leninists on, 113
  Marx on, 91
  in Russia, 107
  See also society
Civil War (U.S.), 97–98
class
  alliance, 97–98, 102, 128n
  "business community," 95, 173, 178
  capitalist, 95, 103, 112, 117, 150, 154, 156
  class character of the state, 96, 97, 100, 111, 175
  classless society, 193
  conflict, 38, 95, 96, 98, 100, 104, 110, 121, 128n, 140, 141, 175, 183, 195, 197n
  defined, 127n
  Dewey on, 53, 54
  divisions in liberal democracies, 94, 95, 128n, 144, 149, 173, 176, 186, 193
  and the family, 109, 130n
  forces, 98, 100, 103, 110, 111
  and ideology, 120, 123
  propertied, 57
  Rorty on, 95–96, 156, 173, 177, 193–94, 197n
  rule, 98, 99, 101, 103, 104, 111, 117, 118, 128n, 130n, 154, 156, 175, 177, 183
  ruling, 97, 98–99, 102, 103–104, 109, 111, 123, 131n, 157
  and state power, 97

subaltern, 98, 99
"subjectivism," 119, 120
working, 37, 110, 120, 143, 150, 153, 157, 175, 187, 191
working-class pride, 150
Clinton, William J., 186
coherentists, 26, 44n
cold war, 12, 16, 86, 125, 148, 171, 180, 185, 189, 194
  liberals, 105, 162n, 170, 196n
  post-, 12, 85, 102, 151, 152, 154, 189, 190
commodification of labor, 172, 176
common sense, 123. *See also* good sense
communism, communists, 132n, 148, 153, 158, 164n, 165n, 176, 181
  anti-, 89, 165n
  "communist oligarchs," 105
  Communist Party of Great Britain, 89
  Communist Party of the USSR, 115, 185
  of Russian Federation, 180–81
Communist Manifesto, 96, 146, 156–57
communitarians, 28, 84n
Condorcet, Marquis de, 120
Constitutional Convention (U.S.), 97
contingency, 29, 54, 119, 181
  of selfhood, 27, 29, 92, 138
Critical Legal Studies Movement, 24
Critique of the Gotha Program, 157
cruelty, 16, 65–68, 70, 76, 78, 136, 138, 154, 183. *See also* humiliation
Cuba, 157–58
"Cultural Left," the, 124, 169, 191
Czechoslovakia, 107
Czech Republic, 67, 68, 83n, 191

INDEX

Darwin, Charles, 31, 188
Davidson, Basil, 137
Davidson, Donald, 22–23, 26, 28, 33, 42n, 123, 133n, 168
decolonization, 152, 195
democracy, 12, 36, 39, 47, 57, 73, 77, 90, 131n, 139, 157, 164n, 186, 188, 191, 200n, 201n
   Arendt on, 58
   bourgeois, 17, 149, 182, 184, 191, 200n
   Dewey on, 57, 63, 77, 84n
   as Dewey's social ideal, 58–61, 84n
   egalitarian, 57–58
   Jefferson on, 30
   Lenin on, 131n
   liberal, 17, 36, 67, 69, 88, 115, 136, 145, 149, 153, 168, 182, 184, 187
   liberty and, 59
   Marx and Engels on, 157
   participatory, 84n, 115
   political, 57, 58–59, 62
   Poulantzas on, 108;
   representative, 36, 57, 115, 131n
   Rorty on, 63, 67, 77, 84n, 158, 168, 188
   Rorty's utopia, 17
   Rousseau's followers on, 58
   as threat to common weal, 57
   Western-style, 12, 65, 88, 180
   See also bourgeois liberal democracy; "rich North Atlantic democracies"; social democracy
Democratic Party (U.S.), Democrats, 153, 169, 196n
Denmark, 190
Derrida, Jacques, 12, 31, 76, 183
Descartes, René, 14
Dewey, John, 11, 17, 30, 31, 37, 45, 48–54, 56–62, 63, 66, 73–77, 78, 92, 101, 102, 104, 122, 126n, 143, 163n, 164n, 167–68, 174, 177, 185, 187, 188, 192, 194
   accused of being a totalitarian, 126n
   on autonomy, 62, 76, 77
   on class, 54
   on community, 48–50, 50, 52, 53, 54, 58, 66
   compared favorably to Hook, 163n
   contrasted to Jefferson, 56–57
   contrasted to Locke, 57
   contrasted to Rorty, 39, 46, 47, 74, 75, 77–78, 79–80n, 84n, 102, 143, 188, 194
   on democracy as a social ideal, 58–61
   on democratic states, 57–58, 104
   on egoism and altruism, 61–62, 73–74, 75
   on the Great Community, 53, 78, 93, 156
   on habits of loyalty, 122
   on individuality, 49–50, 61–62, 101
   and Marx, 198n
   Marxist views of, 200n
   on means and ends, 61
   on negative liberty, 56
   on philosophy, 46–47
   on the political state, 52–54
   on positive liberty, 58, 77
   on the public/private split, 49, 50, 51–55, 92, 93
   on public schools, 76, 77

INDEX

reaction to imperialism, 184
Rorty as a follower of, 16, 39, 45, 49, 62, 63, 66, 73, 74, 75, 167–68, 175, 187
Rorty's admiration for, 184, 187
and Weber, 174, 175, 187, 198n
dictatorship of the bourgeoisie, 175. *See also* capitalists; class: rule; dictatorship of the proletariat
dictatorship of the proletariat, 157. *See also* dictatorship of the bourgeoisie; socialism
Dissent (magazine), 32, 70, 84n, 103, 145, 165n
Domhoff, William, 175
Donzelot, Jacques, 130n
Drakulic, Slavenka, 190
Dryden, John, 37
D'Souza, Dinesh, 169
Dulles, John Foster, 112
Duma (Russian legislature), 180

Earth Day, 112
East India Company, 148
education
 cuts in, 151
 Dewey on, 59, 60, 62, 75, 76, 77
 differential per-pupil expenditure on schools, 172–73
 liberal, 11
 and more inclusive conception of "public," 147
 as part of the state, 93, 99
 public school curricula, 100, 124
 public schools, 60, 62, 75, 77, 100, 130n, 186
 schools and class domination, 101, 102
egoism, 61–62
Egypt, 156
Elchibey, Abulfez, 67
Emerson, Ralph W., 113
Engels, Friedrich, 128n, 146, 157, 159
Enlightenment, the, 13, 14, 28, 106, 184, 192
epistemology, 14, 15, 128n
essentialism, 14, 73, 167. *See also* antiessentialism
ethnocentrism, 147, 169
ethnos, 31, 75
Eucharist, 23
Eurocentrism, 169

family, relationship to the state, 90, 99, 100, 102, 130n
 Althusser on, 100, 109
 Dewey on, 48, 59, 60
 Donzelot on, 130n
 Hegel on, 93
 in the Soviet Union, 107–108
fascism, 189, 202n
FBI (Federal Bureau of Investigation), 103, 110
feminism, feminists, 11, 30, 134n, 169, 190, 196n
feudalism, 101, 145, 146
Filmer, Robert, 13
Fish, Stanley, 12
Foucauldians, 82n, 118, 123
Foucault, Michel, 14, 76, 100, 106, 111, 112, 116–18, 123, 136–37, 144, 156
foundationalism, 14, 22, 40n. *See also* antifoundationalism

France, 98, 109, 130n, 139, 151, 171, 184, 192
Frankfurt School, 13, 106, 200n
Fraser, Nancy, 66–67, 68, 69, 72, 149, 178, 187
freedom. *See* liberty
French Revolution, 58, 71, 188
Freud, Sigmund, 22, 31, 37
 Davidson and Rorty's interpretation, 28, 42n, 74, 168
Fukayama, Francis, 88, 92, 125n, 153, 195

G-7 (conference of leading industrialized countries), 112, 145, 150
Galeano, Eduardo, 137
Gamsekhurdia, Zviad, 67
Gannet, 198n
GATT (General Agreement on Tariffs and Trade), 142
Geras, Norman, 41n, 150
Geuss, Raymond, 81n, 120, 122, 132n
globalism, 93, 144, 145–46, 190, 195
good sense, 41n, 123
Gorbachev, Mikhail S., 106, 114, 115, 130n, 131n, 151
Gramsci, Antonio, 99, 103–104, 129n, 192
 on civil society, 103, 129n
 on good sense, 123
 on ideology, 121, 123
 on the state, 99, 100, 103
Graves, Michael, 12
Great Britain, 89, 139
Guatemala, 90, 157
Gypsies, 83n

Haber, Honi Fern, 192, 194
Habermas, Jurgen, 119, 120, 121
Haiti, 144
Hall, David L., 33–34, 35, 77, 116–17, 141, 144, 177, 193
Havel, Vaclav, 68, 83n, 132n, 169, 191
Hegel, G. W. F., 92, 131n, 170, 184
 on democracy, 77
 on the state, 52, 93
Heidegger, Martin, 12, 14, 34, 148, 162n, 192
Heidelberg, University of, 65, 148
Helsinki Declaration of Human Rights, 144
historicism, 49, 71, 92, 182, 183
Hitler, Adolph, 66, 189, 201n
Hobbes, Thomas, 56, 92
Hollis, Martin, 42n
Hook, Sidney, 77, 126n, 135, 163n, 165n
Howe, Irving, 70–71, 84n
Huber, Dr. Wolfgang, 65
Hume, David, 27, 170
humiliation, 65, 66, 68, 70, 74, 75, 78, 122, 138. *See also* cruelty
Hungary, 107, 179

Ideologiekritik, 116, 118–24, 132n, 134n, 141, 196n
ideology, 38, 116, 118–24, 126n, 164n, 169, 176, 179, 183, 185
 alternative definitions, 120–24
 and the family, 130n
 functional definition, 122
 and good sense, 123
 Havel on, 132n
 hegemony, 38

INDEX

liberalism as, 179
  and the private sphere, 126n
  Rorty on, 118–20, 133n, 164n, 172, 176, 183
  as *Weltanschauungen*, 121, 132n
IMF (International Monetary Fund), 112, 145, 162n, 195
Immigration and Naturalization Service, 110
imperialism, 95, 141, 154, 175, 183, 200n
  anti-, 191
  cultural, 112
  Soviet, 151, 176, 182, 183, 184
India, 98, 156, 161n. *See also* East India Company
individualism, 62, 73
  liberal, 92
  narrow, 75
intellectuals, 15, 98, 163n, 164n, 183, 184
  dissident, 67–68, 87, 180, 199n
  leftist, 169, 171, 176, 197n
  liberal, 31–32, 147, 178
  romantic, 25, 67
Iran, 185
ironists, 17, 65, 76, 167, 183, 188, 191, 192
  liberal, 184, 192, 194
  post-Soviet, 190
  and the public/private split, 65, 71–72
  and Rorty, 17, 167, 183–85, 188, 192, 194
  theorists, 72, 136, 188, 193
Italy, 98, 129n, 151

Jacques, Martin, 89, 111–12, 113
James, William, 26–27, 30, 41n
Jameson, Fredric, 175
Japan, 86, 87, 98, 148
Jefferson, Thomas, 30, 45, 52, 69, 83n, 163n, 184, 188
  civic humanism, 58
  Dewey's differences with, 56
Jeffersonian compromise, 69, 102, 189
Jim Crow, 103
justification (of beliefs), 23, 26, 44n, 121, 154, 168
  circular, 33, 178

Kabul, 86
Kant, Immanuel, 18n, 28, 31, 46, 64, 170
Kapital, Das (Karl Marx), 123, 133n, 171
Kaplan, Robert, 144, 145
Karadzic, Radovan, 67
KGB, 105
Kissinger, Henry, 201n
Kolakowski, Leszek, 119, 126n, 155, 170, 201n
Korea, 152
Korry, Edward, 158
Kosovo, 105
Kuhn, Thomas, 12, 23, 24, 73, 135
Kundera, Milan, 88, 92, 117
Kwasniewski, Aleksander, 181

laissez-faire policies, 56, 73, 143, 185
language games, 23, 43n, 74
Larson, Eric, 110
Lasch, Christopher, 161n
Latin America, 138, 152, 158, 186

INDEX

Lenin, V. I., 66, 96, 113, 131n, 163n, 171, 189, 197n, 201n
Leninism, Leninists, 113, 131n, 171–72, 183, 197n, 201n
liberal democracy, 36, 67, 69, 88, 115, 136, 149, 153, 168, 187
  bourgeois, 17, 149, 184, 191–94
  ideals of, 145
  See also democracy; liberalism
liberalism, 12, 13–14, 15, 17, 21, 28, 33, 46, 54, 55–56, 62, 63, 65, 73, 95, 118, 136, 137–43, 142, 150, 155, 156, 159, 167, 175, 177, 180, 181, 186, 188, 191, 192, 194, 195
  alternative to, 155, 156
  American, 139
  and autonomy, 78–79
  of Bentham, 63
  bourgeois, 95, 113, 149, 179, 182–84, 191–94, 194
  classical, 55–58, 59, 62–65, 143, 188
  cold war, 105, 162n, 170, 196n
  and community, 49, 64, 66, 68, 70, 96, 136, 146, 182
  conditions of actuality of, 137, 142, 154
  and consent, 30, 50, 55, 57–59, 99, 107, 144
  conservative, 57
  of Constant, 63
  Dewey on, 58–59, 143, 185, 194
  economic, 88
  ideals of, 35–36, 63, 66–72, 78, 125, 136–37, 139, 140–43, 145, 151, 153–54, 157, 159, 167, 173, 178, 183, 184
  and imperialism, 141
  and individualism, 62, 73, 92
  institutions of, 13, 17, 36, 45, 67, 69, 78–79, 106, 124, 137, 138–43, 143–54, 155–59, 167, 172, 173, 177, 178, 183–84, 186, 188, 190, 191, 193
  and ironism, 184, 185, 192, 194
  Merleau-Ponty on liberal ideals, 154
  of J. S. Mill, 63
  of James Mill, 63
  neo-, 38, 78, 188
  "nonideological," 176, 179
  opponents of, 139, 154, 155–56
  philosophical, 13, 33–34, 46, 72–73, 75, 168–69, 172
  and the public/private split, 17, 92
  and romanticism, 65, 82n
  Roosevelt on, 185
  Rorty on, 13–14, 15, 17, 21, 28, 33, 38, 46, 47, 54, 63, 66, 95, 96, 125, 138, 143, 153, 194
  and suffering, 137–43, 147–49, 155–59, 172, 193, 202n
  See also democracy; individualism; liberal democracy; liberals; utopia
liberals, 13, 30, 31–32, 39, 48, 60, 63, 64, 68, 72, 76, 126n, 130n, 140, 147, 150, 163n, 165n, 175, 178, 185
  classical, 57–58, 63, 143
  cold war, 105, 162n, 170, 196n
  and community, 49, 64, 66, 68, 70, 96, 136, 146, 182
  Dewey, 58
  English, 55, 56

INDEX

as ironists, 184
Rorty on, 16–17, 136, 138, 175
Shklar's definition of, 16, 66, 136, 143, 202n
See also liberalism
liberty, 39, 47, 55, 63, 65, 77, 137, 143, 151
  abridgements of, 140, 186–87, 195, 201n
  as autonomy, 58, 62, 77
  Dewey on, 58–50, 60–61
  "European spirit of freedom" (Kundera), 88
  as free trade (Marx), 146
  Hobbes on, 56
  as legacy of the West, 113, 136, 168
  as a liberal ideal, 150–51
  Locke on, 55, 57
  J. S. Mill on, 55, 63–64
  negative, 55–57, 58, 59, 63, 64, 68, 70, 72, 78, 111, 113, 118, 136, 143, 190, 194
  as personal freedom, 16, 26, 33, 36, 38, 61, 63, 111, 117, 125, 135, 144, 154, 172–73
  positive, 58, 77, 78
  and private autonomy, 78
  as recognition of contingency (Rorty), 29
  Rorty contrasted to Dewey on, 47, 77, 84n, 143
  Rorty on, 64, 77–78, 143–44
  Rousseau on, 58
  as sole purpose of liberal community, 66, 136
  universal, 137, 141
  See also autonomy

Lincoln, Abraham, 106, 130n
Lippmann, Walter, 84n
Locke, John, 13, 14, 45, 55–58, 92, 188
Lubyanka Prison, 201n
Lukacs, Georg, 120
Luxemburg, Rosa, 25
Lyotard, François, 12, 13, 123

MacIntyre, Alastair, 32, 199n
Macpherson, C. B., 57
Madison, James, 97
Mannheim, Karl, 122
market, the, 12, 78, 88, 101
  automobilization as a market-driven process, 161n
  consumer, 87
  economies, 78, 140, 143, 144, 153, 155, 162n, 164n, 194, 199n
  free, 12, 65, 88, 143, 152, 180, 191
  labor, 94, 101, 146, 150, 190
  mechanisms, 114
  reforms, 12, 180, 186, 191
  stocks and bonds, 94
  Western, 191
  world, 146
  See also capitalism
Marshall Plan, 152
Marx, Karl, 30, 31, 64, 82n, 86, 87, 91, 92, 100, 119, 120, 121, 128n, 133n, 146, 154, 155, 156, 159, 170, 171, 175, 180
  and Darwin, 188
  Dewey and, 198n.
  See also Marxism; Marxists
Marxism, 64, 65, 96, 122, 156, 159, 164n, 171, 177, 180, 194, 201n
  Fraser's "quasi-Marxian view," 149

Rorty on, 66, 82n, 132n, 142, 157, 164n, 170, 171, 186, 188, 202n
See also Marx, Karl; Marxists
Marxists, 64, 82n, 92, 118, 119, 120, 121, 150, 154, 155, 156–57, 157, 170, 173, 181, 183, 193, 197n, 200n
  on Dewey, 200n
  self-proclaimed, 65
  See also Marx; Marxism
Mead, George H. 49, 80n, 165n
Medellin drug cartel, 186
Merleau-Ponty, Maurice, 150, 154
metanarratives, 13, 145
metaphor, 22–25, 28–29, 35, 67, 133n, 183, 185, 192, 198n
"methodolatry," 181
Mexico, 156
Militant Tendency, the, 153
Mill, James, 57, 63, 92, 188
Mill, John Stuart, 25, 29, 45, 55–56, 57, 63–64, 68, 89, 92, 148, 170, 172, 188
  on "internal culture," 66
Miller, Richard W., 41n
Molière, 184
Montaigne, 184
Montesquieu, 57
Moscow, 105, 130n, 157, 158, 185, 189
"movement politics," 75, 84n, 140, 152, 170–71, 201n
  progressivism, 185
  proletarian, 171, 197n
  See also Black Power movement; New Left; Zionism
Munkirs, John R., 162n

Nabakov, Vladimir V., 74, 87
Najibullah regime (Afghanistan), 86
Nation, The (magazine), 165n
National Defense Education Act, 152
National Defense Highway Act, 152–53
NATO, 176, 186, 191
naturalists, 124
neoliberalism. *See* liberalism: neo-
Netherlands, 190
New Deal, 45, 152
New Left, 84n
New World Order, 89
New York Times, 11, 94, 127n
Newton, Isaac, 22, 31, 37
Nicaragua, 90, 157
Nielsen, Kai, 79–80n, 120, 122, 123
Nietzsche, Friedrich, 14, 76, 188, 192
nomenklatura, 185
nominalists, 27, 72, 145, 164n, 181, 182
  historical, 92, 141, 171
  linguistic, 41n
nongovernmental organizations, 102
Novack, George, 200n
Novosti Press Agency, 107, 120

Orwell, George, 67, 74, 105, 113, 185, 189, 194

Pacific Rim, 87
Pakistan, 86
Parenti, Michael, 161n, 173, 175
Paris Commune, 131n
Parsons, Talcott, 122
patriarchy, 128n, 140, 196n
Patrice Lumumba University, 201n

INDEX

Paul, St. *See* Saint Paul
perestroika, 114
Perlo, Victor, 175
Philippines, 156
philosophy, 14–15, 21, 23, 25, 31–33, 35, 39, 46, 83n, 119, 121, 181
   analytic, 14–15, 21, 22, 33, 34, 47, 199n
   argumentation, 43n
   Dewey contrasted to Rorty, 45–78
   Dewey on, 74
   as a *Fach*, 182
   of language, 14, 15
   left-wing intellectuals and, 197n
   Lenin on Hegel's philosophy of history, 131n
   Marxists and, 170–73
   of mind, 14, 15
   natural, 184
   during the New Deal, 45
   pragmatism and, 168, 200n
   priority of democracy to, 63, 160, 168
   Rorty on, 15, 34, 63, 181
   of science, 14, 128n
   Sellars's definition, 14–15
   social and political, 12, 18n, 74, 174
   Wittgenstein on, 39
Plato, 22, 31, 64, 74, 175
Plekhanov, Georgy, 121
pluralism, 12, 70, 112
   pluralistic civil society, 89
   See also pluralists
pluralist sociologists, 128n, 161n
pluralists, 149, 178. *See also* pluralism
poets, 24–25, 28, 67, 75
   "nonpoets," 66

strong, 28–29, 55, 64, 66–67, 70–72, 73, 75, 78, 102, 104, 136, 155, 159
   See also metaphor
Poland, 67, 86, 179
political power, 17, 38, 54, 56, 98–99, 101, 104, 111, 113, 131n
   bourgeois, 194
   centralization of, 101
   and class rule, 99–100, 102
   conventional model of, 85–86, 89–90, 182
   powerlessness, 36, 186
   public/private split as effect and instance of, 100–103, 104, 109
   state power as a special case of, 97–99
   See also class: rule; state power
Popper, Karl, 82n
positivist, 26
postmodernism, 12–14, 18n
Poulantzas, Nicos, 107, 109, 112–13
Pozner, Vladimir, 179
pragmatism, 26, 41n, 167, 177, 200n
   American, 26
   Dewey's, 200n
   Jefferson and, 30
   Marxists and, 200n
   misgivings about, 41n
   public, 70
   Rorty on, 26, 167–68, 171, 177
   See also pragmatists
pragmatists, 26, 30, 39, 41n, 47, 49, 122, 178
   Dewey, 39, 46
   differences between Rorty and Dewey as, 46–47, 55, 74–78
   Rorty, 39, 45, 46, 150, 178, 181, 188

themes, 12
See also pragmatism
privacy, 90–91
private enterprise. *See* "free enterprise"; capitalism
private property, 100, 114, 117, 155, 171
private selfhood. *See* selfhood: private
private sphere, 17, 22, 33, 62, 69, 70, 73, 85, 87, 92, 111, 115, 159, 173, 183, 192
   "apolitical," 88–94, 117–18, 182
   "civil society" and, 113
   conventional view of, 38, 85
   as an effect of politics, 104
   Hegel and, 92–93
   "inviolable," 56, 92, 173, 182, 186, 192–93
   J. S. Mill and, 55
   not pure illusion, 114, 117
   objections to the conventional view of, 113, 118
   political character of, 183
   political power and, 17, 100–102, 103–104, 109, 111, 115–16, 182
   and private selfhood, 17
   "public sphere" as contrast term, 39, 76, 111
   Rorty on, 56, 76, 117, 181
      autonomy limited to, 76–78, 117, 181
   in Russia, 108, 115
   violability of, 87, 88, 109–11, 112, 192–93
   in the West, 109–13
   See also public; public/private split; public sphere; selfhood: private

privatization, 90, 139, 194
   as response to powerlessness, 186
   in the Soviet Union, 107–108, 109, 114–16
proletariat, 13, 119, 120, 157
Proust, Marcel, 28
public, the
   and the democratic state, 57
   Dewey on, 51–55, 57, 58–59
   and Dewey's Great Community, 53
   as government, 52
   inchoate public, 52, 54, 95
   as political construct, 104
   politically organized as a state, 52–55
   Rorty on, 70–78, 158
   and the state, 53–54, 60–61
   the state as a precondition of, 100
   See also Dewey, John; public/private split; public sphere
public/private split, 47, 49, 70, 72, 89, 92, 101, 111, 117, 143, 175
   as component of individuality, 101–102
   as contrast-term for "private sphere," 111
   Dewey and, 49–52, 62, 77
   differences between Dewey and Rorty on, 188
   distinguished from the state, 111, 117
   expansion of private sphere at the expense of, 115, 126n
   Poulantzas on, 109
   Rorty on, 65, 68–69, 70, 71–72, 75–77, 92, 127n, 158, 188
   and the state, 117

INDEX

state power and, 101–102, 103–104
two spheres not necessarily opposed, 192
See also private sphere; public; public sphere
public selfhood. *See* selfhood: public
public sphere, 22, 56, 62, 69, 70, 73, 103, 115, 117, 192
   components of, 93
   contrasted to private sphere, 39, 76
   as an effect of politics, 104
   should not encroach on the private sphere, 56
   See also private sphere; public; public/private split
Pynchon, Thomas, 12

Quine, W. V. O., 33

Rabelais, 184
racism, 128n, 138, 140
Radio Liberty, 87, 126n
rationality, 23, 31, 33–34, 40n, 43–44n, 73, 181
Rauschenbusch, Walter, 165n
Rawls, John, 31, 92
Reagan, Ronald, 130n, 151, 185, 186
Reformation, the, 71
relativists, 36, 39
Renaissance, 71
representationalism, 14, 25–26, 118.
   See also, antirepresentationalism
Republic of South Africa. *See* South Africa, Republic of
Resentment, School of, 169, 196n
"rich North Atlantic democracies," 17, 31, 36, 54, 85, 90, 94, 113, 125, 136, 141, 142, 144, 147, 155, 157, 159, 182, 194
Rio Summit, 112
Roman law, 121
Romantic movement, romanticism, 68, 71, 82n, 187
Roosevelt, Franklin D., 185
Rorty, James, 165n
Rosenblum, Nancy, 65, 186
Rote Armee Fraction, 65
Rousseau, Jean-Jacques, 58
Rushdie, Salman, 12
Ruskin, John, 148
Russia, 67, 86, 90, 98, 103, 105, 121, 130, 158, 179–80, 189–90, 202n
Ryan, Alan, 156, 187

Said, Edward, 112, 147–50
Saint Paul, 22, 37, 64
samizdat, 87, 108, 185
Sandburg, Carl, 184
Schiller, Herbert, 173
School of the Americas, 158, 201n
selfhood, 15, 27, 75, 101, 168, 181, 199n
   centerless self, 127n
   and community, 80n
   contingency of, 28, 29, 92
   Dewey on, 62
   distinction between public and private persons, 47, 70, 75, 124–25, 192
   G. H. Mead on, 49, 80n
   modes of subjectivity, 101
   nonessentialist conception of, 181
   private, 17, 68–69, 70, 102, 116, 159, 192
   and ideology, 118

INDEX

public, 101–102, 116, 192
Rorty on public and private selfhood, 72, 75, 102
Rorty's Humean notion of, 27, 199n
self-creation, 17, 49, 58, 187
   the Davidsonian-Freud account, 28
   freedom for self-creation, 63–78
   ironic self-creation, 184, 192
   theory of, 168
   true self, 27
Sellars, Wilfred, 19n, 33
Sharansky, Natan, 67
Shari'a, 121
Shlapentokh, Vladimir, 126n
Six Tigers, 87
Shelley, Percy B., 40n
Shklar, Judith, 19n, 70, 138, 143, 202n
slavery, 46, 50, 130n, 137, 138, 139
Slovakia, 179
Slovenia, 179
social democracy, social democrats, 31, 151, 153, 158, 168, 169, 181, 187, 198n
socialism, socialists, 116, 139, 150, 179–81, 189, 190
   in Cuba, 158
   defined as workers' power, 156
   New Socialist Man, 64
   nominally socialist states, 105, 106, 107
   privatization and, 105–16, 139
   Rorty on, 155, 156, 165n, 179, 180, 189, 196n
   triumphalists, 106
   See also dictatorship of the proletariat

society, 41n, 67, 76, 89, 90, 104, 112, 131n, 149, 158, 173, 177
   alternative conception of, 80n
   bourgeois, 140, 141, 144, 146, 154
   capitalist, 31
   classless, 193
   Dewey on, 48, 53
   liberal, 25, 68, 117, 140, 153, 177
   political (Gramsci), 99, 129n
   See also civil society
Solidarity (Polish union), 179
South Africa, Republic of, 185
Soviet Union (USSR), 86–87, 89, 98, 105–108, 114–16, 126n, 185
   centralized economic planning model, 162n, 195
   Communist Party of, 115, 131n, 162n, 185
   Constitution of, 131n
   "Evil Empire," 151, 152, 153, 186
   people of, 107, 131n
   post-Soviet era, 98, 156, 179, 202n
   Soviet threat, 105–106, 151–52, 176–77, 182, 183, 185–86, 195
Stalin, Joseph V., 66, 90, 121, 185, 189, 201n
Stalinism, Stalinist, 180, 183
state, the, 74, 85–8, 97, 124, 128n, 131n, 183
   Althusser on, 96–97, 99–100
   and civil society, 89–90, 91, 103, 111–12, 113, 129n
   class character of, 95–99, 100, 111, 128n
   coercive character of, 96, 99, 107
   Dewey on, 52–55, 56–57, 59–62, 93, 104

definition, 52
in the East, 85–105, 90, 103–104, 107–10, 114–16, 125
elements of, 93
the family and, 109, 130n
Fukayama on, 88, 92
functional description of, 97
Gramsci on, 99, 100, 103–104, 129n
Hegel on, 52, 92–93
imperialist, 182
institutions as sites of class struggle, 98–99, 110–11
intervention in the economy, 78, 126n, 162n, 173
liberal conceptions of, 55–59, 61–62, 78, 85, 88–94, 136, 190
liberal democratic, 36, 91, 112, 150
Marxists on, 96–97
J. S. Mill on, 56, 63–64, 89
pluralists on, 128n, 161n
Poulantzas on, 107–108, 109, 112–13
private sphere and, 85, 100–105, 108–109, 111, 112–13, 117–18, 124–25, 126n, 193
Rousseau on, 58
surveillance and control by, 85–105, 112–13, 136
in the West, 90, 98–100, 103, 108–11, 113, 125
workers', 87
See also class: rule; class: ruling; political power; state power; welfare state
state power, 36, 38, 96, 97–100, 108, 110, 115, 116, 121, 133n, 143, 144, 159

corporate capitalist, 176–77
definition, 97
ideology and, 121–24
Lenin on, 113
not confined to state institutions, 98–99
working-class, 37, 116, 143, 156, 157, 159
See also, political power; state
stoics, 72
Suslov, Mikhail A., 148
Sweden, 190

Tajikistan, 68, 105
Talibanis, 67
Tanzania, 156
Telecommunications Bill, 111
technocrats, 88, 176, 178, 187, 195, 201n
Tikopia, 91
Tiles, J. E., 46, 47
Time Warner, 198n
Tito, Josip Broz, 190
Tlingit, 91
Tocqueville, Alexis de, 57, 92, 192
"total revolution." *See* Yack, Bernard
totalitarianism, 90, 126n, 130n, 186
Trans-Dniester, 68
transcendental philosophy/conditions, 39, 140, 141, 154, 170–71
non-, 38, 154, 171
truth-as-correspondence, 19n
Tsetung, Mao, 66, 90
Tuareg, 91
Twain, Mark, 180, 184

Ukraine, 179, 180, 199

Unger, Roberto, 24, 31, 156, 168, 169, 182, 201n
United Fruit Company, 142, 161n
United Nations
  Charter of, 144
  Human Rights Development Committee, 94
utilitarianism, 66
  greatest happiness principle, 66, 70, 71, 172
utopia, 64, 68, 136, 144, 184
  liberal utopians, 68
  Rorty's 16, 17, 33, 47, 63, 70–71, 77, 141, 159, 167–68
  utopianism, 159

Vietnam, North, 152
Virginia, University of, 83n
Voice of America, 87
Voltaire, 184

Walesa, Lech, 97
Wall Street Journal, 68, 146
Warsaw Pact, 12, 113
Weber, Max, 129n, 142, 174, 175, 187, 198n

welfare state, 144, 151, 153, 188, 190, 191, 195. *See also* state
Weltanschauungen, 121. *See also* ideology
Whigs, 57
Whitman, Walt, 70, 184, 192
Wilson, Woodrow, 184
Wittgenstein, Ludwig, 23, 26, 33, 39, 119. *See also* language games
World Bank, 145, 162n
World Trade Organization, 145

X, Malcolm, 64

Yack, Bernard, 64–65, 84n, 159
  total revolution, 70, 75, 153, 158–59, 175
Yeltsin, Boris, 98, 130n, 180, 202n
Yerevan, 190
Yugoslavia, 67, 190, 202n

Zedong, Mao. *See* Tsetung, Mao
Zhirinovsky, Vladimir, 181
Zionism, 84n
Zyuganov, Gennady, 181